CRITICAL ACCLAIM FOR *KIN TO THE WIND* AND *MORO*

"A most diverting and picaresque tale, one that reads like a sentimental journey of a hundred years ago."

—*Norman Cousins*

"Highly entertaining . . . spins an enchanting effect . . . among the cream of his ilk . . . huge potential."

—*Billboard Magazine*

"Like roots growing and spreading in the earth, Moro Buddy Bohn tells his story, digging deep into his childhood. The branches reach out, taking wing upon the wind, the trunk thickens and strengthens. Moro's is an innate aptitude and love for music, played to the accompaniment of a spice of life garnered the world over, inspired and nurtured by love. The fruits of labor and freshness of youth blend to a satisfying adventure of wild success, played out by his fingers, his heart and soul, upon the melodies and harmonies."

—*Diane Buccheri, Publisher, OCEAN Magazine*

"Extraordinary on every count. Moro takes the reader on a thrilling journey. I couldn't put it down!"

—*Norma Paulsen, wife of the late perpetual presidential candidate Pat Paulsen*

"Enthralling."

—*San Francisco Examiner*

"During the two centuries in which they flourished there were about 400 of these troubadours. Today, there is roughly one. His name is Buddy Bohn."

—*TIME Magazine*

" . . . Beautiful . . . his performance was a model of pure, harmonious playing. His tone sings. . . ."

—*San Francisco Chronicle*

"He's tall and handsome, with the magnetism of a Pied Piper. Everywhere he goes people gather around. For life is all harmony in the company of Buddy Bohn.""

—*London Daily Mirror*

"The guitar of Moro travels the world; a touch of flamenco, a hint of classics, some new world, and always gently expressive with warmth and romance . . ."

—*The Christian Science Monitor*

"*Kin to the Wind* is a highly improbable-but-absolutely-true tale of a modern troubadour who made his way around the world relying solely on his musical performances to obtain food, shelter and transportation. It's an enchanting and fascinating chronicle filled with adventure, courage, romance, and ultimately, wisdom."

—*David W. Moore, author and Senior Fellow, Carsey Institute, University of New Hampshire*

"Nathaniel Hawthorne wrote, 'a happy person is such an unaccustomed and holy creature in this sad world!' Moro is deservedly one of those happy people. Through his travels, not merely geographic but also psychological, emotional and spiritual, we're provided a glimpse of his development and a totally new outlook on things. Those who value freedom and love in their purest form will find much to treasure in this incredible, unique adventure."

—*Lori Tunnell, PhD, USPTA certified tennis professional*

"A mystical journey made more so because it is true!"

—*D.P. Sanfilippo, public relations consultant, commercial writer*

"*Kin to the Wind* is a tale told with honesty and ecstasy, lovely and full of love. Moro's musicality transforms prose into song and makes irresistible the charm of the troubadour's travels. It is an enchanting story through to its final wistful notes."

—*Derick Tasker, classical pianist*

"A must read! Moro's story speaks to the innate goodness of all humans. It shows that regardless of background, people are the same. And when you speak the universal language of music you can often overcome even the most significant of cultural barriers. Some will read this story, set in the '60s, and think it isn't possible or even relevant today. I disagree. This story needs to be told today more than ever. We need this reminder that we're all in essence cut of the same cloth, and our differences should be celebrated.

Whether it's a musician playing for his keep, or someone offering a smile to a stranger, faith and love are exchanged and all are richer for the experience. As a survivor of the 2001 attack on the Pentagon, I saw the worst of humanity—and on the same day saw the best of humanity. Complete strangers gave me assistance, even hugs. They didn't ask about my religion, politics or anything else. They just helped. Their kindness fills my memories of that day, just as Moro remembers all the wonderful people he met on his inspiring journey."

—*Lieutenant Colonel Jill Higgins, U.S. Air Force*

KIN TO THE WIND

A troubadour's magical journey
around the world with no money

KIN TO THE WIND

A troubadour's magical journey
around the world with no money

Moro Buddy Bohn

Travelers' Tales
An imprint of Solas House, Inc.
Palo Alto

Travelers' Tales and Solas House are trademarks of Solas House, Inc. 853 Alma Street, Palo Alto, California 94301. www.travelerstales.com

Cover Design: Kimberly Nelson Coombs
Interior Design and Page Layout: Scribe Inc.
Production Director: Natalie Baszile

Library of Congress Cataloguing-in-Publication Data pending.

First Printing
Printed in United States
10 9 8 7 6 5 4 3 2 1

THE SAILOR

My old friend is a sailor
From the crew of many boats.
In his face shine the answers
Taught by visions and horizons
Lit with precious understanding.

He's learned so many nameless lessons
From the risings
And the settings
Of the sun—this vagabond in me.

"What you see in me is you," he says,
"For we never see each other—
Only ourself who is the other.

"And the sense of one and other
Cannot stand before the vision
In the mirror
One could think to be another."

TABLE OF CONTENTS

PREFACE

Being kin to the wind, I've been driven to travel, discover and be discovered. And this tale is about my worldwide family of folks, both rich and poor throughout 50 nations, who've helped me as I came their way.

I'm very grateful. For without connections or referrals, I set out with a backpack and guitar to circle the world at 21 as a troubadour—to play in royal courts and get along without ever using money as a means of exchange.

Other than with the exuberance of my youth, enthusiasm, guitar music, and my desire to see and learn, I had nothing with which to pay anyone. But by trusting, and simply putting one foot in front of the other, I discovered my huge worldwide family. All, even the terrorists among them, saw that I be given food, lodging, transportation, love and encouragement, advice and education. They also taught me philosophy, took me sightseeing, and showed me the lay of the land.

I crossed the Arabian Desert with a camel caravan of champagne-smuggling Bedouins, played for Pablo Picasso in France, was a circus act in Italy—guitar-accompanying a dancing midget horse—and performed with gypsies in Spain. The Communists in Berlin offered me $100 a day to defect. I was attacked and nearly killed by Tunisian beggars, met a ghost in the Himalayas, and was court troubadour to the king of Siam.

If my narrative reads a bit like the tales of Sinbad, I believe it's because there was a beautiful charm at work, born of my trust in love and my faith that love governs. This charm generated an invisible shield, protecting me when dangers became life-threatening and creating what seemed a worldwide conspiracy that I get looked after.

For most of my life I've been known as Moro (Moorish root of Morrow) my legal middle name. It suits the Moorish flavor, probably stemming from blood ancestry, that seasons my guitar composing. But during my troubadour years they called me Buddy Bohn.

Kin To The Wind recalls the events of those years—the people, conversations, and facts just as they occurred—assisted by journals and a big scrapbook of media coverage, documents and photos. The media coverage, including a feature in *TIME*, became so intense in 1963 it was turning my travels into a publicity stunt though. So I had to stop.

But it's a tale that cries out to be told. For my memory of the way I was treated—and what this tells me about the presence of love—has so warmed my heart over the years, I've come to realize it's too precious not to be shared.

My story discloses that amid the world's frailties, insanities and horrors, there's a limitless treasure of deep love abiding in us—a treasure so bountiful as to make all else seem paltry. It further reveals that if any of us goes around reflecting love with a mirror even so crude as a guitar, we can find it everywhere in abundance. For our world is truly the Eldorado of legend. Though it's not mere gold that paves the roads. It is love.

ACKNOWLEDGMENTS

My high school English teachers, Jack Cody and Elizabeth Girdler, taught me to spell and compose sentences. My Creative Writing instructor at Principia College was Welsh poet Godfrey John. He taught me to always be as good as possible at being what I am. That was very important. Then there was my good tennis friend, *Saturday Review* Editor Norman Cousins, author and visionary, who took the time to read my early attempts to write this story and encouraged me to approach a publisher with it.

Thanks also to my old high school chum Dave Moore, author and Senior Fellow, Karsey Institute, University of New Hampshire. Like Norman he read my early attempts, felt there was potential in this true story, even offered to write it for me, and wouldn't leave me alone about it year after year. Then he kept on encouraging me during the writing.

Along the way a pair of redoubtable writers and thinkers, James and Sean O'Reilly, took an interest in the project. My thanks to their associate Larry Habegger for presenting my story to them. Further support came from my friends Chris Rankin, Mary Barnett, Tomislav, Nicky Beach, Jill Higgins, Tony Amendolare, Ted Wildhage, Diane Buccheri, my dear sister Dina, and, so importantly, my adorable lady Simine. Their clear and positive thoughts, warm encouragement, advice and assistance, have been invaluable.

Finally, there would be nothing to write about were it not for the world's good people who picked me up as I stood by the roadsides, took me across oceans on their ships, saw that I got enough to eat, shared with me their eye-opening points of view and attended to all my problems—all in trade for a little music. Their love has enriched my entire life beyond description—such riches as can never be taken away.

1

Becoming a guitarist and deciding to be a troubadour

Mom poked her head through the door of our forest cottage and peered through the trees.

"Bud," she called in her cultured, resonant stage voice.

Though only six, I knew what she wanted and remained silent, hidden behind a tree.

She called louder. "Bud! Garbage!"

I closed my eyes in a desperate attempt to hang onto the music I was at that moment inventing in my head, for I'd come to a very nice passage that needed to be remembered.

But she persisted at full volume, "BUD!"

That did it. My inspiration was gone. My beautiful private symphony was lost.

Sadly I rose to my feet, emerged from behind the tree and confronted her.

"Hmph," she said. "Come here and take out the garbage. Are you deaf? Why don't you answer when I call?"

Sun rays filtered artfully through the treetops. I allowed them to soothe the pain of this confrontation and would've told her, had my wit been developed, "because I need music. My soul requires these musical moments for sustenance. Subconsciously I know this to be so. Thrilling musical inspiration comforts me, and you're always taking it away."

But I was only six, and life was a dream. I could only stare at her helplessly.

She glared at me. "I'm going to instruct the school nurse to examine your hearing. You might be deaf, like Dina says."

Dina was my older sister. She always insisted I was deaf, dumb and blind, for I didn't respond to her very well either. I lived in a beautiful astral-like world of my own making. No one anywhere seemed to understand. I didn't know how to explain and hadn't really figured it out myself.

Without a word, I took out the garbage.

Then I sat in our sun-drenched garden patio, holding my velveteen panda, and once again immersed into my astral-like world.

Fortunately Mom had her moments when she relaxed and got into my world with me a little. She sat inside a half-opened door and listened as I improvised a song for my panda, borrowing the phrase, "A tiskit-a-tasket" from somewhere . . .

A tiskit-a-tasket,
I'll carry my own basket
And travel the whole world with my house on my back.

There was more to the song, but that's all I can remember. Mom wrote down the whole song and showed it to me in later years. It was my first outwardly expressed song and probably the start of my being a troubadour. And it turned out to be a song of prophecy.

Around that time, my divorced mom's boyfriend, Jack McCoy, a fine and giving man who'd been a world-class champion bike racer, took me with him to visit some friends who had a guitar on their hearth. It leaned there temptingly, inspiring a deep longing I can't explain. I'd never played a guitar before, but I intuitively knew I could make music on it. The lady of the house had been friendly toward me, so I asked her for permission to play it. She was cautious.

"Do you know how to play?"

"I've never played, but I can. I just know it!"

She was impressed with my enthusiasm. "Yes, all right then. Go ahead."

I carefully picked up the huge instrument. It was very bulky. But I was tall and long-limbed for my age and was able to tenderly put my arm around it and pluck my first notes. It sounded rich and fine. It resonated like a cat purring, and I could feel it vibrating. Utterly entranced, I began experimenting. Within seconds I made up a tune, my own song, and played it.

She appeared amazed, as were her husband and Jack. Their attention felt good. I elaborated on the tune and played it over and over. When it was time for us to leave, I put the guitar down reluctantly. The thrill of that experience kept me awake all night.

We lived in Carmel-by-the-Sea, California. Among the artsy little shops, sheltered by tall pine trees, we had the Browse Around Music Store with a few dozen guitars on display for sale. The next day, during my walk home from school, I went in and began playing my tune on one of them without permission because I felt at home there.

The blond saleslady listened. She knew me because I'd been there before and bought a Burl Ives album with all my savings. "That's a pretty tune. What is it?"

"My own song," I said, still concentrating on the music.

"I see, but what's its name?"

I thought about it, decided, and then declared its title. "*My Own Song.*"

"Well it's just lovely. But I think Burl Ives might've played it a little differently.

Do you mind if I show you how he'd have played it?"

"Yes, please." I handed her the guitar, grateful for her friendship.

An expert guitarist, she played the same passage I'd just played. But she used all the fingers of her right hand, adding counterpoint with her thumb. It was fuller and richer.

I was very excited. "That's beautiful! May I try it?"

She handed me the guitar, and I played it just as she'd done. We were both delighted, and I kept returning to her for a year during which she taught me a lot. I decided I liked the guitar and her very much, and that I liked making up tunes and playing them.

During those magical days, I often visited my secret quiet place beneath a sprawling, gnarled old cypress tree growing in the silky white sand of Carmel Beach, gazed at the ocean, sniffed the salty breeze, and listened to the powerful music of the surf rolling in. To me it was an infinite orchestra that stretched for miles in all directions. The awesome power of it filled me with a rapture so intense as to make me think of brand new musical works. They were often endless melodious journeys I could hum mentally.

I'd heard many symphonies of course. Mom had a phonograph with lots of Beethoven, Mozart, Brahms and Chopin. A busy actress, she was out of the house a lot. And Dina was generally over at her friend Sally's place. So I had our little forest cottage and those fine recordings to myself most of the time. I wore out the records, playing them until I could hum my favorite symphonies note for note.

By learning these fine compositions, I unwittingly taught myself form and structure. Then, buoyed by a serenity inspired by surf sound, I began giving structure to my musical journeys. My own sonatas emerged, fresh new ones, though only in my head. For I didn't know how to write. I imagined them being played by an orchestra so large as to fill the sky with billions of musicians. A pretty tune made me happier than anything. I liked Burl Ives' public domain folk tunes, as well as those of Stephen Foster. Dina would sing these songs with me while we washed the dishes.

The kindly old widow Mrs. Kelly lived across the street. She had a grand piano on which she'd allow me to play and compose whenever I visited. She also had a couple of old unwanted tennis racquets in her attic, and she let me have them. The frames were made of steel, and they had steel strings. You could hit rocks with those racquets and not worry about breaking a string. Amid a fragrant old pine forest, a block away, there was a pair of city tennis courts where I spent countless hours.

The courts were dug into the side of a hill, and the Carmel stone-surfaced retaining wall was generally my only available tennis partner. Hitting the grouting produced a crooked bounce, making me run too much. But soon I found that if I really focused and watched the ball, I could substantially improve my percentage of good bounces by aiming my shots, causing the ball to hit a smooth area of stone. This learning to focus was vital in helping me to concentrate on my guitar and composing work at the Browse Around.

Mom hired some carpenters to build an extension onto our living room. They built a space for grandpa's baby-grand piano that belonged to her by virtue of her divorce settlement. It was a big day for us when the piano arrived. Now our baby sitter, Margaret Clark, was able to give both Dina and me piano lessons.

Margaret began a special learning program with me. It was a kind of challenge game. I would turn my back to the piano, whereupon she'd play a note and dare me to name it. Then she'd play two simultaneous notes and have me name both. After that, she'd play a whole chord, have me tell her the notes in it, and identify the chord. It was easy for me after awhile. With this and other techniques, she helped solidify my comprehension. But she was elderly and passed away.

So Mom hired Bessie Frazer to teach me. Bessie made me play Bach compositions, insisting I cup each hand face down over the keys as though holding a plum. And she demanded I play the music exactly as Bach wrote it. I found it agonizing and insufferable—not only the hand posture but the reading of notes. It gave me headaches. I insisted on playing the music my way, from my heart, taking liberties with the notes and meter so the music would sound prettier to my ears.

One day we reached an impasse when I simply refused to obey her order to play what I saw on the page. She angrily got up and stalked out of the house. As she passed Mom, who was out watering the lawn in the front yard, she declared, "that boy will never be a musician!" She never returned, and Mom wisely allowed me to just drift on my own.

Inside the back page of a Scrooge McDuck comic book, a year later, I found an ad that said if I would sell 12 cans of their Cloverine Brand Salve at 25 cents per can and return the money to the company, they would send me a small guitar—a kind of jumbo-size, cardboard ukulele. It sounded like it might be easy and fun. There was a coupon in the ad, and I needed only remove it, fill it out and send it in to get the salve. All excited, I approached Mom about it. Would she help me fill out the coupon, address an envelope, find a stamp and . . .

"No!" she said. Mom was very dramatic.

Every encounter was a scene in a play for her. To her all of life was a stage. She was so very talented, winsome and stunningly attractive, she starred or co-starred in a procession of standing-room-only hit plays at the local Golden Bough Theatre for almost ten years.

She proceeded to put on one of her characters. "You'll never be able to sell all those cans of salve. And when you don't send them the money, they'll come get you and take you to jail." She pointed to a place off in space with absolute authority. There was no contesting the point. "And that's final!" she said.

Sad and crushed, I took the precious comic book to my cabin Jack had built for me in the backyard where I was allowed to live alone. I sulked there for a long time. I had no one else to consult, for Jack wasn't around. I just had to find out from someone if they could really send me to jail, or if this was just another one of Mom's theatricals.

The next day, I dropped by the two-room, board-and-bat cottage of my best friend Red Eagle, adopted son of Buffalo Bill Cody. I'd met him while selling the town's weekly *Carmel Pine-cone* newspaper at the post office entrance. He'd bought one, offering to pay double if I'd deliver a copy to his place every Thursday afternoon.

His cottage stood alone amid an otherwise undeveloped, forested city block behind the Texaco gas station, corner of 7th and San Carlos, and was so thickly surrounded by wild juniper bushes and pine trees you could barely see it from the street. He really enjoyed his privacy in there. The only clue to his presence was the broken down, chain link gate out front.

Inside, he kept his spartan, impeccably dusted quarters in perfect order. He'd always welcome me with such warmth I felt like I was in heaven with him. He'd serve me a glazed donut and some milk and tell me of his days as an Indian scout with the U.S. Army. Occasionally he spoke of his glorious days as a performer on his dad's Wild West Show where he'd been an equestrian and snake dancer. He was very wise and knew the answers to all my questions about everything. I found I liked him so much that my Thursday business visits soon became almost daily social calls. He didn't mind at all, and we would go out for walks sometimes.

This particular day, we went for a walk along the divided dirt road east of his house. Cars rarely went along that road, for there were no destinations along it. There was only thick forest on either side, and it didn't lead anywhere you couldn't go using nearby paved roads. As we walked, I showed him the ad that I'd torn from the comic book and carried in my back pocket.

"Could they put me in jail?" I asked him.

He was silent for a long time, as was his way. Finally he said, "you need to listen."

"To what?"

"Listen, just listen."

I listened really hard but could hear nothing. The ocean was too far away to be heard, as were the hustle and bustle of the nearest street. We had the entire divided road to ourselves. But then I heard what seemed to be the sound of a squirrel chewing on an acorn and pointed to it.

"No, not that," he said.

At length I gave up. "I can't hear anything."

He beamed with satisfaction, for he'd heard them—riders on horseback approaching us from the south. Though he was 77 years old, his hearing was better than mine. He knelt to the ground, put his ear right into the dirt of the road and listened for what seemed to be a long time. Then he stood up and announced four riders on four horses were trotting (not walking or galloping) toward us. He added they were on our southbound lane, not the northbound lane as would be normal, and would appear over the hump ahead of us in just over a minute. He checked his watch, and we waited.

In about 70 seconds, the four horses, each bearing a rider, did indeed appear. They trotted toward us on our lane just like he'd predicted. He'd known from the hoof sound that all four horses were bearing riders. The sound had told him it couldn't be Bettie Greene mounted on her horse with three riderless horses in tow. (She often hand-towed her horses back and forth along that road to and from her pasture and riding stable.)

His chest puffed out with pride. His handsomely chiseled old face glowed like John the Baptist beholding Jesus for the first time. For he'd known how many horses and riders, their speed, direction, and exact time and location of arrival.

Supposing he'd detected not four but forty armed hostiles. How precious such information could be to the leader of a small army patrol touring hostile territory. He'd have had 70 seconds to muster his men behind a huge rock or clump of bushes and save their lives. Red Eagle was still a scout at 77, and I felt very lucky to be his friend.

When we returned to his cabin he examined the comic book ad for me. "This is a good plan," he said. "Go ahead and order the salve."

Elated, I told mom of the day's adventures and repeated his advice. She respected him, as did the other few townsfolk who'd met him. So she helped me with the coupon, envelope and stamp. The salve arrived. I sold it all in a single afternoon, going door to door around our neighborhood. She helped me send in the three dollars I'd gathered, and in a week or two my little cardboard guitar arrived complete with pegs, set of strings and instruction booklet. What a joy! I spent hours and hours with it. She was proud of me, and I often caught her playing it.

On a subsequent visit with Red Eagle, I thanked him for helping me with Mom over the guitar. I told him my only disappointment with it was that when I played a composition on my guitar it didn't sound as nice as it did in my imaginings of my billions of musicians playing it. He thought about it for a long time and then regarded me soberly.

"If, when you practice on your guitar, you will pretend that it sounds like it does in your heart, then one day it will!"

At first I thought he was just mollifying me like all the other grownups. But he continued gazing at me with a sober face and looked me straight in the eye for a long time. So I realized he was saying something important and resolved to remember what he'd said.

One day in school, during the weeks that followed, I found myself dreaming about music, behaving distantly and being unaware that this was so. Accordingly I was harassed by a group of my schoolmates. "You don't have any friends. None of us likes you," they chided. I couldn't understand why they were being this way. They said I was different—not like them or anyone else—which is why I would never have a friend. It was awful.

I told them they were wrong because I did indeed have a friend.

They laughed and laughed. "Who?" they chided. "Who would be *your* friend?"

I told them I had an Indian friend who lived in the bushes behind the Texaco gas station and learned things by listening to the ground.

At this they laughed even louder. Our teacher came over to see what the joke was, and they told her about my Indian.

She smiled patronizingly at me. "Indians live on special Indian reservations. They don't live here in town with us."

"Well, maybe so, but this one lives here in town," I maintained. And I stuck to my story with such vehemence she was very concerned. She threatened to go to those very bushes I described and prove there were no Indians in there. Right in front of my fellow students, she said it was important to confront me with my overactive imagination so I'd understand my imaginings weren't real. The kids snickered and chided some more at this, and I was very embarrassed and upset.

But I refused to back down. So that night, just after sundown, she went to Red Eagle's bushes. Thank God he was home, and a light was on! She could see a faint glimmer through the bushes, decided to take a chance, made her way to the cottage and timidly knocked on the door. Red Eagle received her with a pot of tea and accepted her proposal that he come to school the next day and entertain the class.

He arrived wearing his moccasins, leather snake-dance outfit and flamboyant feathery headdress he'd worn for his performances in his dad's Wild West Show of the 1880's. He'd always kept this wardrobe, together with his long hair he'd cut off when he came to live among white men, in a coffin-size wooden box at the foot of his bed.

He walked right into our classroom and took over. I was completely absolved. The kids were quite surprised. He took us out to the playground and taught us some Indian dances, telling us their purposes. He even showed us how to listen to the ground. He was teaching us beautiful things, but the boys behaved insanely around him, whooping, hollering and gaping at him like he was a freak. I was so embarrassed for them, I went over to the far end of the playground and sat against the stone wall there. I didn't want him to think I was like them, and was relieved when it was all over and he left.

Red Eagle and I grew very close in the precious couple of years that followed. Then one morning while I was in school, he went to work with his horse, a beautiful pinto stallion he kept at Bettie Greene stables, and the horse kicked him for the third time. Twice before, this spooky animal had warned by kicking him gently, but he'd thought his love for the horse would prevail.

He knew everything about horses, but about this horse he was wrong. That third kick was a mean one. He fell to the ground, unconscious and bleeding internally. Bettie, mom's closest friend, found him and phoned for an ambulance which took him to Monterey County Hospital.

That same afternoon, I happened to go by the stables to see Bettie. For I often spent my days there, helping her with the stable chores and eating from the 200-pound pile of grotesque but delicious and fragrant organic carrots she kept for the horses. I loved listening to music on the radio in her office where she would sit with me reading her *True Confessions* magazines.

Like her horses, she was a radiantly healthy vegetarian. Her tack room was filled with horse medicines that cured human ailments also, and she was a walking encyclopedia of information on what to do in any sort of contingency. She had more common sense in her little finger than all the legislative bodies in the land.

Very sadly, Bettie told me what had become of my best friend. She'd tried to convince the ambulance drivers to take him to Carmel Memorial Hospital where wealthy folks were taken. But the drivers saw an old Indian in old clothes, figured he had no money, and insisted on taking him to County Hospital—not as well equipped or staffed and popularly known as the "pest ward."

So Red Eagle lay unattended in the Emergency Room at County Hospital until he breathed his last. There were just not enough doctors there, Bettie said. She'd closed up the stable, followed the ambulance and done what she could there to get him some medical attention. But there was none to be had. He was 79.

"Why didn't they take him to Memorial?" I asked in tears. "He was the richest man in Carmel. No one else knew how to listen to the ground. No one else knew about music the way he did," I sobbed. Bettie hugged me, but even she had no answer. I cried all afternoon and evening and far into the night, unable to eat or sleep.

The town of Carmel is very proud of having been Red Eagle's chosen place of final residence. And though, over the years, they've torn down his cottage and bushes, paved the entire lot with asphalt and built a shopping mall on it, they've erected a fine plaque there that says, "Red Eagle Alley." And a splendid portrait photo of him hangs in the Carmel City Library.

There was no one to console me over Red Eagle's loss but Bucky, the big loving black dog who lived next door to us. He was a cross between springer spaniel and German shepherd and had the most soulful eyes of anyone. His owner, Mrs. Beaudeau, an aloof old Frenchwoman, didn't appreciate him much and made him live outside. Mom was so busy with her theatre rehearsals, I lived pretty much on my own too. So Bucky and I got together and were fellow outcasts.

He was closer to me than anyone. Though he had one other friend, a little brown mouse who lived in the tool shed in Mrs. Beaudeau's front garden. Bucky would lie down on his stomach when he saw the mouse coming, and the mouse would climb up and sit on his extended huge downy paws. Bucky would rest his snout upon his legs, and the two of them would confer. The mouse would shake and move to and fro, as though telling a tale by charade, while Bucky would make sympathetic whiny sounds in response, his soulful eyes showing the deepest sympathy.

Mice and dogs don't generally relate, but these two found each other bewitching. Several times I found them thus engaged in conversation as I would drop by. Many special souls like these two lived in Carmel. That's just the way things were.

Bucky and I made countless trips to the nearby city dump finding treasures. And when I would come home at night and find Mom still out, our cottage dark and empty, it was all right. For Bucky would be there, lying down under his tree between our two little houses, and he would eagerly jump up to greet me.

But it was cold at night when I got home. Our cottage had no heat source but the fireplace, and I could never learn to get a fire started in it with the green firewood Mom got for free from a friend. And the lights didn't work, for Mom was too poor and busy to replace burned-out bulbs. Only she knew how to get one or two of them lit.

So I'd generally leave and go down to the manure box at Bettie's. The deep, 8-foot- square box had an outside entrance. She always locked the stable but left the manure box unlocked. If anyone wanted to steal the manure, it was all right. Though no one ever did. A filled manure box is warm, like a sauna bath, even on the coldest nights. So I would sit in there and get warm very quickly. I liked the smell of manure. Betty smelled of it, as did the horses and everyone else around the stable. I didn't realize I smelled of it too.

Mom, when she had the time, would try to get me to take off my clothes—which I slept in because it was so cold—and take a bath. I always refused because it was so cold in our bathroom my teeth would chatter. When necessary I would bolt and escape if she became too insistent. I learned to hate being cold, and my nose ran almost constantly.

But being allowed to meander and discover the world by myself, in the sparsely populated pristine Carmel Woods of the 1940's, was a great boon. A half-dozen or more neighborhood dogs walked me to school each day. If hungry, I'd eat what the neighborhood kids referred to as "sourgrass." It grew in abundance along all the roadsides and on all the town's empty lots. These tall, juicy stems of grass had bright, yellow-petal blossoms. One could gather a fistful of these stems and have a feast of tart, delicious, fruity-tasting food and juice. There were probably more vitamins, minerals and good things in a fistful of this grass than in a whole plateful of ordinary food.

Allowed to meander and discover the world by myself in the sparsely populated pristine Carmel Woods of the 1940s.

Sougrass and Bettie's horse carrots were the extent of my diet much of the time, other than for school lunches. We kids were allowed to eat as much as we wanted at no extra charge during those years at Sunset School. I took them seriously and spent my entire lunch hour filling and emptying my plate at least three times, while the other kids would quickly wolf down a single helping and then go play football. One day the worried school nurse came to chat with me as I sat alone in the cafeteria eating my third or fourth helping.

"Young man, you certainly have an appetite. You may have a tapeworm. Do you know what that is?"

"Uh, no."

She gazed at me with loving concern. She was most definitely worried and very serious. She never did find out from me that this was my one hot meal of the day, because I didn't think to tell her. For it never occurred to me that there might be anything unusual about my life. But I did tell her I played the guitar and liked Burl Ives. She was a Burl Ives fan too. So we had much in common, and we talked about music until I'd finished my fourth helping of beans.

I'd never thought of being a public performer. But one evening Mom took me along to the cast reading of her new play. It was held at the magnificent Kuster stone castle on ten spooky acres of deep forest at the edge of the beach near Carmel Point. Ted Kuster, Mom's producer-director and owner of Carmel's Golden Bough Theater, was respected worldwide. He was known as "Mr. Theatre" in the loftiest circles, owing to a personality so powerful that when I close my eyes, even to this day, I can see the wrinkles in his smiling face.

He sat in his jumbo-size, very comfortable leather-upholstered chair. Beside him stood his old wrought iron standing lamp with a softly glowing, translucent leather shade. The cast all sat around him with copies of the new play, Arthur Miller's *All My Sons*. Kuster had brought in the enormously gifted veteran actor, Forest Barnes, all the way from New York to co-star with Mom as Joe Keller. Mr. Barnes was a blend of James Whitmore and Edgar G. Robinson, and the equal of either. The reviewers used to remark that Mom looked a lot like Greer Garson, possessing similar poise and eclat.

The players read their lines with such power and clarity, such perfect timing and expertise, and the script was so well written,

I was very taken by it all as I sat quietly in a corner. Mom read with awesome brilliance, making me feel very proud of her. The chemistry between her and Mr. Barnes was perfect. But suddenly the actors stopped.

Silence.

Kuster looked up, momentarily lost and helpless. "We need a 9-year-old boy. Where's a 9-year-old boy?" He seemed to be mentally groping, trying to remember where he'd put his pencil. He looked around the room, and his gaze fell upon me—a boy of nine years. His face brightened.

"Bud, how would you like to be in the play?"

He'd forgotten to cast a small role, that of a boy named Burt, and the reading had stopped because they'd come to the place where Burt makes his entrance. I was speechless. Kuster looked over at Mom who shrugged. He looked back at me. "Can you read, young man?"

"Sort of."

"Here. Take this book. See where Burt speaks? Try reading it."

I stammered through the first line. My scene was with Mr. Barnes. He read his line in response, and I continued. We got through the entire scene, and Kuster was pleased. He smiled at me—a most significant and loving smile. That felt good, for he'd never before treated me as much more than a piece of luggage Mom occasionally brought around to the rehearsals.

"That'll do," he said approvingly. "It might work. Would you like to be Burt in the play?"

"Sure, O.K."

"Well, we'll see."

Mom worked with me the next day. I learned my lines and was given the role. I had two scenes, both with Mr. Barnes. On opening night every seat in the theatre was filled. I found the large Golden Bough audience frightening, but Mr. Barnes was a solid professional. Sensing my problem, he stared hard at me as we did our scenes. He stared so hard that all my fear disappeared in the wake of my wonderment at his behavior. It was clever of him. How else does one get a non-actor kid to become an actor in one split second? Surprise him. It worked beautifully. The reviews were super, and the play was held over for several extended runs.

I would generally get sleepy, being up so late every night. So I formed the habit of dozing between my scenes atop a dusty, folded, quarter-ton pair of velvet stage curtains out of sight high up in the backstage loft. One night I fell so soundly asleep I missed my cue, and Mr. Barnes had to ad lib. Somehow his ad libbing woke me up, perhaps because something was different. What a blessing! I scrambled down the loft ladder and got onstage so fast the audience never knew.

But Kuster knew. After curtain call he stalked backstage and roared until everyone shook, "Where was Burt? Why was Burt late?" He found me and scolded so harshly I'll never forget. He made me sit up in a folding chair between scenes after that.

I got so tired during this period, that one day I left my little guitar out in the patio unprotected. Then, of course, it rained. The least expensive replacement guitar at the Browse Around was 50 dollars, far too vast a sum for me. But there was a guitar offered in the Montgomery Ward Catalogue for only 10 dollars including shipping. So I found another comic book ad offering a money-making scheme that involved selling seeds. I ordered and sold the seeds, and got a real, full-size, wooden guitar from Montgomery Ward. I was lucky, for it had a clear resonant tone. I was so happy with it I increased my practice time, and my skill grew exponentially.

A few years later, Mom took a hiatus from her acting. We rented out our Carmel cottage and moved to Laguna Beach for a few months. Mom rented us a beach apartment right on the sand at the foot of Thalia Street. I was twelve. The weather was much warmer than in Carmel, and the ocean was warm enough for swimming. So I swam a lot out in front of our apartment, enjoyed gathering hordes of seagulls with stale bread, got suntanned, and washed away the sea salt in our landlady's unique outdoor steam shower. Once a dirty stable boy, I was now a clean, tanned, freckle-faced kid.

There was an annual music festival there for young musicians. I took my guitar to the tryouts and was accepted. The show was held at the high school auditorium. Mom attended and was so pleased with me she wrote a letter to Grandma about it. For some reason the letter got returned, somehow saved, and then it fell into my possession. I recently found it in a pile of old papers. She wrote,

Wednesday, May 23 . . .

We just got home from the music festival—finale for the whole year—and I am frankly so flabbergasted that I feel like calling you long distance and asking you what to do now. I must have mentioned to you at various times Bud's ability on the guitar and how he plays for groups whenever they ask him. But I had never heard him until tonight and I almost didn't go tonight. As Dina says, it gets so monotonous hearing him work, work and work on his music at home that we often feel relieved when he's off playing for somebody else. Sometimes we even make him go in the garage to practice.

Tonight was a huge program of very talented children on whom fortunes had undoubtedly been spent. They were so darling. Each piano student seemed excellent to me—much better than I could do—which isn't saying much I know. But instead of being bored, I was fascinated and the enormous audience seemed fascinated too. There was even a nine-year-old accordion player that was out of this world—and all kinds of instruments and singing, etc. Then, without any warning, I saw Bud sitting casually on some box with a spotlight on him and everything else dark. My heart pounded with fear for him. It seemed cruel to me to put him on a program with finished children artists. He smiled a crooked little smile so that the audience laughed before he played his first note, which also scared me. But then he started playing, and *filled that auditorium* with the sweetest tones I've ever heard him make. I still can't understand it and neither can Dina. We both think we must be crazy or something. Every note was distinct. The music came from inside him and he played with infectious joy. That audience went wild. They shouted, stomped and cheered. Bud said that he had been told before that there were so many children to perform that no encores were allowed. So he tried to get back through the curtains as best he could—bowing, walking a few steps, bowing again. I counted at least six bows. He was squeezing the rag dry, I was afraid. But they chuckled and clapped long after he had disappeared.

After the performance enthusiastic admirers surrounded us and I was wishing I had at least bothered to dress up. They told me Bud was a natural showman with rare ability, and they couldn't believe he had never had any lessons. Maybe Jack is right. He's been saying for two years now that Bud will never have to work for a living. Fortunately I know the dangers of what Bud overheard tonight and know how to combat it. Children are natural artists, if they are artists at all, and it is cruel to give them heady wine that they can't stand up under. But people don't think of that and ruin many a budding genius by thoughtlessness.

It's a shame you couldn't have been there. No audience ever cheered me that way. A few of them have rolled in the aisles so that I went crazy ad libbing, but they never clapped like that.

It was quite an experience for mama—and a shock.

A kindly couple, who'd been in the audience at the music festival, contacted me at school the following week and offered me my first professional concert. It was an evening performance, held in their large living room, for about 50 or so in rows of folding chairs. I wasn't all that nervous and found it kind of fun. They sat quietly and listened to me play my guitar compositions for more than an hour. They also paid me nine dollars which I used as down payment for a Martin classical guitar, a true concert instrument.

I spent my afternoons, after school, playing tennis with members of the high school tennis team. On weekends, I figured out how to raise the money to pay the balance of what I owed on the guitar by selling laundry soap gotten from a chemical company. It was really good soap, better than what you could get at the supermarket. So I developed a return trade and soon earned enough for a sturdy case as well.

When we returned to Carmel, after some months in Laguna, we found the Golden Bough had burned down. There was no more theatre, so Mom and Jack decided to move to Los Gatos where he could find work. For while we'd been in Laguna, he'd gone to Arizona and lost everything in a failed flagstone quarry enterprise with his Uncle Roy.

So we sold our Carmel Woods cottage and bought an empty lot located on a tree-festooned hill above Los Gatos, a small, inland town about 60 miles north. The site commanded a view of distant Stanford University's Hoover Tower, and Jack spent a year building us a fine house on it. During construction we rented a house on another hill that adjoined the picturesque unfenced Novitiate wine grape vineyard where I would often take my guitar to practice, the better to be alone with my music and not disturb Mom.

One warm golden afternoon in the vineyard, as I practiced a difficult passage on my fine new concert guitar, I looked up in surprise to see a tall smiling priest in dark clothing standing over me. I think he'd been standing there for some time. But I hadn't noticed him, being so focused on the intricacies of the music. He saw, from the bare grape stems next to me, that I'd been sampling some of the Church of Rome produce.

I don't remember our first words, but he seemed tolerant that I'd been trespassing and stealing. He seemed to understand that he'd come upon a dreamer who was truly unaware that this bit of earth and its contents were Church property, not quite the same as public property. After making these facts quite clear to me, he then said, to my amazement, that I may have as many grapes as I wished.

He invited me to walk with him to a nearby venerable garden where there was a statue of Jesus in the middle of a fountain pond. He pointed to the holy words carved into the stone base of the statue, "The truth shall make you free."

"What does this mean to you?" he asked.

I wrestled mentally and observed, "well, lies make us their prisoners, and truth frees us. But I think Jesus was telling us something more than that. I think He was saying that when we understand the truth of our oneness with God, we're automatically free of our mortality."

He appeared both surprised and impressed. "That's quite good, my son. You have a fine understanding, don't you." Shrewdly he then asked, "and why are we mortal?"

That was tricky, and I wrestled with it several seconds. "I think we're not really mortal. We're only dreaming."

He looked down into the pond, smiled and chuckled. Then, putting his hand on my shoulder, he invited me to follow him to a fine patio where we sat and chatted, and he asked me to play him some more of my music. The acoustics were very good in this patio, due to some high stone walls, and my guitar sounded rich and warm.

After perhaps a half-hour, I stopped playing. For I sensed he might have more to do in life than sit and hear me play. We introduced ourselves. His name was Father Charleton, and he was in charge of the Novitiate.

"Do you know what a troubadour is?" he asked. I didn't know, and he began to instruct me. He had an impressive knowledge of music and music history. And he seemed imbued with his devotion to God and his faith that love is the answer to all things. His love and faith were so pure and strong that he seemed a kind of angel with much more to him than the black-clothed figure that sat before me. I felt so loved by him, so honored to be in his presence and have his attention, that it all began to overwhelm me. And I'm afraid I couldn't concentrate on many of the words he spoke.

I told him how I'd often dreamed of visiting exotic places in far off lands.

"Do you believe the people in the places you dream of are motivated by love?" he inquired.

"Sure," I said, "because they have good in them. And they're probably sitting there as curious about me as I am about them."

He liked that so much he musingly repeated it. Then he laughed and said I could be a troubadour. He referred me to the Britannica Encyclopedia article on the subject and told me troubadours traveled around playing their music without using money as a means of exchange. They played directly for everything they needed. A troubadour may possess money, even earn it, but may never spend it else he forego a chance at enjoying the pleasures of guest friendship wherever he eats, sleeps, or rides on a conveyance. The second principle that distinguishes a troubadour, he said, is that he's not just a vagabond who plays his music for his keep. He is, in addition, a court performer who entertains kings and other royalty in their palaces.

That impressed me so much I've never forgotten. He gave me a huge bunch of grapes as we parted. "It's only for a moment," he said, for he saw that I was sad at parting company with him. He invited me to come again very soon and sent me on my way.

I could speak to my family of little but Father Charleton long after. Father Charleton this and Father Charleton that. I began thinking I might really like to be exchanging music directly for everything and playing for kings in palaces. What a truly special life it would be! I began contemplating a life lived purely by this "troubadour code," unblemished by even a single payment of money for anything. I envisioned living this life until I could make it all the way around the entire earth at least one time, surrendering myself to whatever adventures this life might bring.

Father Charleton warned me I would find insanities and paradoxes, but I could always deal with them using my two most powerful weapons, love and faith.

"No matter what your predicament," he said, "if you can give enough love, you will find it in others, and you'll be all right. And you must use your faith to believe this to be so."

This exquisite man further told me that if I could give enough love to stay free of predicaments, I would become an ambassador for love. And that, he said, is the highest post anyone can achieve. Then, most helpfully, he added that any adversary, no matter how repugnant, is made in God's image. And therefore if, remembering this, I could feel sufficient faith in the wisdom and love that guided even my adversaries, they would cease to be adversaries at once and become allies.

I knew I'd been very privileged to meet such a wise man, and that there was little but fear and doubt standing between such a glorious adventure and me. I also knew fears and doubts have no power other than that which we give them.

We moved into our house on Live Oak Avenue that Jack built for us, and Mom married him there. We had a Mormon priest friend of Jack's come and perform a simple marriage ceremony in the living room. Mom and Jack remained steadfastly in love—and together—for the remainder of their years.

I attended Los Gatos High School, never forgetting Father Charleton's counsel. During those 4 years, I found the time, despite being in training for a procession of tennis tournaments, to play Monday nights at the Kerosene Club, a showcase nightclub for musicians in nearby San Jose. You had to be 21, and I was only 16. But I got to play for several months before the local inspector from Alcoholic Beverage Control happened by one night and put an end to it.

I was accepted at Principia College where I studied drama and journalism. During one Summer Break, the Summer of 1959, I took my guitar and rucksack to the Hawaiian Islands, hitchhiking to six of the islands by private airplane. I found I could walk into an airport coffee shop where the pilots ate, play a little and quickly gather an audience. After the applause, I would announce that I was looking for a ride to another island.

Sometimes two or more pilots would offer me a ride. When I got to an island, I'd sit in the park, play, gather an audience, and announce that I needed a place to stay. People would invite me to their homes where I would often give another concert for them and their friends. People took turns looking after me, and there was plenty to eat. It was all happening just like Father Charleton said.

I was on the floor shows at Waikiki's Don The Beachcombers, Hilo's Lava Pit and Kauai's Club Jetty in Nawiliwili Harbor. Some archaeologists took me to Kauai's Valley of the Lost Tribe in Nualolokai where we got stranded without water and faced certain death for a couple of days. A Bishop Museum expedition rescued us, and I wound up at Wailua Beach where beach boys took me in. They gave me delicious food and allowed my sleeping in their beach shack at night in trade for guitar lessons.

Honolulu Advertiser columnist, Bob Krauss, wove it all into an adventure tale that filled an entire day's column, saying my Hawaiian travels were, "as romantic as anything you'll find in Robert Louis Stevenson."

I became so encouraged that in the Summer of 1960 I visited several European countries with similar results. In Paris I traded away my Martin guitar for a handmade masterpiece by Parisian luthier Jacques Camurat. It had better action, character and depth of tone. Later, in London, I found a 70-year-old, Madrid-made, Casa Gonzales guitar that sang even better than the Camurat and traded into that. It had the finest mother-of-pearl inlay of any guitar I'd ever seen. Discovering music on this guitar was such pure joy I would lose all track of time.

My love for music took over my life. I was so obsessed with it, both night and day, I was barely able to complete my studies at Principia in June of 1961. So I got a Kelty pack and visited Mom and Jack, who'd sold our Los Gatos home and moved to Bodega Bay, California, telling them of my resolve to make it all the way around the world as a troubadour. I planned to play for royalty and such potentates who could grant me transport across oceans. I would not use money as a means of exchange for food, lodging or transportation even once, until I had made it clear around the world back to California again. They liked the idea.

"It's something you can only do while you're young," Jack said.

"Do it now while you can," Mom added. "When you're older, you'll never do it. Always remember, it's the man you perceive in the man you speak to who speaks back to you. You're at home, wherever you are, because God is there."

Jack made me a strong polyethylene sack big enough to hold all of me, my guitar and Kelty pack on rainy nights. Mom made me a chest pouch, with a neck strap, to hold my passport and other valuables. They drove me to nearby U.S. Highway 40 that would take me eastward for the first 3,000 miles. They parked in the shadow of a tree and watched tearfully as I stood and thumbed my first car. It was an emotionally trying moment for us all. But it proved to be an important one, for it marked the beginning of a world tour so enchanting it has haunted my life.

That first car was a VW Beetle driven by a 30-year-old American war vet. His shoulder-length hair was all white, and he told me a bizarre story en route to Reno. One night, somewhere in Southeast Asia, as he and his small patrol of war buddies were asleep under the stars in hostile jungle, they were attacked by an enemy patrol who'd quietly slit the throat of their man on watch. They then fell upon the rest of his party who were zipped up in their mummy bags asleep and helpless.

My white-haired host woke up in time to see what was happening and roll himself underneath a thick bush where he lay undetected, watching his buddies mercilessly bayoneted to death as they screamed in pain for mercy. The enemy patrol then looted the carcasses and left as my host watched, paralyzed with terror, safely hidden under the bush, but in such a state of shock his hair turned all white in the following weeks.

Since that time, he said, he'd never felt he could trust anyone. And with that, he quickly produced and brandished a chromed, Smith & Wesson. 44 six-shooter from the car door pocket. But I allowed myself to trust him and didn't flinch. He was pleased.

"I'm always prepared," he said darkly. Re-pocketing the gun, he told me stories about frailties in our government, human foibles and dark deeds he'd seen. I inwardly affirmed the love in him, and he grew friendlier as he talked.

Father Charleton had told me to trust in the love that guided others. "If you can give enough love, you'll find it in others and be all right," he'd said.

We had a harmonious journey as far as Reno. I was so grateful, both for his having defended America and for giving me this first ride of my world tour, I felt sad to leave him. But Reno was his destination, and he let me off in the middle of town.

My new Kelty pack felt light as I strapped it on. I carried it and my guitar along a Reno avenue and entered an intimate sidewalk casino that emanated a nice vibration. Folks were pensively engaged in both blackjack and roulette. I sat on a barstool among them, began playing background music, and got some approving glances. So I stepped up the energy level by playing some flamenco, and the entire casino broke out in applause. I climbed off the stool. As I put away the guitar, an older man approached me.

"You can play a little can't you," he said.

"Thank you, sir."

He was the club owner. He invited me to have dinner with him, and I accepted his offer of a free hotel room, meals, and a job playing there for the upcoming weekend. I told him of my quest to see the world without using money as a means of exchange. His eyes glowing with enthusiasm, he asked how I planned to get across the Atlantic when I got to the East Coast. I didn't know yet.

"Tell you what. I'll give you a ticket on Icelandic Airlines."

It was truly beginning to look as though the whole world was in a conspiracy to see that I got looked after, and I could hardly believe my good fortune.

It took only three or four rides to make New York. As I hitchhiked across North

America, absorbing the awesome beauty of the Rocky Mountains, I felt the expansive sense of freedom you feel having your "residence" on your back so that your address changes minute to minute as you go along.

My troubadour life combined this freedom with that of being independent of money. Whether I had little or lots of money, it didn't matter because I was on a different standard. It was like visiting legendary Eldorado where the streets are paved with gold, and heartfelt love is the medium of exchange. Troubadours enjoy a very special niche where nothing costs money. A troubadour gives of himself instead. In response, things are done for him out of love and not for money. This exchange is arguably the greatest charm of the troubadour experience.

But certainly not the least of the charms is that the troubadour, always a stranger who's just arrived in town, loves and trusts his audience just because they're people. He knows or cares little about people's character weaknesses or past sins. The audience responds with the same attitude, and the troubadour is enjoyed on the grounds that he's a fellow human—one with a tune who is free.

And free I was, destined to make this exchange with ruling, palace-dwelling monarchs, hashish-smoking Bedouins, custodians of castles, terrorists, Casbah-dwelling Arabs, and a whole camel caravan of desert-dwelling champagne smugglers. I found them mostly good and with much in common.

2

Performing in the palace of
HM King Frederick IX

The plane took me to Amsterdam, and I wandered over to Rembrandt Square. It was a warm Summer evening, and there were gondolas floating in a pretty canal. Bearded artists displayed their paintings along the cobblestone streets, and amorous couples lingered in the shadows of hand-sculptured 17th century buildings. The numerous little outdoor cafes, filled with customers, presented a bohemian appeal with their crooked little wrought iron tables and chairs among colorful potted plants. It was the perfect setting for a troubadour.

I was still new at being in places where English was not generally spoken and still felt a little lost at not being able to speak with anyone I pleased. But I was starting to learn that I could ease this feeling by playing music. I sat down at one of the tables and began to play, lifted by a budding awareness that music speaks to everyone.

Some elderly women were particularly appreciative. They brought me some paper money, putting it on my guitar case and placing an ashtray on it. I felt grateful and played them my new sonata in four movements. When the elder ladies left, an unescorted young woman, who'd also been listening, invited me to sit down with her. I was about to oblige her when two very tall, very angry policemen came up from behind me. One of them grabbed me by the ear and spun me around to face him.

"Passport," he ordered with a scowl.

"But officer, what is the matter?"

"Passport," he repeated. The young lady looked nervous.

I produced it, and he glanced at its pages briefly. "You must come with us to the police station."

With a regretful wave to the lady, I went with my two captors along a canal lined with outdoor art galleries to the Rembrandt Square police headquarters. They made me sit in a holding cell pending the arrival of the supervisor who spoke better English. I was allowed to keep my belongings, so I used the time to practice my sonata. I was sad but not afraid. For I sensed that these men were very bright, and that the problem, whatever they perceived it to be, would be ironed out soon. I resolved to have faith in the wisdom and love that guided these Dutch police, for Father Charleton had said this would cause adversaries to become allies.

The supervisor arrived, found me playing and listened. He sat with me and explained about the local "beggar law." One had to be a licensed beggar to do what I'd done. To get a license one had to be a Dutchman and be able to prove inability to get a job. He decided to let me go with a warning since I hadn't solicited money, and the money the ladies had put on my guitar case was totally volunteered. Next time though, I would be fined 25 guilders. If unable to pay I would have to spend 30 days in jail. And as I didn't use money as a means of exchange, it would be the latter for me.

He most lovingly concluded our interview by shaking my hand warmly and telling me ("off the record") to play only when his officers weren't looking. For it would be their obligation to arrest me again if they saw me playing in the street.

I was grateful for his kindness but sorry at the state of things. I could see the wisdom of this "beggar law," as it helped clean the streets of panhandlers. But the law is crude and cumbersome, I thought to myself, for it cannot discriminate between artists and beggars.

At a nearby produce center I met a farmer driving a truckload of hay, and he took me with him all the way to Scandinavia where I spent a few weeks. One of the kind souls there, who picked me up as I stood thumbing a ride, was Rynar Evenson, harpsichordist for the Copenhagen Symphony, who took me to his home in Fredrickstad.

A magnificently talented musician, he played for me on his fabulous harpsichord. I played for him too. He arranged that I ride on a train to Oslo and tape a one-hour radio special of my compositions in Studio A at Norsk Rikskringkasting, Oslo's finest recording studio.

The man in charge was very pleased and told me the special would be aired all over Scandinavia. As though all this wasn't enough, he paid me 150 Norwegian kroner for broadcast rights. I now had a nice little stake of money to keep in my chest pouch next to my passport—not that it mattered of course.

And soon I found another appreciative audience in Scandinavia—a quiet group of philosophical sailors at a seaman's mission in Sweden. Among this audience was another Rynar—Rynar the fisherman—who took me across the Kattegat Channel to Denmark early the next morning in his boat.

A cold, stiff morning breeze whipped our faces and stirred the sea, creating swells that dumped water over the bow as we motored past Elsinore Castle.

"There's the castle where Hamlet saw the ghost," Rynar yelled to me, laughing over the salty wind that cut like a knife, his half-frozen, weathered face shining in the sun. He pointed over his pile of fish to the cannon-festooned ramparts that grew like a blossom from the rocky cliff on the Danish side of the channel.

"Ah. So this is Elsinore, home of Hamlet, the royal Dane—victim of indecision. I too, Rynar, will grapple with indecision one day. I feel it in my bones."

"No, it is all Shakespeare's invention," he protested, steering the boat.

"Yes, but I'm told that he based his Hamlet story on historical fact—that it did actually occur here in ages past."

The castle appeared bright and clear in the morning sun as the surf lashed at the granite rocks beneath it—a truly magnificent sight.

Rynar stood beside me and viewed the scene philosophically. "When you see it every day, as I do, you get used to it. You, being a visitor, are happy because the castle is beautiful. But the beauty of this castle does not put food on my table, so it does not make me happy at all. I am happy because my boat is full of fish, and the price of fish is high. So I will eat good."

"Rynar, you are a pragmatist. I am an artist, and in the beauty of this castle I find sustenance. So we are different. I'm glad that we're not all the same."

"But how are you going to eat?" he inquired with concern. "You have no money."

"Oh, I have a few shekels, but I don't spend money for things. Troubadours don't do that."

"Then, in effect, you have no money," he maintained in his practical way.

"True, but I'll play until someone offers food as people often do. That's why I love people so. They're kind."

He shook his head. "No one in Denmark will feed you unless you pay them."

"But I do pay them—with music."

He grinned. "Because you gave our group an evening of free entertainment at the seaman's mission and then said you were hitchhiking to Denmark, I invited you to come in my boat. But people generally are not that way. They will take your free show, then walk away and leave you."

I was surprised at his pessimism. "I do hope you're wrong."

He adjusted our speed and then pointed in the direction from which we'd come. "You could easily have charged fifty kroner for that show you gave, paid two kroner for the ferry to Elsinore and gotten to Denmark with a 48 kroner profit."

"But I'd not have met you and ridden on your fishing boat. You did me a service out of kindness and generosity. This means more than money to a troubadour."

He saw my point and thought about it. Then he said, "Maybe you will play for our King Frederick. His Summer palace is in Fredensberg, and he's there now. His Majesty might enjoy hearing you. He's very liberal, up-to-date, and might even feed you."

It sounded like a good idea, and I began thinking about it.

It was a great relief when we entered the harbor at Helsinger, got out of the wind and gently motored through a nest of other boats toward the unloading pier.

After we docked, I checked in with immigration at the nearby ferry landing and headed for Copenhagen, its cold-water flats, statues, fountains and museums.

I found the place where Rynar had said there was a pretty outdoor café in a vast flower garden. It was a large café, full of happy customers, and it was a splendid day. Putting on my guitar with a shoulder strap, I began strolling among the tables and playing. Per

European tradition, people put coins in my pockets as I passed by. In five minutes I'd worked my way from one end of the café to the other, and my pockets were bulging with these coins.

A pale and rotund man in his mid forties, who looked a tiny bit like the actor, Charles Laughton, was seated alone with a mug of beer. At his invitation, I sat with him. His suit was very worn and ill-fitting, and he wore a soiled, tattered hat that he'd propped on an empty chair.

"You appear to be a shrewd young man. That was the quickest, easiest, legally made money I've ever seen made," he said with a nod at my pregnant pockets. Smiling, he sat back in his chair and studied me as he clasped his hands together beneath his heavily pocked face accented by a bulbous Roman nose. ". . . But then you are an artist. One can easily see that—a true artist."

I noticed the hole in the elbow of his suit jacket. His shirt cuffs were hopelessly frayed. He took a hasty look at his watch, grabbed a paper from his bruised and dirty briefcase, put on a pair of old, bent spectacles and perused it importantly. I think he was just pretending to be busy.

"Hmm," he said, turning back to me. "Now then. I haven't much time unless you are willing to cooperate with my plan completely. I have an idea for you to better yourself to our mutual benefit. My name is Christian. I am Danish, although I've been to school in England. I have several contacts among important restaurateurs about town, and I believe it would be to their advantage, mine and yours, if you were to place your art at their disposal during certain hours of the day."

Such a pompous talker he was, with his queen's English accent. "You want to be my agent?" I asked.

"Yes, for a price—a high one. My time is too occupied at the moment for me to even bother with a hundred percent of your profits, but I'm interested in you as a person. Therefore, as impetus for you, I will take only fifty percent commission for myself." He folded his hands once again and placed them under his chin with elegant poise. He could have been posing for a portrait photograph.

"But agents usually take only ten or twenty percent," I gently protested.

"Fifty," he maintained with authority, raising his nose with an attempted air of dignity that came off as comedic. (That nose was just too bulbous!) "But if you'll obey me explicitly, I can assure you that fifty percent of your earnings under my management will be tenfold times a hundred percent of your present earnings. Well?"

I found him amusing, though he didn't intend to be so. Figuring the worst he might do would be to show me the town that I wanted to see anyway—and he might just lead us to something interesting—I consented. He told me that a gentleman was a man of his word. And as we were both gentlemen, there was no need to have a written contract. Half of my earnings, from this moment on, would be his, as long as I was under his management. He stood up, picked up his briefcase, donned his raggedy hat gingerly, with respect, as though it were made of platinum brocade on velvet, and walked out of the café like a prince. I followed.

He led me through archaic and crooked little streets past mildewed seventeenth-century tenement buildings. Odors of sweating mortar mingled with those of stale sewage. But to this man who led me, they might well have been rose-strewn perfumed paths to glory. His posture was impeccable—his chest inflated. Eventually we emerged into a better section of the city where he found our first restaurant. The main approach was up a gigantic marble stairway, beneath a crisp, purple canvas canopy and past two footmen who wore uniforms with gaudy cords and brass buttons.

Christian mounted the thickly carpeted stairs as though this was his own home. He pranced gallantly, smiled cordially and properly at the footmen, who were exchanging concerned glances at our approach, and entered the glitzy foyer where a massive, half-ton chandelier glowed softly above us.

A receptionist took possession of his briefcase and my knapsack, and a maitre d' escorted us to an impeccably set view table covered with a starched, white linen tablecloth on the far side of the room. We were each given a crystal-embossed, leather-bound menu.

Christian sipped some water, rattling the ice in his goblet with delight, and dabbed his lips with his white linen napkin. "Now then," he said in a low tone, "take out your guitar."

"Here? Now?" I felt intimidated by our surroundings.

He placed his folded hands on the table and assumed a stern face. "Do as I say. One of my conditions is that you must obey my instructions explicitly."

I got the guitar and put it on my lap.

"Now begin playing softly. Remember, *softly,*" he whispered.

Figuring the worst they could do was to throw us both out, I began playing a gentle, low-energy improvisation with long-sustained notes. As it was a quiet restaurant, my notes were clearly heard throughout the grand room.

He looked around impishly at the other patrons who were studiously ignoring us. "Not that softly. Give it more volume."

So I leaned a bit harder on the notes, and a nearby party of four in bow ties and fancy dress began frowning at us. Another table of elegantly dressed businessmen stopped eating, raised their eyebrows at each other and smirked derisively with nods in our direction.

I began to weaken and stopped playing.

"Continue!" he doggedly instructed. His face assumed a zealous glare. "Louder!"

Our waiter bustled over to us in haste. "I'm sorry, gentlemen, but you'll be disturbing the other customers with the music."

"Quite to the contrary," Christian protested with a confidant, engaging smile. "I think they would enjoy a bit of music. Let the young man play. He doesn't mind. Everyone is enjoying him."

"I'm so sorry, sir. He must stop playing."

"Where's your initiative, young man? You've a good thing here, and you don't know it."

The waiter turned to me. "If you insist on making music, you must leave."

"Why then we *will* leave," Christian angrily snapped. He stood up and ordered me to gather the guitar into its case. I followed as he grabbed his briefcase rudely from the receptionist and glided from the room with his huge nose so high it almost pointed to the chandelier.

As he walked down the posh steps, the outer sole separated from his left shoe and began to flap with each step he took. When we reached the sidewalk out front, the flapping got worse. It kept flapping for a block or so as he continued along the sidewalk without a word to me. He stopped, angrily tore it off and cast it into the gutter. Then he walked on. His clothes and hat were those of a bum and now his shoes as well. But he wore them all with the dignity of a marquise.

"Come," he said at last. "My friend owns another place down the street. I won't have those plebeian bourgeois pushing you around."

His friend's restaurant was packed with a boisterous private party eating spaghetti on linoleum tables. We sat down, and he wrote something on a scrap of paper from his briefcase. "Here. This is my mother's address in Odense. If you ever go to Odense, she'll care for your needs. I've written her a note on this paper, and it's valuable. Don't lose it." He handed it to me with tender care.

His friend then came over, and Christian introduced us. "This lad will play for the customers and charge you nothing for this first performance," he explained, "and music calms the savage beast."

The manager surveyed me and gave us a worried smile. "I do not think so. It might not be a good idea."

"What about in the bar?"

"You'd best ask the bartender," he advised.

Christian turned to me. "You stay here. I will go alone to the bartender and negotiate a palpable business arrangement." He got up and left.

My agent safely gone, I felt safe in asking the manager to give me paper bills in exchange for the heavy coins that were stressing the fabric of my front pockets and making me uncomfortable. He agreed. I poured the coins onto the table, and we began counting, organizing them into piles of five kroner.

Christian returned. "Ah, you are counting the money. How much is it?'

We ignored him, absorbed in keeping track of the amount. "Thirty-seven-sixty, seventy, thirty-eight-forty." The coins clanked and glittered as we pushed them into piles. "Sixty- five, seventy, eighty, eighty-five and twenty. Eighty-five kroner and twenty cents."

In full sincerity, Christian showed the whites of his eyes, behaving as might a hungry dog watching us eat steak. The manager gave me paper notes, gathered the coins in a bag and left us.

Christian's face glowed. "Ah, you're a rich young man. Come along to the bar with me, and you can buy me a drink."

"I'm a troubadour and therefore never buy food," I explained gently.

He laughed. "Well, just give me my half of the money, and I'll buy our drinks myself."

"But I had this money before we ever met and made our arrangement," I calmly reminded him.

He became very angry, and his veneer slipped. He lacked dignity for the first time. "The money is mine!" he whined.

"No, I'm sorry it isn't," I replied gently and with considerable regret. For I liked him and wanted in the worst way to make him happy. But I knew it wasn't right that he take my money. We both stood, and he faced me with an expression of both disregard and despair.

"Give me the paper."

"No. I have just explained to you. It's mine."

"No, the note to my mother."

I handed it to him. Very upset, he took the note in his hand, tore it into several pieces, crumpled them vigorously and put them into his pocket. Then, wearing a sneer so bitter as to be worthy of Charles Laughton's Captain Bligh, he wheeled about on his one good shoe and glided into the bar. I never saw him again.

Such a powerful scene he put on. I was very moved by it as I walked out into the street. I felt deeply sorry that such a noble soul was disappointed with me—even if it was only because of his warped view. I'd clearly had a narrow escape. I could see that my trek around the world had hidden dangers and realized that troubadours and agents belong to different worlds. As I walked along and discovered a centuries-old, dimly lit cobblestone alleyway, I resolved that if I met any more agents I would protect myself by telling them up front that I was a troubadour.

I was now in the Stroget, a bohemian part of town where artists lived in garrets and women sang out of their windows as they watered their flower boxes. The smell of good cooking attracted me to an intimate if expensive-looking bistro on the ground floor of an artfully gabled building along the old alleyway. It was half-full of quiet customers—a perfect place to play. I put my knapsack in a corner, sat at an empty table and began playing flamenco. There was immediate rapport. A well dressed old gentleman came over and gave me a 10-kroner note as he left.

In the far corner, a youngish man, also well dressed, was seated with two attractive ladies who kept looking at me and jabbering excitedly as I put my guitar away. The man rose and came over.

"Pardon me fellow, would you care to be our guest for dinner, or are you otherwise engaged this evening?" He seemed a bright, cultured and pleasant person. "Your music is very tasteful, and we thought we'd like to meet you." He was full of confidence and poise. I looked over at his table, and the two young ladies smiled in unison.

"I'd be delighted, sir."

Together we joined the ladies. We all introduced ourselves and had a scrumptious dinner, over which we talked of troubadours and kings. I felt soothed as the evening wore on—the encounter with Christian thankfully becoming a distant memory—and then the youngest, prettiest lady told me I was handsome.

Daybreak brought with it a host of Summer dragonflies. I found myself miles out of Copenhagen, abiding with this pretty lady in her country home. It's always sad when leaving your hostess, particularly such a friendly, talented sculptress as she with her quaint, garden cottage. But like Rynar the sailor, she'd talked to me about the king.

"He rides about in his gray Jaguar," she said. "He is, how you say, a horticulturist—he grows his own flowers. He is a swinger. He loves music and fun. Everyone loves him, and he would love you. You must go see him and play for him."

I stepped out to the main road that passed her cottage, and a farmer driving a small truck stopped to give me a ride and practice his English. "So you are going to Fredensburg, yes? To see the royal palace of course."

"Yes, sir."

"Ah, she is the most beautiful in the world. You must see the change of the guard. Everyone goes to see that. It is most impressive. And our King Frederick IX, he too is impressive. His Jaguar goes 150 kilometers an hour past my farm as he is driven from his headquarters in Copenhagen to his castle. He goes so fast that he is only a gray blur. But he is a kind man."

We came to a fork in the road. "I go left here. You go right. It is five kilometers to the castle. Good luck, my friend," he said as he drove off.

The road sign said "Kongsvey" (king's way), and I followed it on foot through several kilometers of lush meadows, glens and forests. Fresh water streams gurgled hither and yon between small ferns and hyacinths. Finally I arrived at the tiny village of Fredensburg, climbed the crest of a small hill and saw the palace for the first time. I couldn't believe how big and tall it was.

It was all white except for its tall, green, copper-topped minarets that protruded and shone dramatically in the sun above a layer of morning mist that partly clouded the lower portion. The front courtyard encompassed several acres. The grounds occupied mile after mile. Impeccable uniformed guards stood at the gate at stone-like attention, and a few early-morning tourists milled around taking snapshots.

It was an imposing and challenging sight for a troubadour to see. I looked at one guard standing at the magnificent iron gate, and the thought of making my intention known to him filled me with panic. But my young lady had been so sure it was the right thing for me to do. Father Charleton had said I should see friends in people I meet. "It's the man you perceive in the man you speak to who speaks back to you," Mom had said.

So I swallowed a lump, perceived a friend in this guard and said, "I would like an interview with His Majesty, King Frederick, in order to perform a concert for him. How would you suggest I proceed?"

Amazingly, the intelligent-looking guard surveyed me and looked downright interested. But he wasn't allowed to speak on duty. So he just pointed to a small, inviting white house about 50 yards inside the gate and ushered me in through a little door next to his guard box. It was a pleasant-looking cottage—nicely furnished and neatly maintained. I pressed the buzzer, and a short, wrinkled man answered dressed in vest and sport coat.

He gave me an unfeeling smile that showed all of his front teeth and gums. He seemed the kind of man you hate when he's opposed to you and worry about when he's with you.

"Yawse?"

On hearing my request, he blinked thoughtfully and surveyed me several times, perhaps unsure he could believe what he'd heard. "Well now, I don't quite know. I'm only the gardener—well, I am the landscape supervisor. I would suggest you inquire at the chancery in Copenhagen. His Majesty isn't here anyway. He's away in Arhus. In any case, please move along, young man. You have done a rather improper thing coming inside the gate." He gave me another large, gummy smile, and I headed for the gate feeling both put down and embarrassed.

But as I passed the guardhouse, a guard who'd been watching me emerged and invited me in for a chat. He looked friendly. "What happened over there?"

"He said King Frederick was in Arhus, and that I have to go to the chancery."

He grinned. "You want to play for His Majesty with that?" he asked, pointing to my guitar.

"Yep."

He kept grinning and stroked his chin. "Would you like some coffee and a biscuit?"

I was hungry and thirsty from my long walk, and the coffee smelled good. "Sure, thanks."

We chatted awhile. Then several more guards entered, after a change-over, and I played a ballade I'd composed—a simple one. The first guard told me His Majesty wasn't in Arhus at all, but in Copenhagen, and was due back around 6 p.m. They all snickered when they heard what the gardener had said, and I gathered they didn't like him very much. It was probably that gummy smile.

"Come back around 6:00," the first guard told me. "The guard on duty then will try and help you. That's all I can tell you right now. O.K?"

I understood completely and promised to return right at six. These guys were all right. Such good people! They gave me a whole sweet roll to put in my knapsack. I was delighted and walked out filled with optimism.

The midday crowds had now arrived to watch the changing of the guard. The entire front area was lined with busses loaded with tour groups. I joined one of them as they listened to their tour guide speak in broken English.

" . . . And these grounds," he said, pointing to the miles of royal real estate inside the gate, "have seen some of the most illustrious noblemen of all Denmark. Generations of kings and princes have lived out their privileged lives here. Hamlet's blood may be mixed into this very soil."

"Ooh!" chorused some of the tourists.

"Queen Elizabeth has passed through this gate, as have dozens of crown heads from Europe, Russia and Asia."

"Ah!" they sighed.

I went off to explore Fredensberg, the quaint old village down the road, but returned at 6 p.m. Rain was starting to pour, but a guard standing at attention in his wooden cubicle saw me, stepped out and let me through the gate without a word. He pointed across the 300 yards of open courtyard to the right wing of the castle. Then, like a robot, he marched back to his wooden box and resumed his rigid pose.

If I was afraid of what I was attempting, the fear was smothered by my haste to get across those 300 yards to the shelter of an eve or doorway. I got under the eve of the right wing and followed it around to the rear. The rain became so intense I actually ran to a garage-size door I found there. It was ajar, so I stepped inside before thinking one way or the other about it.

The massive door closed behind me with a creak and loud latch click. I was now safe from the rain in a dark old stable that had been converted to a garage. And there in front of me was His Majesty's famous gray Jaguar.

Then I heard what sounded like a dishwasher or compressor. I investigated and found it to be only a noisy pipe. Imagine. Noisy plumbing—even in His Majesty's castle.

There were two opposing garage exits—the first was a staircase, probably leading to the royal chambers. I peeked through the second, to my left, and found the royal kitchen. I opted for the kitchen—the scullery maids and the cooks. Here was a place to play, gather an audience and perhaps something to eat.

I entered the kitchen as though I were a new staff member, walked straight to one of the kitchen sinks, washed my hands with soap and warm water and dried them using a clean hand towel hanging there. After all this, I was still unchallenged and my confidence grew.

So I uncased the guitar and sat with it in a chair next to a pretty pair of scullery maids engaged in peeling potatoes. I began playing a soulful study I'd written in the tune- structure style of renaissance Granada and quickly became absorbed in it. The maids listened and kept peeling. I built the piece to a climax that ended with a flamenco rasqueada flourish.

"Ole!" shouted a cook in the distance. That broke the ice. The two maids giggled, stopped working and sat down to watch and listen. Then both cooks and His Majesty's chauffeur joined my audience. I played an intricate bulerias that started slow and became bouncy toward the end, at which point the maids began clapping.

Things couldn't have been better, but it didn't last. A Herculean hulk of a man came downstairs from the royal chambers, angrily shouting orders and admonishing the staff for being late with the dinner preparation. In terse Danish, he demanded from the cook to know who I was and what I was doing there. They all chimed in and told him I'd come in out of nowhere, was a "fantastique" player and that he should listen.

"Humph!" he huffily said, and walked back up the stairs.

The chauffeur clapped his hands and laughed uproariously. Then he picked up an intercom phone, dialed His Majesty's extension and spoke excitedly in Danish. One of the maids, a tall, blue-eyed blonde with classic, Nordic features, seemed delighted at his words.

"Can you play something else?" she asked.

I nodded.

"Well, play! Play!" she commanded urgently. It sounded like she meant King Frederick might be coming, and I began playing an alegria.

She was right. King Frederick appeared, stood at the door and smiled approvingly at me, listened for a few minutes, and then returned to his chambers ordering that I be given dinner and looked after. As it happened, His Majesty was entertaining some foreign diplomats. And as they were amid important and urgent discussions, he had to return to the meeting.

The hulk returned from upstairs and delivered His Majesty's orders in a mellow and friendly voice. My blue-eyed friend squealed in delight, rushing over to shake my hand.

"Congratulations," she said. "I'm Nina."

I was glad to meet her and thanked her for her help. She was a beautiful girl with such warmth I wanted to pack her away in my knapsack and take her along on my journey.

"That took a lot of nerve," she said. "At first I thought you were a kook."

"Are not we all?" I answered.

The other maid appeared with two autograph books for me to sign. I ate with them in their staff dining area while they questioned me about my music and philosophy. They told me stories about their fascinating lives. Several hours with them seemed like a few minutes. They asked me to play again because His Majesty didn't need them the rest of the evening, being so busy upstairs with his foreign diplomats. They were so appreciative I played for them far into the night, and they found me a roll-away bed in one of the pantry rooms where I slept until midmorning.

A bright sun awoke me. Nina had made me some sandwiches which I packed into my Kelty pack. I walked out into the warm day to find a pretty garden. Strongly attracted to the spirits in residence, I thought no harm in sitting on the white bench I found among the blossoms. I was in no hurry to leave such a pretty place and began playing some notes on my guitar. I wanted to hear how they would sound mixed with the heart-dappling enchantment I felt in response to the beauty there.

Many minutes passed. Then, feeling I was being watched, I looked around to find an utterly charming, smiling, middle-aged couple holding hands and regarding me and this quiet garden with delight.

"Good morning," I said, smiling back at them. "It sure is nice here."

They sat down with me on the bench, and we began chatting. This was the West German Army-Navy Attaché, Theodore Von Mutius, and Mrs. Mutius, who'd been among the group of diplomats the night before in His Majesty's chambers. After some minutes, we found we enjoyed each other very much. So they decided to take me to Berlin as their guest. And an hour later I waved a thankful farewell to the friendly castle guards as I rode through the front gate with my German hosts in their large black Mercedes with a flag on the front fender.

They were monumentally congenial company. I was a good listener, and they told me many stories to pass the time as we rode along. Having always been interested in Russia and Russians, I asked Mr. Mutius about his relations with the Russian military attaches.

"Do the Russian attaches act just like the others?" I wanted to know.

"Oh, indeed they do not," he replied grinning. "I probably shouldn't tell you this, but recently I attended a banquet for all attaches and noticed that my friend, the Russian attaché, was missing. Later, as Mrs. Mutius and I returned to our car, we saw him. He was dressed as a taxi driver and huddled in an open black Mercedes, listening to the conversations of all the embassy people as they went to and from their cars. His face turned red when he saw us."

"Did you exchange any words?"

"No. We just smiled, waved and walked on."

"So he knows you're on to him! When you do talk with him, what do you generally discuss?"

"Mr. Michailov and I avoid current affairs, politics and philosophy, for a misinterpreted statement in one of these areas causes a rift in our relationship. Your American attaches have the same policy with the Russians. We talk mostly about our World War II experiences."

"When you're tired of reminiscing, what then?"

He thought for a moment and smiled. "Then we often play our little game. Instructed by the Kremlin to use all means of getting information on the latest Western military developments, he always questions me about West Germany's new weapons, troops and ships. I know the answers but always give him the wrong ones. He knows this, of course, but continues to ask questions. So it's all a type of much-needed game. Dwelling on the day's weather or the quality of the bourbon is so shallow."

We all laughed at that. And thus the long trip melted, save for those hours going through Communist Territory. For the roadway that had been smooth became rutty as we entered the Russian Zone where bitterness clouded the faces we saw. But my hosts shared with me the joy of their love, each of them winking at me as they nodded toward the other. I felt we were a kind of lightbulb in a zone that was darkened, through no fault of its own, by the whims of politicians. Mr. and Mrs. Mutius were so warm, I was sad when, at Friedrichstrasse Station, they bought me a ticket and put me on the train to West Berlin.

The train just sat for several minutes, and I began looking around. There was an undecorated and humbly furnished train station coffeehouse filled with patrons. I thought I'd try playing some music, here in the Russian-controlled part of the station, to see what would happen. So I got off the train and went into the coffeehouse. Using the shoulder strap again, I strolled and played, and people filled my pockets with money.

A bald, middle-aged German soldier greeted me like an old friend and invited me to his table. As I sat down, he apologized that he couldn't buy me a drink. I didn't have the proper papers. Before being served, every customer of an East German restaurant had to show a card proving citizenship in the Russian Zone. Any East German restaurant serving an American risked being closed down by the police.

Just as he was telling me this alarming story, a smiling waiter came over and gave me a tray of tea and sandwiches that hadn't been ordered. Glowing, he put a finger over his lips. Then gesturing with both hands as though to push me away, he shook his head, indicating he wanted no money, and quickly went away. The soldier and I were amazed and grateful.

We were both philosophers and dreamers. I mused to him that one day I might be in the U.S. Army and we two might be fighting each other and shooting to kill if Khrushchev gave the word. He nodded and answered, "I wish there weren't any governments."

Unbelievably, he then handed me about $5 in East German Marks—a week's wages—and said, "You take this. I like Americans ever since the war. I was a prisoner of war in your country for two years and treated well. Now I want to repay." Then he quickly got up, repeated with much emotion, "I wish there weren't any governments," and ran off, disappearing into a dismal alley.

As I looked back and forth between the money and the alley where the bald head had disappeared, I heard a loud "halloo" but couldn't find the source.

"Halloo!" the voice said again. I looked to my rear left. There she was—a young German matron wearing a suit. "Will you sit down with me please?"

I took my tray to her table and sat down with her.

"I see you are treated well here in the Communist Zone," she smiled, with an approving glance at the food on the tray. "Your performance was well received. I enjoyed it thoroughly. I am hiring agent for the Deutsche Konzert-Und Gastspieldirektion (East German Concert and Artist Management Association)."

She showed me her credentials—an automatic reaction, for I'd not even thought of asking her. Expressing her surprise that the waiter had brought me food, she confirmed the soldier's story that the reason the waiter had not taken payment was because I was a Western "alien." One could not dispense food to my kind without a special permit. Food was precious and not to be given out to imperialists.

She warned that the People's Police would arrest me for playing in cafes (a foreigner on tourist visa may not work at any employment without official sponsorship), and the U.S. Consulate would be powerless to help me. But she said her organization could give me sponsorship and a contract to play at political gatherings in East Germany.

"Imported artists are always bigger drawing cards—especially when they are from America," she warmly explained. "Would you come with me and allow me to introduce you to my superior, Fraulein Unga? Our office is very near."

Here was my experience with Christian repeating itself in slightly different form with new characters. I'd already learned how life repeatedly throws us the same experience time after time until we learn to deal with it.

Reluctantly I told her, "I'm a troubadour. I don't think it would work, because it might interfere with my current pursuit."

She sensed I was torn and continued her warm coaxing, "You could explain this to Fraulein Unga, and the two of you could surely work something out that would suit both your purposes."

She was so nice, and I wanted to please her. "All right," I said.

For half an hour she led me through unrepaired ruins of the 1945 Allied bombing. After 16 years, there had been no repairs. Walls were missing from some buildings, but they were inhabited nonetheless.

We arrived at her building, and she led me up several flights of stairs to a cold, utilitarian office where sat Fraulein Unga, an emotionally callused, hard woman of tragedy and broken dreams. She was dressed in a military uniform, looked through me rather than at me, though she was not blind, and asked me to play. She depressed me and I played listlessly, hoping to flunk the audition.

"Yes, I can send you on concert tour," she said dryly. She reached into her bottom drawer, pulled out a thick black book and began thumbing through it. "I can get you $100.00 in U.S. hard currency per day. My fee for handling you will be five percent. Are you interested?"

I gently explained to her about my being a troubadour and the fragmentation of purpose this tour would represent.

"You can live like a king on that money here in East Germany," she coaxed lightly. "Money always prevails over purposes."

I took a deep breath, I do confess. That was more money than I'd ever made or even thought of making in my entire life. So I asked, "would I have to sign a contract?"

"Of course." She looked pleased. "I can have it prepared by Monday at two o'clock."

I groped for a catch. "Would I be allowed to take the dollars with me back to the West?"

"Naturally. I would arrange this for you."

"How long would this be for?"

"I don't think we could bother with anything under ninety days. Once you've been with us that long and seen how nice life is under communism, you'll want to extend indefinitely."

I admitted to her that life would indeed be nice on $100 a day. "But would I be working against my country?"

She smiled grimly. "Is that important?"

I took another deep breath. "Well, it seems a sound proposal, but I'll need time to think about it. This has all happened rather fast."

She nodded and said, "opportunity knocks only once, you know."

"But the devil knocks many times."

She pretended to look offended. I felt like apologizing but didn't.

"Shall I write up the contract or not?"

I squirmed with indecision.

"I must be reasonably sure of you so I can safely make out the contract knowing you'll return at two o'clock on Monday."

"This isn't a guarantee, but I'll try and come by this afternoon and give you a decision."

She gave me some train coupons with which to go to West Berlin and return later should I decide to put my troubadour life on the shelf and do this thing. She also gave me her card so I could find my way back, and suggested I stop by the office of the People's Republic downstairs if I wanted true facts and figures concerning life and economy in East Germany.

"Remember," she said, as I descended the stairs, "what you read in the capitalist press about two thousand East Germans coming to West Germany each day is misleading. For they return to their homes in East Germany at night after work."

"But what about the East German refugees in the American Sector at Marienfelde?" I called back.

But she'd returned to her office and didn't hear or answer.

I asked the same question of the official I met at the People's Republic Office.

"They are lazy fortune seekers," he droned casually from behind his chipped desk. "Every country has them. They know they can get free food from the imperialists without working. Nobody wants such bad people. It's a boon to us that they're leaving. They're a drag on the West who accepts them only to make propaganda."

He talked as though he answered this question several times a day. But he was destined to eat his words. For within a week of that day, communist workers began building the Berlin Wall to stop the "bad" people from defecting.

He gave me some propaganda pamphlets to read. Carrying these, I took the train to West Berlin, found a beautiful park and sat down on a bench to read them. I envisioned my appearance at their political gatherings with a loud orator introducing me as a young American who'd seen the light, defied capitalist temptations and so on. I saw that for $100 a day they had valuable propaganda.

Still I headed back to Fraulein Unga's office to tell her I would do it. I actually went on the subway to the transfer station and stood at the entrance to the eastbound train. Then, unable to enter it, I turned around and used her last coupon for the next train west.

Riding westward on the train, I felt I'd shed a heavy weight from my shoulders. I was free again, still a troubadour, and excited once again about my freedom. Looking around in East Berlin had helped me to better appreciate the freedom Americans enjoy. The fact that my country was free allowed me to choose my free way of life.

It occurred to me that I could, in a small way, thank my country for that freedom, and all the young Americans who'd relinquished their lives that I might have it, by helping get out the word about the way America's Cold War adversary operated. So I decided to write a letter describing my experience with Fraulein Unga and send it to both of my media contacts, Art Volkertz and Dwight Pennington, managing editors of the *Santa Rosa Press Democrat* and *Kansas City Star Times*, at my earliest opportunity.

That opportunity came within 24 hours. I happened on a nice nightclub in Berlin that very evening—The Lido. It was late at night. The musicians had all left, but half the audience was still lingering. It was a perfect setup. I climbed onto the still lit stage and began playing. The audience livened up and applauded. The club owner enjoyed it and bought me a hotel room for the night. The next afternoon, he connected me with his friend, Abe Zwick, an American comedian who was director of entertainment at another Berlin night spot, the Wannsee Hotel, an American military officer's club.

One of the finest mansions in Berlin, the magnificent old Wannsee Hotel-Resort stood on the shore of beautiful Lake Wannsee. It had been Hitler's old hangout until the U.S. Army took possession of it in 1945. Now it was the pride of the U.S. military and boasted a nightly dinner show. Abe was in charge of it. He sent a military courtesy car to get me, and we met upstairs in the Wansee's luxurious mezzanine beneath the massive open-beam ceiling. He had more energy in him than a three-year-old.

"I'm told you just wandered into Berlin's best civilian nightclub and took over. That's pure show business." he smiled, incandescing like a light bulb.

We liked each other right away, and he made me a guest artist on his dinner show. He gave me board and room, with a typewriter, a box of hotel stationery, and all the postage stamps I'd need to write and send out my story about Fraulein Unga's offer.

Both the *Press Democrat* and *Star Times* printed the story with banner headlines, and the wire services picked it up. The American Forces Network, AFN-Berlin, invited me to record a one-hour special program of moromusic and tell the story. The program was aired throughout Western Europe. I never checked to see if the Communists tried bribing any more American musicians after that.

3

PERFORMING FOR PARLIAMENT, PABLO PICASSO, THE GYPSIES AND THE DUCHESS

After about a week at the Wansee, my feet were itching to move on. It was pretty there, but I felt separated from the world I'd undertaken to see. Abe understood. A noisy truck picked me up near the hotel and took me through the pretty countryside of Bavaria into France. The driver let me off at his destination, a picturesque old city called Strasbourg, among gothic-inspired churches and cathedrals. It was very pretty here too, and the beauty exhilarated me. But what excited me even more was the fact that it was a warm Saturday night, and there was a festive mood in the streets and outdoor cafes.

I was particularly drawn to a Victorian hotel in the town square—the Des Vosges. It was so Old-Worldly and quaint I wanted to see what it was like inside. There was a private party in progress in a banquet room off the rear of the lobby. I peeked in at a couple dozen happy, smartly dressed men and women seated at a pair of long banquet tables. From their behavior I sensed they were more educated, cultured and into art than most. This and their happiness drew me to them. I found a barstool, set it up near the head of the pair of tables and sat on it playing a calypso tune. I was right about them. For they stopped chatting in order to listen, becoming attentive and curious.

"This is better than Maverick," declared a rotund gentleman near the head of the first table. His double chin wobbled, and his eyes twinkled. Those seated near him were enjoying his reactions to me more than my performance. I continued with a sonata I'd written, introducing it with a brief speech. They really got into that, and you could hear a pin drop in that room. Applause rippled when I finished the piece.

"Maverick," repeated the rotund man, full of cheer. He put money in an ashtray for me and started it passing. The sound of rattling coin purses filled the room.

A self-assured Frenchman was seated at the second table's lower end barely six feet from me. He smiled, "may I offer you your dinner tonight, young man?"

I hadn't eaten all day. The smell of the food tantalized me, and I eagerly accepted.

He was a reporter from the Paris News Service. "I am covering this I.C.E. convention," he said with an air indicating the event's importance.

"I.C.E.?"

"Yes, the International Council of Europe, a gathering of parliament members representing the major republics of Western Europe. In case you weren't aware, nearly everyone in this room, except you, me and the waiter, is a Council member. You've performed for a highly select group—one of the most important official gatherings in the world."

Puzzled, I asked, "where are the security guards, police, media cameras and limousines?"

He laughed. His dinner wine had relaxed him. "Things are somewhat less formal and exaggerated here than in your country, my friend."

After some conversation I could see this man wasn't kidding me. Europe was certainly full of surprises. No wonder troubadours thrived in Europe, I thought. In such environs one could make an occupation of crashing these affairs and interviewing premiers, prime ministers, presidents and kings over a bottle of scotch.

"A point of interest," my reporter friend continued, nodding toward the rotund man who'd dubbed me Maverick. "That man is Professor Carlo Schmid of Heidelberg, vice president of the Socialist Wing in West Germany. He's the head of this convention."

Schmid seemed to know we were discussing him and called out to me. "Young fellow, you are American, are you not?"

"Yes, sir, from a place near San Francisco."

"Splendid." Do you know the *Yellow Rose of Texas*?" He began humming the tune.

I handed my camera to the waiter, sat with Schmid and played him the tune. He waved his finger, conducting. Everyone knew the old Texan melody, and they started singing along. The waiter took our picture.

"Vive l' Amerique!" exclaimed a French delegate, and there was a round of applause.

"How are things going at the council sessions," I asked Schmid.

"Slowly," was his reply, and he grew serious. "As you have probably heard, we are attempting to establish a United States of Europe—a Common Market with a common currency. We meet with resistance, problems and more resistance."

I didn't know he was a father of both the new German Constitution and what was destined to be the European Common Market. But one could sense his brilliance and the adoration he enjoyed from the Parliament Members. I asked him why this Common Market thing was such a good idea. This launched us into philosophical discussion. We talked of capitalism, socialism, and the strengths of commonality versus the virtues of individuality. His arguments for commonality were the most imposing I'd ever heard. And though he had problems, he was optimistic. He was close to getting President De Gaulle of France, Prime Minister Macmillan of England and Chancellor Adenauer of West Germany to agree with him on precursory steps.

He looked over at my guitar and said whimsically, "Someday I will learn to play that instrument. It has a beautiful sound. You must cover the world, my young friend, and play. Make so many

He waved his finger, conducting.

friends and stay in so many homes you cannot remember them all. Then you'll have established a unique commonality among the friends you've made in all those countries, bringing people together in peace through their love for your music. None here will forget your music this evening." His passion was heartwarming.

"You're very kind," I replied, smacking my lips. That lasagna was delicious! I finished the last morsel and soaked up the sauce with a piece of bread.

Then a NATO interpreter from London came over and sat with us. He heartily said to me, "Pardon, old boy. I don't mean any effrontery, but if you lack a place to sleep tonight, my wife and I have a spare couch in our suite." I liked this English couple and accepted.

Schmid was pleased and thought my situation very funny. "How can we put a tax on a troubadour's income?" he laughed as he shook my hand.

My hosts were generous, allowing me to shower, shave and wash my clothes which I hung over the radiant heater to dry overnight. And they sent me off with a big breakfast.

My plans were vague as I begn thumbing a ride. For a troubadour is flexible, taking opportunities as they occur. But my tentative thought was to see the south of Spain, birthplace of flamenco and much of my musical composing style, after which I would skirt the south side of the Mediterranean, heading east along the northern coast of Africa.

So in the following days, I headed south and played the outdoor cafes of the Champs Elysees in Paris where I met a fine pair of French teenagers, Dominique Jamet and her brother. They took me to their parents' palatial home in Versailles where they organized and sponsored a concert for me.

It was held in their courtyard surrounded with very high stone walls and covered by a heavenly canopy of thousands of fragrant roses that grew from an old, old vine—old as the centuries-old chateau itself that was host to a world of spirits. It was an elegant affair, attended by about a hundred family friends of all ages who listened to me play with rapt attention. There were sumptuous refreshments at intermission, and these folks made me feel like I was indeed an artist.

Dominique introduced me to a polished young man from the audience who was an executive at the Savarez Company, a French guitar string manufacturer. He inquired about the strings I used. When he learned I already preferred and used a brand of strings made by his company, he was so delighted he came around the next day and took me to the Savarez wholesale outlet in Paris. He worked out the details, and I was given fifty complimentary sets of strings which I packed away in my backpack.

Buoyed with newfound confidence, I headed still farther south to Aix-en-Provence, arriving at dusk on a balmy September evening. Along the main boulevard there were many outdoor cafes. I picked a quiet one, sat down at a table and began playing. No one took the slightest notice, so I was thinking of packing up and moving on.

But then a radiant, suntanned old gentleman, wearing a short sleeve, brightly polka-dotted shirt, sat down with his smiling lady at the table next to me. He'd come over specifically to hear me. He and his lady concentrated on my music with energy and purpose. The old gentleman was completely focused, and when I would finish a piece he would ask me to please continue. By the sheer force of his energy directed at me, he got everyone listening. Soon I had a large audience, with this old gentleman at its head.

I felt very grateful for his interest. He seemed to respond most keenly to the passionate moments. So I decided he might like to hear a version of *Malaguena* I'd developed. It had rasqueada passages that called upon the guitar to gather force from deep in the ground beneath my feet and bring it up through me with a deep thunder that danced around the café. The piece built from near silence to a grand flourish at the end.

The old man jumped to his feet clapping and shouted, "OLE, muchacho!" The entire café audience broke out in frenzied applause during which the old man stepped over to talk. I stood up to receive him. He started to talk but couldn't find the words, being either too moved or unable to speak enough English. He took a shiny five-new-franc coin from his pocket. Grabbing my hand, he plopped the coin into my palm.

"Buena Fortuna," he said lovingly, looking straight into my eyes. Then, with the audience still applauding, he took his lady's hand, and they walked down the street.

A large group of thrilled French people gathered around to explain what had happened to me. That old man was Pablo Picasso, the famous painter who lived and worked nearby.

While everyone stood around staring at me, I had to choose between a number of dinner invitations. I chose a young Spanish doctor and his lady who said they were traveling to Spain. During dinner they invited me to go along with them in their luxurious Mercedes.

They took me to San Sebastian, Bilbao, and then to Madrid where I went to play for Tico Medina in his office at the *Pueblo* newspaper. I'd been referred to him by a patron of a remarkable jazz club, The Cave, in Heidelberg where I'd performed a year earlier.

Tico was pleased and tickled by my short flamenco rendition. He assigned his entertainment reporter to look after me—a kind young man whose name I cannot now recall. Tico also saw to it that I had a place to stay as guest of his friend in a beautiful house while he arranged that I perform on Spanish National Television.

It was a venerable house—that of Pepe and Senora Bienvenida—on Via Alcala, a street lined with tall mature trees and gracious old homes. Pepe was the only remaining son of Senora Bienvenida who'd lost all but one of her sons, and her husband, to the horns of the bulls during their efforts to please the afternoon crowds at the Plaza De Toros.

Pepe was a charming young banderillero, possibly the most talented of the Bienvenidas, and enthusiastically explained that Spanish bullfighting is the noblest of all spectator sports. It's ennobled not only because it's the only surviving one in which only the victor lives. It's noble because it demands the ultimate courage and grace.

He and Bernardo, his Cuban novilliero friend, demonstrated the beauty of the sport in the Bienvenida backyard bullring. With the grace of his stance and sweep of his cape, the matador is an artiste who faces paying the ultimate price with each pass of the bull.

"A man of courage dies only once. A coward dies many times," Bernardo said.

Senora Bienvenida had the noblest of visages born of courage. She'd sacrificed all but one of her family upon the altar of art and bravery. Having given this gift had opened her eyes to the sacredness of life and to the presence of all the love that had filled her heart in order to make and keep her equal to the great task of her sacrifices. It all showed in her precious face so venerable as to inspire me to want to be her best friend, even her son if possible. For hours each day she knelt and prayed at the altar of the intimate church they maintained in their home.

None of them minded the sound of my practicing flamenco. In fact they seemed to enjoy it. I prepared my music

Bernardo

diligently, for this was my very first television appearance.

But I was nervous the day of the show. My hands were so cold, and my case of butterflies was so intense at the television studio, I was in no condition to play. I told the director I needed a sink full of warm water for my hands. He seemed gruff and unsympathetic—of the sort who didn't relate to artists—and he told me there was no time for this. We were about to go "live" on the air, he told me.

But I could see there were at least ten minutes. I got the young reporter to intercede for me and was given leave to put my hands in warm water. What a blessing! I got my fingers clean and warm. And when they began working, my confidence grew. I was able to play just in time.

It went beautifully. The entire studio staff broke into applause when I completed my mini concert of three pieces—about 11 minutes. That's unusual in a big-city studio, but here was an American playing their own style of music. The director came over and apologized tenderly.

"Now that I've seen the way you play, I understand why you must care for your hands," he said. Vindicated, the young reporter beamed with pride. He wrote a large photo-illustrated feature story about my travels that appeared in the *Pueblo*. He included a review in the story and dubbed me "un maestro consumado."

As I made my way south toward Africa, I got to thinking about that review. I decided that while I was grateful for the young reporter's enthusiasm, I had a long way to go before I could really be what he said I was. But Red Eagle had told me that if, when I practice, I would pretend it sounded like it did in my dreams, then one day it would.

So as I climbed into a topless car that stopped and took me to Granada, I resolved to write a new piece. It would be the finest I'd ever written. I would play it like a maestro and justify that young reviewer's faith in me. I began composing it in my head as we rode among Andalusia's very old fragrant trees growing on hills of burnt orange that were caressed by Autumn sunlight.

At dusk I was let off in a nice section of downtown Granada and began walking along to see what destiny would put in my path. I didn't have to wait long. A raggedy-clothed, dark-faced old gypsy approached me. He smelled of stale tobacco and a bathless lifestyle.

"Hola, Senior," he said with a salesman's smile. Looking around to make sure no one was watching us, he pulled a golden ring from his pocket. Its large jewel of cut glass sparkled and glittered in the light of the shop window next to us. He held it in cupped hands, so none but me could see.

"Es de oro." (It is of gold.) he said. "It is yours for only one thousand pesetas."

I wasn't fooled but was curious about the man. I didn't feel at all threatened by him, though he clearly belonged to that special gypsy culture who live their lives on the cusp—in that gray area between crime and honesty. His gold ring ruse has been used by con men for centuries in big cities where foolish foreigners never seem to learn. "That is too much," I said, testing him.

"But it is a diamond," he protested in broken, poorly accented English. "I stole it today. I must go to Barcelona. I need quick money bad."

Two of Franco's Guardia Civilla Police were in the next street, and they knew this gypsy all too well. They appeared out of nowhere and grabbed him. Brutally, they began to subdue him in handcuffs, jerking and twisting both his arms. Though horrified, I was calmed by the serenity in the gypsy's face. There was something spiritual, noble and good about him. He wasn't afraid of the arrest, and he had the knowing look of one who is confidante to many.

I knew a little Spanish from school. "Wait!" I said. "What's the matter?"

"We have caught him cheating you," said one officer. "You must come with us and file a complaint."

I replied that the gypsy and I were just talking about the ring. I added that I couldn't be entirely certain he'd have sold it to me for more than its value and would therefore not sign a declaration that this was his intent.

Frustrated, the officers exchanged angry glances. This American did not wish to press charges, and there were no other witnesses to the conversation. So the little con man had escaped them again! They verbally abused him, flung him roughly against a post and stalked away in anger.

He was badly shaken.

"Are you all right?" I asked, almost as agitated as he.

Recovering quickly, he stared at me appreciatively and evaluated me a moment before he spoke. "Gracias, muchacho. I am sorry to have disturbed you. See here." He reached into his pocket and pulled out a handful of rings identical to the one he'd shown me. "But you were not fooled. You did not buy from me or the Guardia." He bestowed upon me a warm, congratulatory and grateful smile, told me he was the father of a daughter and son my own age and invited me to dinner.

"My home is humble, but it is good there," he said. His neck was wrapped in a moth-eaten scarf. His filthy, bushy hair was gray at the temples. He led me a mile or so out of town to a limestone hill. We climbed it along a narrow winding path until we came to his cave dwelling where we found his wife, son and daughter to whom he introduced me. In rapid pidgin Spanish, he related to them our adventure together.

His teenage daughter had been lucky that day, begging on street corners with her doll wrapped in a baby blanket, and had made a whole bull durum sack full of change that she added to her father's pocketful. He too had been lucky, having sold a few rings. They were in high spirits as they invited me to sit and eat.

The ring seller's gypsy wife wore bracelets, necklaces and ostentatious earrings, and she prepared us a delectable community dish of corn mixed with green vegetables, onions, potatoes, some delicious herbs and God only knows what else. We each took from the dish with our fingers, putting the food between layers of bread. They told me they were richer than clerks and bank tellers in Spain, and far happier. This wasn't true for them though, until they'd come to Granada and secured this cave during the previous year.

I was offered a bowl of water and a towel for my hands, and I played for them by the light of the fire. The women danced, and a few neighbors joined us, clapping to the flamenco rhythms, their faces shining in the firelight.

The old man asked me, "Where do you live?"

"I live wherever I am," I said, feeling very mellow with them.

They all laughed and understood. "But tonight. Where will you sleep tonight?"

I shrugged. "I haven't decided yet."

They held a quick discussion in rapid pidgin and decided to buy me a hotel room.

"I will find you a place," declared the old gypsy. He led me back down the winding path to a nearby hotel and began bargaining with the propietor. As I walked around reveling in the many objects d' art, I heard them settle on a price of 12 pesetas, about twenty cents U.S. currency, for the one night's lodging.

The room was clean, with clean sheets, and had a pitcher of water and a bowl. The old hotel had been much grander in its heyday, for it was floored with broken, hand-painted tiles and studded with the remnants of masterful sculpture. The old man came to inspect the room with me and was satisfied.

I thanked him.

"It is nothing. If you ever are in trouble, please come to me or to my son. We will always help you."

From a gypsy, that commitment is for life and is very meaningful. With a lump in my throat, I assured him the feeling was mutual, and that I might return to see him even if I needed nothing. He nodded appreciatively as we shook hands and parted.

I slept until noon and stayed until checkout time. I didn't want to leave until absolutely necessary, for I felt a loving vibration in this hotel that had hosted travelers for centuries. The spirits of many adventurers, both noble and ignoble, came alive in the aura of these broken but still beautiful mosaic tiles. A rich if faded history was subtly written here, and the only sound was that of an aged arthritic horse munching hay in the courtyard below.

I used the time to change guitar strings. I also practiced and developed the new piece I'd been mentally composing—the piece I sensed was going to be my finest ever. As I worked on it, I imagined all the guitarists in Andalusia were performing it with me.

Then I sat back and reflected on how that communist booking agent had called me a Western "alien." I'd also seen that word printed in large letters at immigration checkpoints where visitors are greeted. I decided I didn't like that word. It seemed poisonous and not a polite word with which to describe a brother or sister human being you've not yet gotten to know. Father Charleton had said I would encounter insanities.

This was certainly one of them, and I'd seen others. One couldn't be a street artist until he was first a beggar. And Western visitors in the East needed a license to eat.

It was late in the afternoon when I left and ambled into the artful cobblestone alleyways of Old Town Granada. I wandered around until after dark and found a very old arcade where a large crowd was gathered around a most unusually plump, flamenco-dancing gypsy. I would estimate her weight at about 300 pounds, though her height was well under 5 feet. Her body moved like a two-legged cannonball, and she was blessed with the most expressive, rubbery, deeply characterized face I'd ever seen. She used her face to the hilt as she danced a soleares, regarding the world around her with a soulful gaze so intense as to be capable of exorcism.

Sweat rolled down the rivulets in her face during her dramatic pause while the hushed crowd watched her with bated breath in awe of the immense power her soul displayed. Then she began to pound her heels on the tiled arcade, very slowly and deliberately at first, while her guitarist gradually quickened the tempo. At length her heels began moving so fast that they became blurred, and they shook the tile pavement. It felt like a large tractor was roaring past at top speed.

For the coup d' gras, she took her fellow dancer (a 90-pound man whom I later found out was her husband!) by the wrist and twirled him over her head, like a lasso, with ease.

Meanwhile her guitarist played rasqueadas at lightning speed as fleas actively hopped about on his forehead.

An emotional hurricane of applause followed. I was so excited I pushed my way through the crowd to meet them—particularly her. Her name was Dorotea Estampio, a great mime, dancer and thespian. As soon as the crowd dispersed, I played for her, her troupe and a handful of hangers on. She decided she liked me and caught my eye with hers in a tenacious gaze. She began to jabber at me, and then laughed when she realized I couldn't understand a word of her gypsy tongue. I also laughed, for I was so pleased with her I didn't know quite what to do about it. Then she grabbed and held me in a long bear hug.

With Dorotea and her two partners, I spent several of the most enjoyable evenings of my life. I played duets with her guitarist as she danced on Granada's many streets. Her husband passed a pan among our crowds for money with which he paid all our expenses. We stayed in nice places and ate at pleasant inns.

Finally it was Saturday night, balmy and warm for October, and we gathered a very large, post-dinner crowd in the grand old arcade. A Rolls Royce gently drove up and parked fifty feet from us. The lady in the back seat began staring at me. I pretended not to notice and immersed into my playing. Dorotea was holding the crowd beautifully. After some minutes, I looked up and found the lady in the car still staring at me. Now she was smiling too, for she saw I was checking on her. So I ignored her until the end of the show. During our lengthy applause the lady sent her chauffeur over to summon me.

"Madame would like to speak with you," he said with a reverent gesture toward the lady. So I walked over to the car window to see what it was all about.

She leaned back comfortably in that spacious, lambswool-upholstered rear seat, her shapely legs folded, smoking a cigarette in a jewel-encrusted cigarette holder. "I don't make it a practice of picking up young men," she said boldly, huskily and crisply, "but tonight you inspire my sense of adventure."

Very few folks could get away with a lead like that. But she did. For this woman was a monument to relaxed dignity and refinement. And she was obviously enjoying a little charade, pretending to be a raving man hunter while she subtly telegraphed, at another level, the noble soul she clearly was. If there were women like this in California, I'd certainly never seen one. She was so alert and aware!

She introduced herself as Her Royal Highness, Duchess Francesca of Assisa, Asorsa or Sissi—something like that. Charming and ageless, she invited me for supper at her villa located miles out of town at the end of her long, long, private road.

I was amazed that she looked so excitingly sensual and attractive as she sat there. So I swallowed hard and quickly accepted. I walked over and told Dorotea I would be back in a few hours but was destined never to see that great thespian again.

For Francesca was far too exciting—too possessive. And she allowed no avenue of escape. After dinner the chauffeur had gone to bed. He arose before anyone, in the morning, to take the car on an errand in Malaga. Then Francesca got involved in helping me plan my upcoming trip. I would require visas for Africa, including a hard-to-get one for anarchy-torn Algeria—impossible for me to obtain through normal channels on my own without her help. And there were delays while we awaited response to the trunk calls she'd made to her high level embassy friends in order to get me this precious visa.

And then there was Francesca herself—so loving and fascinating, like a pretty little girl with an ancient soul, full of stories and thoughts I needed to hear.

"You and your music here among the flowers—together they unite me with all that exists," she murmured the morning of our first day together as we sat and I played in her magnificent garden. "Do you know the story of here and there?"

"Um . . ."

"You are there—you have arrived. Consequently you are here, now."

I was puzzled. "So I'm here because I'm there?"

She laughed like a child, covered my ears with her hands and kissed my forehead tenderly. Then she sat and listened to my new piece as I practiced it.

The hours melted, as did that day and the following days. It was a nice way to be marooned, but my enjoyment of it was clouded by my unvoicable and ungrantable wish to let Dorotea know what was happening. I kept this anxiety hidden, marveling on how, when destiny places such kinds of loveliness in our paths, there's always a cross current.

The strong scent of bougainvillaea in her garden was like a drug. Mostly we sat among the lush flowers or on her nearby canopied featherbed just inside the house behind a pair of open glass doors. My new piece made her smile at me radiantly, and she wanted to hear it over and over. Tenderly she said she loved it, for it reminded her of happy times. It was a slow, haunting kind of tune that suited her exotic tastes, and I loved it because she did. It became our private unique joy never before experienced by anyone but us.

"Such a tune!" she exclaimed. "Where does such beauty come from?"

I shrugged. "From inside you, I think. For I'm told we see only what we have inside us."

"Then you are inside me?"

"What you see in me—that's inside you."

Folding her hands together in rapture, her face glowing, she replied, "and I have discovered beauty in you."

This made me smile at her. "It's nice, being discovered by such an exciting lady."

Each afternoon with her was golden—each evening an enchanting dream. It wasn't the mint tea so much as the tender way she prepared and served it. A strong love quickly developed between us—one that allowed us both to remain free but celebrated the kinship of our two souls. Before meeting her, I'd felt relatively like a lost waif of a troubadour. Now she made me feel like a man who belonged where he was.

But after several days my visa was granted, and Francesca had other business. Heavily into social work, she had to visit Madrid to work with her group of volunteers whom she was helping. She had her chauffeur take me around to the French Consulate and several

African legations for visa stamps. As I was getting into the car, she told me she'd never forget my new piece and our time together. I felt deeply honored.

"Dinner invitations can last for days." I marveled.

"Yes indeed," she said with a long hug.

I got the visas and returned to Old Town, but Dorotea had disappeared without a trace. The bitterness of this loss grew worse by the hour as I spent the day searching for her.

Exhausted and upset, I went up to the Alhambra Castle—a lovingly restored vestige of the grenadine renaissance of art, music, science and architecture that flourished during Granada's golden age between 900–1400 A.D. During those years, Granada was a center of learning and discovery in the Western World. And it was here that flamenco and the grenadine andalusianesque tune structure style were born, blending the noblest qualities of Arabians and Europeans. It was music so powerful as to penetrate all between-life memory barriers and haunt those who in past lives were denizens here.

The Alhambra has in modern times become a museum of sorts. It was closed for the evening. But I sat near the entrance and tried to content myself by playing my new piece that was very grenadine and Andalusian in character.

Practicing is never drudgery when, from the onset of inspiration for a new piece, I exuberantly pretend I'm playing it the way it sounds in my fantasy. This self-delusion continues until my fingers find a way to make it manifest. I keep the picture in focus and let my fingers draw it. As I practiced, I felt a sense of Francesca abiding next to me and decided to call this piece *Francesca's Tune.*

There were two armed guards at the castle gate. They came over to say hello, and I asked if they knew a restaurant where I might play for a meal. They said if I'd continue playing that piece, they'd share their own dinner with me and allow me to stay the night in the castle. They made me all at once an employed musician with an appreciative audience and the occupant of a castle with two generous hosts at my side.

They dined with me in the guardroom and allowed me to explore the castle alone. There was a gargoyled minaret from which I could look out and view the firelit gypsy caves where I'd shared dinner with the old ring seller. So awesomely did Granada's timeless splendor fill the space around me, the sting of losing Dorotea abated. My hosts found me a straw mat for my sleeping bag. And as an October chill had set in, they left an electric space heater going for me all night.

4

"THE ARABS—THEY KILL YOU FIRST AND THEN ASK YOUR NAME AFTERWARDS."

Morning brought the first day of the seasonal rain. Such a day is special anywhere—even at Alhambra Castle. It filled me with energy. And I was further excited by the prospect of visiting the Arab world—the culture that had launched Ali Baba and Aladdin. The great religious conviction and the artistry of the Arab world had always lured me. Arabic innovation influenced even the architecture of this castle where I'd resided for the night.

A pair of pretty American nurses picked me up along the road in their car and took me across the Rock of Gibraltar as far as the roadway outside of Tetouan in Morocco. All the people here wore robes and headdress, and there was even a shepherd carrying a huge staff with which he guided his small flock of sheep along the roadway. I felt like I'd taken a time machine back to biblical times. I was excited at the prospect of meeting my first Arab and didn't have to wait long.

A new, black, swept-wing American Cadillac approached me and stopped. "Going to Tangiers?" asked the driver from within his Arab headdress. "Hop in."

As we drove off, I thanked him for stopping.

"Think nothing of it, my boy. How do you like my car?"

"It seems to ride well."

He gloated. "Tsk, 'tis very common to have a new Cadillac nowadays in Morocco. I am a mere hotel manager, and I afford this car without even feeling the financial burden. You see, I operate two hotels—one in Tetouan and one in Tangiers. I make this trip every day or two."

"Uh-huh."

"So you will go to Tangiers? I can get you a hotel room with a nice view at a specially reduced price."

"No, thank you."

"Then you have a friend in Tangiers?"

"I hope to have fairly soon."

"Ah, but of course. Now I happen to know some lovely girls who will give themselves to you for a reasonable price. I would require only a small commission."

"No, thank you," I replied, alarmed at his ambition. "Not today."

"Very well," he submitted. "Maybe you will need a car in Tangiers?"

I was now in disbelief, but this man was for real. "I don't think so, sir."

"But I have one which I can give you for a very low price."

"No, thank you." And thus went our conversation all the way to Tangiers where I managed to leave his car unfleeced.

Surely, I thought to myself as I walked through the streets of Tangiers, not all Arabs were like this man. He made me feel so lonely in this strange land, for it would seem his only motive for giving me a ride was to profiteer. And I began reflecting on how lonesome my life would be were I traveling alone as a customary tourist who met primarily only those who stood to profit financially from my visit.

Rain began pouring relentlessly. I had a special plastic bag for my guitar case that Jack had made for me, but I had no raincoat. Drenched to the skin, I entered a restaurant that had a large wood-stove at its center, around which sat twenty or so quiet, cheerless patrons. I sat at a table near the stove, and a waiter brought me a menu.

"No, I cannot buy a meal," I told him. "I have come only to get warm and dry. But if you will allow me to sit next to your stove, I will play music for you on my guitar. For I am a troubadour."

He didn't understand English, so I repeated myself in Spanish. Then he understood but looked doubtful, for I didn't look like much of a musician in my drenched condition. So he took the menu and went to the kitchen to summon the cook who emerged from his hot griddle. He looked half-Spanish, half-Arab—a proud, confident, shirtless, hairy-chested man wearing an apron and holding his spatula. Chefs are usually friendly to musicians, for music and food have gone well together since time began. He surveyed my drenched guitar and knapsack.

"You are a wandering troubadour, no? You play music?"

"A little, sir."

"Very good. You may use my stove as much as you like. When you are dry, you may play as much as you like. Very good." With a cordial smile, he hastily retreated to attend his frying food. He was a warm and good man.

Of course every patron had witnessed our negotiation, and all watched with interest as I sat and warmed my hands, removed the plastic bag from my guitar case and prepared to play. About half the people were Europeans, as we were in the French Sector of the city. But a cloud of weather-induced dreariness hung over us all. I was tired, hungry and still feeling abused by the Cadillac driver.

So I turned to my music—my own compositions and family of constant companions—which, to me, is a collection of old chestnuts equally as much a part of me as *Stardust* or *White Christmas*. Each piece, to me, is a living Great Spirit—an individual with a soul and feelings—to be respected, listened to and given freedom of its own individual expression. Just by the way I play its notes, I can make it feel happy, sad or angry. Now I decided my tune was beautiful, and that I would tell it so. I listened to its beauty most admiringly, playing its notes the way that it seemed to want them played.

It worked. My tune was ecstatically happy. It floated like never before, which thrilled me. I too then became happy because my tune was. There was applause when I finished. A dewy-eyed old man—filled with rapture—stepped over, reached out and gently touched my guitar with reverence. Then we all watched as he walked out into the rain without a word.

Everyone was staring at me in silence now, and I was very embarrassed by it all. As it made no sense to run and hide, I had no defense but to begin playing another piece and immerse myself into it. A happy vibration developed and quickly filled the room, propelling me into such an orbit that I gave a half-hour show that was heartily received. The applause was so robust that it drew milord the cook from his hot griddle once again. Pleased, he went back to his kitchen and prepared me a delicious meal.

The patrons were delighted with his generosity. "Good show," happily declared two Englishmen as they left. A young Muslim couple in Western dress came to my table wanting to talk, and I invited them to sit down. It was Mr. and Mrs. Oziel.

"We have a spare bed at our home in the Casbah, and would be most happy were you to stay with us for a few days," said Mr. Oziel. He said he was a watch repairman currently out of work. "But Allah will find me work. Until then, we make do with what we have. Allah gives. Allah takes away. We trust in Allah. He does what's best for us."

That sounded a lot like some of what Father Charleton had said to me, and I wondered why—since we shared common beliefs—Muslims, Christians and other sects had such difficulty getting along, insisting on referring to God by different names. The Oziels were puzzled about that too.

They were nice, so I went along with them past the open marketplace into a labyrinth of cobblestone alleys and tiny bazaars. Their home was small and built of clay. But it was still larger than most of their neighbor's homes, for it had three rooms. I slept in the main room on a flea-ridden couch.

"You looked very wet when you came to the restaurant last night," Oziel observed in the morning. "You must not go in the rain without a rain coat. Have you no raincoat?"

"No," I said, beginning to scratch at some fleabites. But there was no bathing facility in the house, so I said nothing about the fleas. I just told him I wanted to move on to avoid overstaying my welcome.

"Oh, but you must not leave so soon," he protested.

"Well, you know how troubadours are. They're always moving on."

He nodded.

As I was about to leave, he ran to his bedroom, emerged with the raincoat he'd been wearing the night before and began stuffing it into my Kelty pack. "You must take this. You need it more than I do."

"But I will get one later," I replied, removing it.

At this, he looked offended to the core. "I have given you a humble gift. It even has a rip in it, and the bottom button is missing. You must take it or never speak to me again."

I had to accept. Furthermore it was of light, thin-but-strong material that folded into a wad not much bigger than a pair of fists and would easily fit into my pack. "Very well, it's just that I didn't want you to be without it."

"I understand. Be sure and return tonight if you are still in Tangiers," he smiled.

I went away aglow at his kindness, though itching from the fleas. This is truly the way Arab people are, I thought to myself. Arabs are like Mr. Oziel—not like the man in the Cadillac. I was now filled with enthusiasm about the Arabs and my prospects among them, but was desperate to do something about the flea-bites. Now I was just like Dorotea's guitarist.

Wandering around the open marketplace, I searched for a way to play music for a shower. But there were only sandal-wearing, robed hucksters and buyers who heaved with the universal agony of buying and selling. Dozens of camels carried heavy loads. Money changers were everywhere, as were deformed beggars demanding baksheesh as though if you didn't give them any they would surely expire and die within the hour.

Veiled women shoppers perused rows of skinned, blood-stained, fly-infested sheep's heads that lay on counters in the open air. A headdressed Arab crossed my path driving a mule-drawn cart loaded with two giant cauldrons of fragrant sewage from thunder mugs placed in the homes of his customers wealthy enough to afford this kind of service.

After some meandering I found a small dirt-floored teahouse among some palm trees overlooking Tangiers Harbor where pirate galleons from the Barbary Coast moored centuries ago. A rag-hooded Arab was baking bread on a centuries-old barbecue, and a handful of bearded, robed customers were smoking hash-ish to pass the balmy afternoon. Might a potential friend with a shower be among these folks?

I found a chair inside, sat down and played.

A dense Midwestern American accent bawled out from the dark rear corner. "Hey, yank, how long you been playing like that?"

I peered into the corner and saw a middle-aged, pudgy-faced American covered in tattoos. He'd reckoned my nationality by the look of my Kelty pack, and he offered me a pouring from his large pot of mint tea.

He was the ship's cook on an American freighter that had just left for Suez. He wasn't drunk or doped and seemed congenial.

"I just jumped my ship," he confided in a low tone. I was surprised that he would entrust me, a complete stranger, with this information and listened intently.

"I've never done anything before like this, but you know what? I'm happier right now than I've ever been before, to put it plain and simple." He warmed his hands, wrapping them around the tea glass, and sipped just a little. He was obviously delighted with the mint flavoring from the fresh mint leaves in the pot. "Where else can you find tea just like this except here in Tangiers. I love Tangiers. They take regular Ceylon tea leaves, mix them with mint leaves and sugar, chop them together, dump them into a teapot and pour in the boiling water."

He was burly and masculine. Yet he picked up his glass daintily, his little finger extended, and gently sniffed the mint bouquet with such a happy face I couldn't help grinning at him—and with him—though I knew he was in deep trouble for jumping ship.

He ordered a fresh pot as we traded stories.

Then, shaking his teaspoon at me, he gave me a lecture. "My young friend, you'll never stop traveling like you do. If you ever return stateside, I give you six months—a year at most—and you'll pack up again and go. Mark my words.

"You'll remember all the hospitality and friendliness of the folks you've met in your travels, and you'll miss that. You'll miss your freedom from Social Security deductions, income taxes, insurance premiums, rent payments, surcharges for social programs, Blue Chip Stamps, union dues, Selective Service notices, labor benefit deductions, car registration fees and numbers for everything. Each of these things'll be an ulcer in your gut. The minute they begin to hurt, you'll take off because you've known freedom."

Ship jumper in the Casbah (Illustration published with my story in the Kansas City Star, Oct., '61*).*

It dawned on me that perhaps Americans are not all that free— hemmed in as we are by higher and higher taxes in order to pay for our increasingly complex structure that yokes us with these things he mentioned. There seemed to be a growing deluge of laws that restricted and infringed, necessitating that more and more of our decisions and options be dictated by others.

Here in front of me was a man to whom a brief taste of freedom was so precious he'd been willing that very day to jeopardize himself in order to have it. He'd gotten himself into deep trouble with both the Moroccan and Merchant Marine officials in order to experience it—even if only for a short period—until his indiscretion caught up with him.

He and his story made me so intensely sad over the human condition I nearly wept. I didn't say much, being deeply moved.

There was a convoy of three modern cars parked in front of the bistro where we sat, and a crew of robed Arabs was busily engaged tying boxes and muslin bundles to the roofs with hemp rope. One of them had been listening to me play earlier. Just then he came over to our table and charmingly invited me to go with them to Casablanca.

"I hadn't thought of going to Casablanca," I said. "But why not?" I gestured at my tattooed friend. "Is there room for two?"

"Only one," the Arab said.

The American, who never did tell me his name, bestowed a grateful smile, thanking me for my effort to get him passage. "Always travel alone," he said. "Then you'll never be alone, for there will always be a place for you." He shook my hand.

Chefs and musicians certainly do get on well together, I thought to myself as I climbed into the car with the Arabs.

These Moroccans were pleasant company, though they spoke little English. The roadway was very wide and smooth for a Third World nation. The few areas of the countryside that weren't sandy desert were brown and parched after a long, hot Summer. My hosts put me out on a waterfront street similar to the one in Tangiers where they'd found me. There was even a bistro, a bit larger than the one in Tangiers, and I went in to play.

The place was packed with noisy dock workers, but they quieted down when I played. A gruff but benign Moroccan told his friends to shut up and listen, for the guitarist was playing "Europee musique." They applauded and kept listening. But I had an excuse to stop playing when the waiter brought me a bowl of beans.

"No money—no dirhams," I said.

He understood. And in his effort to make sure I understood that he understood, he pulled a handful of change from his own pocket. Smiling, he pointed first to the money, then to the food and then to himself, assuring me in this way that he was paying for it.

Thus assured, I ate the beans, got up to leave and another waiter came over wanting payment. No explanation would satisfy him. The first waiter had left, and there were no witnesses.

"Two dirhams, two dirhams!" he said angrily. He became choleric as I walked out.

Dusk lowered the visibility in the street outside. I walked inland in search of a better section of town, for the port area of Casablanca is known to be one of the toughest neighborhoods in the world. An alley looked like it cut across to a main avenue a block away, and I turned into it. Just as I turned, I heard a missile flying and felt the jolt of a shaft that pierced the bottom left side of my back pack. It was a heavy knife. Had I not happened to turn just as it was being thrown, the knife would have found its intended mark just below my ribcage. I turned again and saw the waiter running away.

I considered trying to find a policeman but thought better of it. The two waiters might stick together and both insist that I hadn't paid for the beans. Could I prove he'd thrown the knife? Assuming so, would it make me happy having a man sent to prison? I extracted and examined the roughly hewn, hand-whittled wooden handle and rusty blade. No fingerprints here.

So I walked back to the restaurant and stuck the knife into the half- rotted wooden frame of the doorway. I had no need for this knife. On finding it, the waiter would know I was unhurt. Eventually he'd also discover my innocence from the other waiter, and all would be healed. I retreated a few feet and looked back to admire the way the knife decorated the café entrance. It was very appropriate for such a pirate-like hangout at the Casablanca waterfront. If I may say so, it was a fine decorative idea, and more rusty knives should have been stuck there around the door.

But I got out of town that very moment and spent the next several hours hitchhiking to Rabat, the capitol city from which led the road eastward across the top of Africa.

I arrived about 2 a.m., and the only place open for me to play was a dimly lit, barn-like club full of lascivious drunks sitting around a completely nude belly dancer. She swiveled like a snake being charmed, while her musicians played three-string mandolin, conga drum, maracas, and a tight-skinned pair of bongo drums with hot red lights burning inside them to keep the skins tight. The red light shone through the skins into the drummer's face, revealing his complete fascination with the movements of the Nubian girl dancing. Every face in the building was similarly hypnotized, including those of the manager and doorman, so I was able to enter and take a seat without being challenged.

A fight started out front that began to distract a few people. But the Nubian dancer countered by twirling her navel like a whirlpool, completely regaining her audience.

Around three a.m. she finished. Half the audience followed her to her dressing room. The other half was stoned beyond saving. Realizing there was no audience for me here, I walked out—straight to a waiting policeman standing at the door who demanded my passport. He read it briefly and put it into his front shirt pocket without a word.

As he spoke only Arabic, I summoned help from a friendly passerby who spoke some Spanish with me. He was a nice old man and took some time to intercede for me with the policeman.

"He says he does not suspect you of anything yet, but he wants to be sure you had nothing to do with the fight one hour ago."

"If it is not too much trouble, please ask him for me how this standing around will help him decide."

"Yes, that is a good point," the kind man said. And he babbled for 10 minutes with the policeman.

"It seems the detective-inspector will be coming around sometime this morning and will be able to answer your questions more fully. Until then you must wait. I do not think he is angry with you. I think maybe you should give him some baksheesh, eh?"

There was no doubt about it. It was a clear case of extortion. My kind friend lost interest and went away.

"No baksheesh," I told the policeman.

He just smiled. He had everything to gain and could lose nothing. It was his duty to stand there all night anyway. So together we waited. After an hour, the detective- inspector arrived, found the club closed and his policeman standing alone with me.

He took us in his car to headquarters where we joined two other officers and sat at a table. I wasn't afraid—just curious about them. Why were they so interested in me?

"Where is your immigration stamp? We cannot find it." They turned on a powerful lamp and shined it into my eyes, but I found the stamp and showed it to them.

"Oh, so you entered Morocco just this week. How long will you stay? What is your purpose here?"

"I'm a tourist and will stay only long enough to get through to Algeria."

"Algeria? Why will you go there? Are you Muslim or Jew?" They adjusted the lamp to shine even more aggressively into my face.

"Neither. I am Christian."

"But a Christian would have no reason to go to Algeria unless he was a member of the OAS (Secret Army Organization). Are you with the OAS?"

"No, I am going to Algeria as a journalist for a newspaper." I showed them a press card that my friend Art Volkertz of the *Santa Rosa Press Democrat* had given me.

"Do you have your Algerian visa? Let us see it. Ah, yes, it says here that you are a journalist. Can you prove you are a Christian?"

"Why is that necessary?"

"Otherwise you may be shot in Algeria. It is very dangerous there. Where were you tonight when the fight occurred?"

"I was inside the club."

"Are there any witnesses?"

And thus the questions and answers flew incoherently. They seemed to be composing the questions in an effort to pass the time rather than to achieve some goal.

Finally I broke in, "Why are you questioning me like this with no apparent aim?"

"These are just matters of routine."

"Routine! To keep people up all hours of the night?"

"Not exactly. But how much money do you have?"

"Not very much."

"If you could give us some money for our trouble, we could be assured you did not need our protection."

So that *was* it! "From what?" I asked, somewhat aggressively.

"Rabat is a safe city, but where you were at such a late hour could be unsafe. But now, of course, you are safe with us."

"Well then, may I go?"

The inspector smiled wanly. "It seems it is almost five o'clock in the morning. It will be difficult for you to find accommodation. Perhaps you would care to sleep in our jail."

"No, thank you."

So they took me to another room and filled out long forms with information about my family. The first question was, "What are the names of all your uncles and their sons?" They ultimately demanded all my male relative's names, ages, birth dates—if known—and occupations.

It seemed so insane, and I began to feel a bit frustrated with them. But then it occurred to me that it takes insanity to see insanity. I knew that if I accepted the notion that they were hustlers, hustling me for money, then I was accepting that as a description of myself. It takes a hustler to know a hustler. A determination welled up inside me to trust them as good and truly wise men who had only my best interests at heart—guardians of the law, truly dedicated to protecting and serving. I knew this might cause my adversaries to become allies, for I had committed no crime or misdemeanor.

Sobered, I went to work with them on the forms with patience and love. After another two hours I was still cooperative and mellow, so they cheerfully let me go with their friendship and good wishes. Patience and love had won. I was still a troubadour, having not used money as a means of exchange for my freedom.

The sun had also risen, and I found a ride to the Moroccan frontier town of Oujda on the back of a truck filled with live sheep—nature's most gentle angels. I had many fleas, but so did the sheep. As we drove along, I patched the hole in my backpack with a needle and thread. The sheep watched me work with loving interest, emitting a powerful vibration of peace that was so soothing and relaxing it made me smile.

These sheep were so humble and peaceful as to be far more pleasant company than many people I'd met. I realized the danger of losing my respect for the law—and for police generally—having witnessed the behavior of those extortionist Rabat police, and the brutal way Granada's Guardilla Civilla had treated the gypsy ring seller. So I decided I'd try to be more like the sheep who forgave and forgot instantly.

But it's hard to be as good as a sheep. I knew I could never measure up to their high level of forgiveness and peace, and was deeply awed as I gazed into their faces. Being surrounded by these woolly ambassadors felt like being in an oasis of love.

Outside the city of Fez, we drove through lovely meadows upon narrow roads. It felt almost like Ireland, though it wasn't as green. We stopped to pick up a pair of hitchhikers who joined me and the sheep in the back of the truck. Young Arabs in raggedy robes and headdress, they wore sturdy boots. They were friendly, rather curious about me, and one of them spoke English. He too found the sheep enchanting and relaxing. With this in common, we exchanged information about ourselves to pass the hours en route to Oujda.

He said they were both on their way to Algeria with plans to steal across the border and support the FLN (Arab Freedom

Fighters). The French still being in control of immigration proceedings, and each of them being Muslim, able bodied and of
undetermined motives, they couldn't get permission to cross the
border officially. They were too likely to be FLN supporters on
their way to join up with Ahmed Ben Bella's brave guerilla ren-
egades who were far from defeat despite Ben Bella's having been
imprisoned by the French.

Grimly, he told me the dire consequences of being caught by
the merciless French border patrols. Each day some illegal entrants
made it across the border, but always a few were caught and shot
on the spot without trial. Their own lives would soon hang in the
balance of a coin toss. But their fathers had freed Morocco. It was
now their time to free Algeria from the yoke of imperialist rule by
France and the French Colonials.

"How far will you go on foot?" I asked, feeling both amazed and
honored that I was being trusted with all this, but a little nervous
about pushing my luck.

"About 80 kilometers must be covered on foot as fast as possible to be safely east of the border," he said. "It means hiking
both day and night without rest. But that is not hard. I have done
it many times," he told me with considerable pride. They both
looked to be in fine physical condition, and I had the feeling they
would be successful. I remarked that were it not for their robes
and headdress, they might have been a pair of young revolution-
aries in America of the 1770's migrating to join their fellow rebel,
General George Washington.

My Arab friend was most interested in learning of this event.
He interpreted for his friend my brief account of George Washington and the Revolutionary War, saw the parallel to himself and
his compatriot at once and smiled triumphantly. "Yes, and General
Washington won. So will we."

In the center of downtown Oujda where the truck stopped to
let us off, we parted reluctantly and went our separate ways after
so many hours of being so closely together. People are a bit like
windblown clouds. They touch as they pass each other and then
move on, each cloud toward its own destiny.

My destiny was the one restaurant within sight. It was tucked
beneath a hotel. I sat and played for the four occupants, a young
couple, a man and the friendly proprietor. They listened with

loving attention—particularly the proprietor, a moustache-wearing Frenchman who wanted to talk. He wanted to know my whole story, so I told them all a little about my travels and recent experiences. They seemed more interested in this than in the music. When I got to the part about the knife-throwing Arab waiter in Casablanca, the proprietor was incensed.

"Ah, you must not go into Algeria alone," he said with deep emotion and concern for me. "The Arabs, they kill you first and then ask your name afterwards. They will leave your body in the street. People will walk around you and let you lie there. They will pay no attention, for everyone is afraid to put their nose in someone else's business. The Arabs are a ruthless savages. They live in casbahs of tiny mud holes and have strange ideas."

I was amazed to hear such words. And, though I didn't tell him, the more he talked this way, the more eager I became to visit the Arabs in Algeria. Even as he spoke, I sensed that the Arabs couldn't be as bad as all that. For I'd just met two of them that afternoon who were very friendly. And the quiet young couple who sat with us looked as though they might be quietly disagreeing with him.

They introduced themselves as Jean and Louis. Jean was a pale, willowy brunette. Her husband was tall, thin and hungry-looking. They offered me dinner, and the proprietor went off to prepare it. The single man also rose and walked out, leaving us there alone.

Jean and Louis then told me their story. They were French nationals recently banned from their own country for publicly sympathizing with the FLN. They were both fluent at speaking and writing in Arabic, were scholars in Arab history, literature and culture, and until recently had been teachers at an Algerian school for Arab children.

"We would like to go back to Algeria and help the FLN effort. But as France still controls things there, we would be arrested and thrown into prison if we were caught. We flew out of France to go teach in Algeria only hours before a warrant was issued to arrest and try us for treason because we helped organize the FLN fund-raising campaign. This is the same as being exiled, for we cannot return to our country," Louis said. He seemed relaxed and objective. There was no bitterness in him, and his attitude was that of a philosopher.

"Even in modern times," added the less placid Jean, "we are exiled for helping children and supporting those who want only to be free!" There was anger in her tone.

These two were so good with shotguns as to be a kind of French version of "Bonnie and Clyde." Not long after their arrival in Algeria, their school had been attacked and bombed by some French soldiers with grenades, and they'd had no choice but to fire back at their own countrymen in order to protect and defend the children.

They'd fought so bravely and effectively as to force the troops into retreating without having killed a single child! So now the charges against Jean and Louis weren't limited to just the treasonable fund-raising in Paris. They were in much deeper trouble, and the French authorities were actively and earnestly seeking to locate and arrest them now.

After I'd eaten, they took me to their huge apartment hideaway—an old storage warehouse they'd remodeled that was innocuously immersed among condemned, deserted buildings. There were a dozen beds kept for refugees, freedom fighters, and adventurers bringing needed if illegal supplies through known gaps in the French-patrolled border.

I told them I had fleas and wondered if they had a shower.

They did!

The shower parted me from Oziel's fleas that had plagued me for days. I washed all my clothes and went to sleep readily and gratefully, after days of being awake, in one of the dozen beds.

"It is best that you take the train from here to Oran," Louis suggested in the morning during breakfast. "You have a proper visa and should be able to go through customs and immigration without more than the usual amount of trouble. I have a railroad ticket I cannot use. It is yours," he said with a hearty smile, handing it to me out of his wallet.

He explained we were nearing the end of seven ghastly years of war for Algeria's freedom. Though the French were still in control of the borders, they were hanging on only by a thread. This was Degaulle's "Last Hurrah." Breakfasts and train tickets, he said, were compliments of Ben Bella's guerrillas who were giving them money for their help in preparing to snatch Algeria from Degaulle.

Such a brave and giving Samaritan, this Louis—a true hero. Anyone who will sacrifice his own birthright, so that others might someday have theirs, is a truly noble man.

"I feel so honored to have met you," I told him.

"We are just doing a job here," he smiled.

I walked over to the railroad station. It was packed inside with small groups that bustled with disorganization as I mounted the train to Oran. I took a seat and began marveling on the way Louis and Jean, as well as the hitchhiking Freedom Fighters and the tattooed sailor, had all trusted me with so much sensitive information about themselves. Why is it that folks seem to trust musicians and bartenders with information they wouldn't dream of telling anyone else?

5

FINDING A FRIEND—ONE OF AFRICA'S MOST BEAUTIFUL WOMEN

It was an old train. It rattled and squeaked to a stop at a small station less than five minutes east of the Algerian frontier where we were to go through French Customs/Immigration and then transfer to another train.

We were herded to an unwalled barn roped off into titled sections where we were to present ourselves to immigration officials. All but me were forced to leave their luggage in the adjacent sheep paddock to be examined at random and whim by rude customs officers. Violently they ripped open bundles and trunks, allowing earrings, and other small items, to fall and get lost in the grass. Wrappings and loose-leaf papers blew away in the wind. Bottled items were opened and sniffed. Powders were tasted, and liquids tested, by insertion of unclean fingers. Bedding, undergarments and art objects were scattered among the tall grass and stepped on as the passengers watched, screamed and complained helplessly from their roped-off areas.

This was wartime, and the enemy was not being nice. The terrible agony that prevailed around the building generated a slaughterhouse atmosphere. I alone was allowed to enter the Immigration Area carrying my belongings. An assistant summoned me to a special room to be personally examined by a polite if slightly nervous French-Arab.

He warmly apologized for the violence. I, being a neutral Westerner, would be better treated he told me. He explained that the

French had just made a successful counter- attack and routed Ben Bella's band of "cutthroat rebels" who were about to surrender. He told me this was a French victory for which I could be grateful indeed, for now my French-issued visa would be honored. He seemed impressed when he read my documents, seeing that I was sponsored by Francesca and her friend Pierre Desseaux, the French Press Attaché in Madrid. I was surprised when he took my train ticket, but he said that was the process.

"All tickets are collected here and given to the railway company. Please do not worry." He stamped my passport and visa, returned them to me, and summoned a customs officer who examined my luggage with little interest and directed me to go aboard the onward train and await the other passengers.

I found a comfortable compartment on the train and watched through the window as my fellow passengers continued filling out forms, chasing their windblown bags and baskets, and desperately searching the tall grasses for missing small items. What a sorry sight!

But after three hours or so, the horror ended. This new train was much better than the first one, and it rattled powerfully through magnificent Algerian countryside. Rich red earth was decorated with green foliage, colored rock formations and exotic gorges illumined by a golden sunset. Small mystical-looking mountain villages were carved into the beautiful hillsides, and lone Arabs traveled by donkey within sight of the train.

Ghostly doubts began entering my head about my future in Algeria. Would folks entwined in a national freedom struggle have time to enjoy a troubadour? What would become of me if they didn't?

My thoughts were interrupted by the conductor who slid his paunch belly noisily through the narrow cabin door and asked for my ticket.

"But I don't have it. The immigration officer took it."

He didn't speak English. So he left and returned minutes later with an interpreter.

"You say the immigration officer took your ticket? But that is impossible, for he does not take tickets," the interpreter declared.

"That's what I thought too. But he disagreed and said not to worry."

The two men regarded me sadly. God knows what they were thinking. When the train stopped at Sidi-bel-Abbes, they tried phoning the immigration office. But the line had been cut by rebels.

"You must buy a ticket," the interpreter relayed.

"But I am a troubadour and don't buy tickets. The one I gave the immigration officer was a gift from a friend."

They shook their heads and frowned. Ticketless travel is frowned upon everywhere. "We must take you to the police," they said.

They grimly escorted me to a special police station at the Oran rail depot where I was taken to a back room and searched for money to buy the ticket, the value of which was about a dollar and a half in U.S. currency. But they didn't find my chest pouch. I fiercely maintained they could retrieve their precious ticket from the immigration officer. My troubadour status was at stake, and I was getting worried.

They did find my 50 sets of guitar strings.

The French police captain became very tense and alarmed. "What is this? What is the purpose of this wire?"

"They're guitar strings, sir. I'm a guitarist."

"But this is copper wire, no?"

"Yes, I believe so. But the central cores are made of nylon."

The captain and his staff had a lively debate in French, after which the captain turned to me angrily. "Did someone give you these strings to bring into Algeria? If you do not tell us the truth, you will be in serious trouble."

"Great Scott, no! I obtained these strings in Paris from Savarez Manufacturing Co."

They all looked skeptical, but there was little they could do but to judge me by my air of innocence. "Please do not give these strings to anyone," said the captain, "for there is a control on copper wire of this gauge. OAS and rebel forces are using it to make plastic bombs."

I agreed. He took my California driver's license, telling me he wanted to keep it overnight while he continued trying to reach the French Immigration Office at the frontier about my ticket. I would have to return to him the next day in order to retrieve the license. I had the feeling this whole ticket thing might have been a ruse designed by French Immigration in order that they, in cooperation with the police, might have an excuse to interrogate and examine me.

I was set free and wandered into the city. Uniformed French soldiers lined the sidewalks every few feet and faced pedestrians with short-barreled automatic assault rifles strapped to their shoulders. The pedestrians were used to this, for the war had been in progress for seven years. But to me it felt like a firing squad, for there was a soldier every ten feet along some streets.

The French Sector of each North African city had its "Whisky A Go Go" club. This night, Oran's was packed with volatile French students from Oran University. It was nifty inside. It resembled the student caves in Heidelberg, with its rocky walls and low ceilings. But they had no live musicians, only rock and roll records to which they were doing a new dance called the "twist," the latest fad. This was the first I'd seen of it.

I had a quick word with the manager and was allowed to play because the dancers needed to rest their feet. My music was a needed change of pace, and the students responded with ear-splitting applause that lasted about a minute. My doubts about being able to eat in Algeria were quickly resolved.

A group of young French Army officers bought me dinner while twisting resumed. One worked at the AFN (French North African) Intelligence Center, and he told me his job was to keep track of all the reported plastic bombings and killings in the city.

"We must keep control, and my work helps us plot the movements of the Arab Freedom Fighters (FLN)."

When I asked him why the Arabs needed controlling, he surprised me. "They should not be controlled. Many of my friends think the same but don't talk."

"But then why do you do it?"

"I'm a soldier, and that is my life. And I am French. I will always support France."

"Even when, in your heart, you feel France is wrong?"

"Yes, because I personally think the Arabs will win anyway."

I thought his situation very funny and laughed. Then he laughed too. We discussed this widespread human behavior. We follow our leaders, whether they are right or wrong, because we belong to them and they to us. We go with the flow and get with the program, so that few of us end up like Jean and Louis, my "Bonnie & Clyde" friends, about whom I said nothing.

A cute French coed came over and invited me to dance. "Danse vous le twiste?" she asked with an alluring smile.

I felt like a giraffe on the dance floor, being taller than 6' 3" and a bit gawky. But I wanted to get a better look at her. So I got up and began learning to twist.

She spoke little English. But melting my heart with her compassion, she took me home anyway.

"Such courage you have," she said as we walked along. "You are so far from home and alone in this harsh land."

I replied that I was right at home, for home is wherever love is and there was much love in her.

As it was a cool mid-November night, and her parents were asleep upstairs, we built a fire in the large stone fireplace, sprawled in front of the crackling flame and forgot the soldiers, plastic bombs and curfew violations. All war intrigues waned in the wake of our need for each other's love.

Her father was a surgeon. Over breakfast in the morning, he warned, "Don't ever walk into the Arab Sector (Casbah) or you will be squashed just like that pancake you are eating. No one will watch for you, and no one will inform your relatives in America when you are dead."

"But surely no one could be that mean. Have you ever been there?"

"Of course not. For I have a family to support, and I value my life." He was very adamant, and well informed on many evil goings on about town resulting, he said, from Muslim intrigues that rooted in the Casbah. He cautioned me to please not take his words lightly. I respectfully took note of his warning and thanked him and his lovely daughter for their advice and hospitality as I left.

Anxious to recover my driver's license, I returned to the French police office to collect it.

A clerk gave it to me without a word as to whether the immigration officer at the frontier had cleared me. I'd apparently passed "inspection" and was free to roam and discover in Algeria.

But now it was the Secret Army Organization's turn to inspect me. About three blocks down the street, I was approached by a pair of sloppily dressed, unshaven members of the "Blackfeet." They were part of the French colonial OAS forces fighting for people born and raised in Algeria who owned property there and were in danger of being dispossessed should the Arabs prevail. One showed me his OAS card ("Organisation de L'Armie Secrete"). Responsible for most of the plastic bombing during the Seven Years' War, the OAS was a terrorist movement advocating Algeria be owned and governed by themselves.

With phony smiles and grim determination, they gently marched me through several streets and alleys to their meeting place, the back room of a dingy, foul-smelling bar, where I was rudely seized by three strong men and pushed toward a corner seat behind a table. When I resisted they yelled an alarm, and about seven more men entered from an adjacent room. All dozen sat around me, motioned that I should sit too, and I cooperated.

They were all sloppily dressed and unclean-looking. When they saw I would be no further trouble to them, they relaxed and began ignoring me, striking casual conversations among themselves. We sat thus for almost an hour until a dyspeptic, oily-eyed little man entered with a briefcase. Briskly he took the empty chair at my table and icily introduced himself as the district supervisor of the OAS Underground. With a very negative bias, he began questioning me.

"We know you are an American journalist," he said, with a note of disgust as he stressed the word, "journalist." (Francesca had told Pierre that so I could get a visa. But to know this, the OAS must've had an informer at the embassy and/or the immigration office.)

"Journalist!" he said again, and spat on the floor with distaste. He glared at me. "What are your leanings?"

I told him the truth. The truth had always helped me in all my 21 years. "I have no leanings, sir."

He looked dissatisfied. "Do your opinions support the Arabs, Degaulle or the OAS?"

Something about his adamancy, and the heaviness in the room, made me chuckle. I often chuckle at seriousness. For how important, really, is anything of this world?

He became furious. "Don't make us angry at you," he warned, his face shaking, "your life is worthless here. You have no rights." His oily eyes began to bulge, and his lips quivered. He was mean-looking. This made the politeness of his threat more frightening.

I sought to soothe him by being specific. "I really have no opinions. I'm neutral."

He squinted his very expressive eyes. "You are just as stupid as the country you come from. Don't you realize you cannot afford to be neutral? Degaulle cannot possibly hold out against this revolution. And if the Arabs take over, they and Algeria's resources will fall prey to the Communists."

He told me America should help the OAS and assured me a French colonial government in Algeria could survive economically without aid from France or anyone else.

I nodded in agreement with everything he said, genuinely admired his wisdom, decided such a wise man must surely have love in him, and I was therefore quite safe with him and his men. But he still suspected me of being anti OAS. He warned I would always be subject to arrest and/or harassment by the OAS anywhere in the world if my articles represented them unfairly.

Another man motioned that he wanted to see my guitar. He wasn't as serious-minded as the others and was getting tired of listening to the long conversation in English.

So I uncased the guitar while the dyspeptic eyed me suspiciously and seemed relieved when he saw it was really—and only—a guitar. The amiable man suggested I play something. The others agreed.

It was a perfectly theatrical setup. Grateful and overjoyed, I played my heart out for them as they sat around me with full attention. You could have heard a pin drop. Rarely have I had so good an audience. The amiable one was delighted, and he gathered a little pocket change from the others to give me, confidently and aggressively telling his friends to "dig deep."

I packed up to leave, and they permitted it. I thanked them for the money, and when shaking hands with the dyspeptic I told him, "Don't drop any wooden bombs."

He chuckled and said he wouldn't. His disposition had turned completely around. And he lovingly advised me, "beware the French soldiers, for they're mean men."

I wouldn't trade having given that performance for anything. The power of music is awesome.

I decided it was time to pursue my eastward course. The road to Algiers skirted a pretty belt of evergreen trees that extended for miles as far as Renault. A truck with two Arabs picked me up, and I sat between them in the cab. They shared with me their thermos of tea as well as their bread, pickles and olives. And they took me all the way to Algiers with only one or two quick stops for examination by French troops.

Algiers was built on a hill facing the Mediterranean and looked much like Monte Carlo. It was a unique blend of Arabic and French architecture. On its surface, it featured organized public transportation, modern, well-maintained wide streets, and expensive shops with the latest clothing styles from Paris. Charming.

But there was an oppressive undercurrent of foments. Plastic bombs exploded in cafes without warning, killing the innocent as well as the intended. Troops lined the streets as they did in Oran, and those entering a fine shop or department store were frisked by weapon checkers at the door. Despite the frisking, over half the women in town carried pistols in their purses—and certainly many men packed them under their coats—all of them with some kind of permit, forged or otherwise, so they could get past the checkers.

Most folks were in trouble with at least one of the three power factions—the OAS, the FLN or the French—because these factions often demanded opposite things from the citizens, and each had equal power. This was anarchy. The general atmosphere reflected the intrigues and traditions one associates with Old World pirate havens where expatriates are involved in nefarious business practices against a background of whores, hucksters of every possible deviation, and the black market. Then there were the hordes of French soldiers and secret agents patrolling the many barbed wire barricades.

My Arab hosts put me down at dusk near the edge of the French Sector. I found a street leading into the Casbah. It was blocked by warning signs and a barbed wire barricade along which patrolled a dozen French soldiers. Parked on the French side, to be used in emergencies, was a pair of old WW II tractor-style tanks.

I approached the soldier who seemed in charge. He was radio-equipped with a walkie talkie and stood near the tanks.

"Excuse me. Is it allowed for civilians to enter the Casbah?"

"No," he said. "The Casbah is forbidden, for we have no authority there."

"But I'm not French. I am American."

"Oui. Then you may enter, but please do not. For you will not succeed in coming back."

"It's that dangerous?"

"Oui," he sadly nodded. The hate for all "Europees" in the Casbah knew no bounds. Only Arabs passed through this checkpoint—never Westerners.

For a few seconds I looked back and forth between the soldiers and this tempting road to the unknown and dangerous. All had warned me against this road. Common sense rallied against it. But I had to take it and walked through to the Arab side. As I looked back to wave goodbye, I was stunned by the pall of silent horror upon the soldiers' faces. They were so afraid for me that I confess I was very frightened. But I was driven by my need to include Arabs—to have love reflected among any evil. That's all I can say.

The street narrowed, twisting its way to a small plaza lined with tiny homes. It was a warm evening for November. A small group of Arab women had gathered in the cobbled plaza to enjoy an evening of gossip. They stopped chattering and watched in silence as I passed. I'd love to have seen their faces, but they were covered by veils.

I chose one of the many cobbled alleyways that led from this plaza and walked on. This alleyway led to another plaza, this one littered with bits of broken glass from a bottle. There was a palm tree under which sat a group of twenty or so robed, sandal-wearing, hashish-smoking men.

They gathered around me at once, preventing my walking forward or backward. They weren't angry. If anything they seemed interested that a traveler had entered their midst. Excitedly they uttered speculations to one another on who I might be and what I was doing there. A few were interested in my Kelty pack with its frame of aluminum tubing. It showed breakthrough scientific design and thoughtful, practical construction. They went over it with their fingers, admiring the skill in its making. One smiling man pointed to my guitar and made strumming gestures.

They seemed to want a show. I was certainly willing and found a stool within the tea-house at the edge of the plaza. This teahouse was surprisingly clean and smelled of mint tea and other herbs. The concessionaire understood when I opened the guitar case and then gestured to him that my hands needed cleaning before I could play. He brought me a bowl of water and a towel. I produced a cake of soap from a handy side pocket of my Kelty pack. That impressed the group.

Then I played. They were quiet and reverent. So many souls had packed into the little bistro that none could breathe without extra effort. But I played for an hour because they applauded long and loud at the end of each piece, way out of proportion to the quality of my performance, for the excitement of our mutual discovery was special and intoxicating. Often it's not the quality of the wine but the occasion and our feeling about it that makes it delicious.

At length I took a break. As the crowd thinned and dispersed, several bought themselves refreshments to the concessionaire's delight, and a husky, middle-aged Arab in ragged headdress invited me to have mint tea with him. His English was perfect.

"Pardon my friends," he said with abundant civility. "They are very friendly and mean well by their gathering around you like that."

"Yes, I was happily surprised by their enthusiasm. For I am told they feel bitterly toward Westerners."

"Toward the French and French colonials, yes—especially the troopers. But you were obviously different. Your knapsack told us that. We don't see travelers on our streets anymore since the war began seven years ago. We go to the European Sector, but they never come to ours. You know it is quite amazing that you have made it through the French Sector and gotten past the OAS intact and alive."

He offered to take me around and show me some sights himself. We walked through crowded labyrinths and remote haunts until we found a bearded Arab displaying and selling about twenty, shiny new watches. Long stringy hair protruded from his soiled headdress, and his eyes gleamed. His gray robe was torn and streaked with smudges.

"Mahabbah," he said in cautious greeting.

My friend talked with him about the watches. "He got these watches from a French jewelry store that was bombed last night by the FLN. Somehow he got them through the Sector Patrol, and now he's in the watch-selling business."

"Doesn't the law stop him? For surely this is illegal."

"Law?" He reflected momentarily. "The law protects him. He is a hero for helping to drive out the French. For he helped them bomb the store."

"But the French law?"

"Ha! He has obeyed the Arab law by disobeying the French law. Here he is a hero. There he is a criminal. One cannot please everyone," he surmised with a shrug.

The watch seller became friendly and presented me with a watch to examine. It had a solid gold face and back, was fully automatic, shock and water proof, and had dozens of jewels. I returned the watch to him with some remiss, as I could probably have bought out his entire collection very cheaply and had enough gold watches to last a lifetime. But then I've never had much use for a watch. For the time is whatever it is. Whatever time it is, it's the right time. And there's little any of us can do about that. I explained this to my host who translated for the watch seller. They both found it funny, and we shared a good laugh.

My host took me a checkpoint where I re-entered the French Sector, waving goodbye with considerable regret. Though he'd repeated his name several times, at my request, I'd found it impossible to pronounce, much to his delight, and it escaped me.

He'd told me about a legendary belly dancer, Sonya. She performed nightly at the Fantasio, "the most opulent nightclub in all of Africa," he'd said. So I walked down to the waterfront, found the club and walked in. Sonya was in the middle of her act.

She belly danced on the large glass stage as multicolored lights illuminated and followed her from beneath the glass. Her face was from a classical painting by one of the Italian masters. Her voluptuous body blended the finest attributes of the Hollywood greats, with long, shiny, black hair, brown eyes, lithe withers, and skin as fair, white and unblemished as a morning dew. She rendered a winsome smile at her audience, openly and frankly. It was a special smile that seemed to say none of us has anything to hide.

One by one, she removed each of her dozen ultra sheer robes until she stood completely nude. Totally relaxed, she rotated her right breast in a counterclockwise direction. Then she rotated her left breast in a clockwise motion. After some seconds, she reversed the direction of each of her firm breasts and put a large silver coin in the top crevasse of her abdomen. She lowered it to the crevasse below and then brought it back up to the top one again. She motored the coin up and down over and over, all the while keeping her breasts rotating and continuing to sway in her most uniquely erotic style.

It was merciless. And it was unfair to any other belly dancer hoping to compete with her for the cream of the bookings and top money. She was the most sought after and highly paid club attraction on the African Continent. The soulful musicians who accompanied her were the finest concert percussionists I'd ever seen. The spectacular lighting and dramatic surround sound were as perfect as you could find at any theatre in the world.

She finished her show and went backstage. I looked around the club and was awed by the splendor. Crystal, rheostat-controlled lanterns lined the walls that were a mosaic of hand-etched glass upon gold leaf. There were many crystal chandeliers. Seated at the linened tables were some of the wealthiest, most worldly aristocrats in and beyond Africa—some of them sophisticated hedonists and aficionados of erotica, including a table of sheiks from Arabia who'd flown in from far away just to see her.

To avoid being challenged and thrown out, I headed straight for the service door that led to the backstage area. It was probably my guitar that caused the security man there to let me through without conversation.

Sonya sat on a black velvet couch in her dressing room, surrounded by her agent, manager and several gentleman admirers—all telling her how marvelous and beautiful she was. I wanted to meet her. So I decided to unpack my guitar and begin playing background music. The plan worked. Sonya peered through all those men and got into my music. I played improvisations I hoped would appeal to her, having heard the music in her show.

There was a particular improv I'd been working on that was inspired by my having watched a stoned young Arab playing a

Moorish lick on his three-stringed oud in the bazaar of Tangiers. I combined it with some flamenco and some Mayan folk music I'd heard. It was a strange hybrid, the likes of which I'd never before and have never since composed. She seemed fascinated by it and came over to sit with me. Her presence felt warm and tender.

"What is that music?"

"Something I'm composing," I replied. I smiled at her, for she made me feel very happy.

She shook her head. "How did you get in here? Who are you? Where are you from?"

She had every right to be cold and defensive. But instead she was toasty warm—almost as though she really didn't care about my answers, because the music was more important. I was a musician with music she liked. So I was a friend.

I couldn't help chuckling at that, and shrugged as if to agree that her questions really didn't apply in our case. She chuckled too. We were like two infants, uninhibited, happy, curious and unafraid. The other men had no chance with Sonya the rest of the evening. It was all Sonya and me. She was queen at the Fantasio, and I was now her king. For we were each an adventure to the other. I was captivated by the strong self-assurance she combined with her demure sensitivity and dependence.

As her shows were over for the evening, it was time for dinner. We ate together—just the two of us at our own table. We were served an elegant meal over which we got acquainted. I told her I'd just that evening been to the Casbah and performed. This fascinated her, for she was also interested in the Arab freedom struggle. Then we strolled along the waterfront. She was my own age. She'd been a ballerina since she was fourteen in Munich, but had worked without much recognition and little pay until she'd gotten into her present "thing." Her mother was pure Moroccan. Her father was German.

She told me she suffered from a hollow void inside that made her lonely.

I was amazed. "But you're a star. Stars are complete. Stars have everything."

She gave me her winsome smile that told me none of us has anything to hide. "There are no stars." That moment was so special, I've never forgotten.

I remarked that a wise old sage once talked to me about loneliness and the void she spoke of, telling me this void in us is God's greatest gift. For it draws us to Him when we come to realize that nothing on this earth can truly and permanently fill that void.

She said she liked that thought because it comforted her.

The moon shone in her face, and I told her I thought her the prettiest critter I'd ever seen. I felt grateful that this pleased her, and she took me home to her room for the night. I'd found myself a friend, and we shared the night in magical bewitchment, taking each other flying beyond reach of the world. There was no void at all.

We didn't have as much time together as I'd have liked. She had to be up early for a conference with her agent and staff about her upcoming tour a few days away. She stunned them at the meeting with news that the two of us had planned an afternoon stroll in the Casbah. They protested vehemently, but Sonya was stronger willed then they.

Before we left for the Casbah, she ordered a brief rehearsal with me, her musicians and the technical director. It went very well, and I was worked into her show. For she wanted to dance to the Mayan-like, "oudish" flamenco piece I'd invented. I routined the piece to suit her and decided to call it *Mosquito's Dream*. I still play that piece today, just as I performed it with Sonya during her last days in Algiers, and it's among the most popular of all my compositions.

"It's true that in the Casbah of Algiers, a man might be murdered for the price of his silk shirt. But that's also true of many places," I assured Sonya as we approached the barbed wire barricade. For though this Casbah visit was something she wanted very much to do, it made her more than a little nervous. We came upon a robed, headdressed Arab also attempting to enter the Casbah. He was being interrogated by the French soldiers. At Sonya's suggestion, I got out my little camera and took a shot of one of the soldiers frisking him. They found a large collection of stolen watches pinned inside his robe.

"He may have been involved in the same looting enterprise, two nights ago, as my friend with the stringy hair," I whispered to Sonya. And well he may have been. A soldier summoned help on his walkie talkie. More soldiers arrived and took the Arab to jail.

Sonya was a German national and I was American. So the soldiers had no choice but to permit us entry into the Casbah. As we

They found a large collection of stolen watches pinned inside his robe.

walked into the winding alleyways beneath arches of stone masonry, we discussed the Arab who'd been taken to prison. The French considered him a thief. But had he made it through the checkpoint to his own sector of town, he'd have been a hero. The SAO would have considered him a thief who'd stolen from other thieves—the whole lot of which should be thrown in jail.

Discussing the pros and cons of anarchy, we entered the bazaar. Merchants everywhere chanted the merit of their wares to strollers like ourselves. No one seemed to be buying anything. There were wicker trays of wheat kernels, dried fruit, seasonings and semi fresh fruit. The odor of human defecation mingled with that of stale blood emanating from the butchered carcasses on display. Equally powerful was the scent of rotting fruit that blended with the fetid essence of the bathless multitude.

The skinned heads of lambs lay in rows on the front shelf of a huckster's booth. The tongues of these unfortunate wooly ambassadors were still intact and hung out limply. Their eyes glared senselessly, and thousands of flies were having a banquet on their bloodstained faces.

Nearby, in a temple beneath a tall muezzin tower, the Muslim priests silently prayed to Allah for deliverance from French oppression. Sonya and I watched as they methodically bowed, straightened and bowed again from their knelt positions on straw mats, always facing Mecca. We weren't challenged and were allowed to stand just beyond the open archway entrance to hear the metrically chanted sermon from the Koran. The temple was brightly painted inside, and the straw mats were laid over a floor of loose gravel.

When the sermon finished, we walked back out among the glittering stalls of cheap trinkets, multicolored imported plastic items and rows of beggars.

In the alley across the square from the rows of beggars, we encountered an Arab dentist going about the removal of a tooth. He'd seated his patient, a strong-looking fellow in his twenties, upon a wooden box on the pavement so that his head faced down. He tied a string to his patient's malignant molar. We watched as he secured the string and then placed a pan of dirty water on a flat stone beneath his patient's head.

Finally, as though in the process of making more preparations, and with no warning whatever to his patient, he suddenly grabbed the string, pulling abruptly and firmly. The young Arab patient uttered a guttural sound, and the tooth popped out on the string followed by a steady trickle of blood that dyed the water in the pan.

Sonya invited me to be her guest at the small teahouse where I'd played the night before, and we sat down. She was grimacing at the sight of the dentist with his pan of bloody water. It hadn't been a pleasant sight. Our attention was drawn to a squabble at the far table. There were about eight Arabs taking sides behind two swarthy rogues engaged in violent argument. Suddenly one of them rose to his feet and drew a knife from a holster strapped to his leg.

His adversary gazed at him menacingly, with a face so evil as to freeze the air in the room. Then he too drew a knife. The pair stood in the center of the teahouse and jockeyed for position—backs bent and knives poised. Both were unshaven and wore ragged headdress. They were both muscular and quick. Each would feign a slice in one direction and then try for blood in another.

The pair of them blocked the only exit. A trapped audience, we sat hypnotized and surprised, for it had all begun with so little advertisement. The first Arab sliced the evil one's robe at the sleeve, but there was no blood. The evil one laughed wickedly. But as he counterattacked, his foot slipped, and he fell to the dirty floor, losing his knife when the first Arab crushed his hand underfoot. Then the first Arab grabbed him by the throat and squeezed hard, poising his knife at the jugular. Slowly, he drew his victim to his feet and led him away into an alley, while the others muttered sullenly and followed.

The evil one's knife was left on the floor. The concessionaire cautiously picked it up and wiped it with his apron. Wearing a pale fear on his face, he carried it behind the counter.

There was the principle war going on. But there were also Casbah intrigues and subplots resulting in such violence as this. Sonya and I were served. Numbed by what we'd seen, we pensively dallied in silence over our tea.

"Will it ever end?" she asked finally.

"Will lust, greed, anger, attachment and pride ever end?" I asked her in reply.

There was an old Arab at the table next to us who was a fellow adventurer, having been trapped with us in the circle of violence, and he heard us talking. From the spaced look on his face, one could see he was a philosopher. I liked him at once and smiled at him. Sonya liked him too, and she offered him some of our tea. He accepted and gave Sonya a bouquet of flowers from a large collection that he had beside him. He was clearly charmed by her and listened attentively as she spoke.

"There are three sets of laws in this town—all of them conflicting. Everyone is a criminal several times a day, disobeying one law in order to obey the other. It's pure anarchy. What are we to do?" she asked.

He told us we should never talk politics in Algeria unless forced to do so, in which case we should speak with triple-forked tongues. It's a cultivated art, more lethal than the sword, he said. And it was developed and honed by the Connecticut Yankees during their mid nineteenth century campaign to exterminate the Mexicans, Apaches, Navahoes and Russians.

He said we were as safe here in the Casbah as we could ever be within the opulent walls of the Fantasio. For the club could be bombed at any time by the OAS.

Safe, he told us. But even so, hundreds of eyes were on us as we passed through the centuries-old alleyways and little plazas. Sonya was so ravishingly beautiful, we attracted many smiles and stares. Some of the smiles were from people who'd been in my teahouse audience the night before, including the friendly man who'd made strumming gestures for me. To Sonya's delight, he smiled and strum-gestured for me again. Then we met a beggar seated alone at the base of a stone wall.

"La illah, il Allah," he whined desperately from his toothless, leprous cavern. His cataract-plagued eyes were the distillation of sadness and remorse. Sonya was very moved. She reached down to the old man and gave him her flowers. This changed him at once. He cried with delight at her attention and wept openly, embracing the flowers as we walked on.

I stayed on with Sonya until the end of her engagement in Algiers, working with her percussionists and performing my *Mosquito's Dream* each night for her show while she danced and swayed to the rapture of our audiences. She was such a treasure!

But we said goodbye as easily as a pair of windblown clouds in the sky that touched only for a moment. For we told ourselves that our friendship was such that our sense of separation by time and space wouldn't interfere. I walked with her to the car that took her to the airport and watched her speed away with a new sadness, for I would now face life without her. Still, I had my round-the-world trip to excite and fulfill me.

Before heading east though, I just had to go play at Algiers' Whisky A Go Go. I was allowed to play for a few minutes during a break in the twist dancing. The feeling was unbelievably warm, just as it had been in the Casbah. The whole club-full of folks gathered around me. I was interviewed and photographed by reporters from the Algiers daily newspaper, *Le Depeche*, who happened to be present.

I also met some American diplomats there, including Mr. Porter, the consul general, who invited me to visit his home the following day for Thanksgiving Dinner. American food. Fellow Americans. I learned the pleasure of touching base with those of my homeland after a long absence. I'd forgotten all about Thanksgiving.

In addition to the Americans, a crowd of French people gathered around for my autograph, presenting me with invitations to functions. I laughed to myself at the pessimistic advice given me by the people in Morocco. I was learning that the tougher the going in a country, the easier it can be to travel in. For the folks become kinder.

Mr. Platt, the club owner, took me to his flat for the night. He was a warm-hearted, stockily built man with a fetish for neatness. Being French, he was loyal to the French soldiers. The OAS was after him to give them money and join them. Any Frenchman who remained loyal to his country was a "Loyalist" to the OAS, and was fair game to be terrorized and bombed. So Mr. Platt carried a revolver at all times.

The front door of his flat had no fewer than five locks. He carried a separate key for each, and it was a lengthy process getting all of them open. When we finally entered, we discovered his side window was broken.

His expression turned to stone. "It's the OAS, the terrible OAS," he said. A plastic bomb had been set off beneath the window, and the entire side of the building had been shattered and caved in. "This is only a warning. Next time it will be worse," he moaned.

He had me sleep in his children's room. They'd been sent off to Belgium, with their mother, to remove them from Algeria's dangers. But since Platt had invested heavily in prewar Algiers, he had to stay and hope for a resurgence of property values before he could sell out and follow them.

Mr. Porter's vice consul came the following noon and drove me to Thanksgiving Dinner. Porter's home was a fine mansion overlooking the scenic Bay of Algiers. Graced with spacious, semitropical gardens that surrounded the courtyard and swimming pool, it was one of Algiers' finest homes and combined French and Arabic design.

As we ate, I asked Mr. Porter what he thought of all this war and anarchy.

"I don't have any thoughts. I have no opinions," he firmly replied. "We of the consulate stay healthy by talking as little as possible. Three weeks ago, an American friend of mine was talking about his opinions. His apartment got bombed, and he had to leave town."

"The French or the OAS?"

"We don't know. But they jimmied open his door and threw in the bomb. The whole front was caved in, and the furniture was ruined. We find that the only way to please everyone is to keep our mouths shut. Whenever President Kennedy says something indicating his preferences and hopes about Algeria, we suffer the consequences here."

A fellow guest, sitting next to me at the grand table, was NBC Radio Correspondent Pier Anderson. We liked each other at once as we got acquainted during dinner. So afterwards he took me to his office downtown and produced a program with me for NBC Radio Monitor. I played and told my stories, and he gave me a bunk there for the night. He returned before dawn and drove me to the city's edge on the road to Constantine.

"The American Consulate here has been assaulted twice recently," he said, "because we're bombed if we do and bombed if we don't."

His arm was heavily bandaged at the elbow. "Just a bit of shrapnel I picked up while covering a story here in Algiers. Are you sure you don't want to take my job for a month while I go to Brussels for the holidays?"

"No thanks. I'm a troubadour, not a journalist." I was very honored though.

He let me out on the lonely highway. It was about 5 a.m. "Don't let them recruit you into the Arab Army," he yelled back to me as he drove off.

Pier is very special.

I got picked up by an English-speaking, French Arab driving an old Pontiac. We drove over 150 miles of twisting, narrow highway over the mountain ranges of the Djebel Djurjura toward the plains of Setif. The high and lonely Djebel Djurjura is a refreshing oasis of evergreens among colorful pinnacles. The roadway winds along the edges of tall cliffs, providing a panorama of breathtaking scenery unparalleled in North Africa.

But then we descended upon—and began crossing—the hot, dusty, spirit-wilting plains of Setif. It seemed to be an endless desert. The world was such a big place, and I found myself wondering if I would ever make it all the way around.

We came upon a long stretch of road purposely littered with millions of tacks. The trucks we passed had heavily needled branches, cut from the local evergreen trees, tied to their front bumpers in such a way that they brushed the road in front of the tires.

"You see these tacks?" frowned my kind friend. "They are put there by Ben Bella's rebels. They think they can win the war with tacks. They are fools."

He had only one spare tire and no tree branches. We had a flat tire in minutes, and I helped him change the tire.

"The rebels will never win like this," he grumbled. "They cannot defeat us with tacks. They will have to come out of their filthy holes and fight."

He cut two branches from a sun-withered bush, and we tied them to the front bumper with a roll of abandoned kite string I'd found in Algiers and had in my pack. He pruned the branches with his pen knife. With some adjusting, our improvisation worked perfectly, and now we too were equipped with a viable set of road brushes.

We were fortunate and made it to the kiln-dried town of Setif, where we left the punctured tire at a service station and went in search of a place to eat while the tire got repaired.

"But you do not need to play for your lunch. I will get it for you," my friend offered.

I insisted on playing. "I want to meet folks in Setif. This is my way of doing it."

He was impressed with my enthusiasm. "Very well. Then perhaps you can play for my lunch also." He lost his nerve though and succumbed to embarrassment. He pretended he wasn't with me when we entered the town's best restaurant. It was filled with chattering Arabs, as it was the peak of lunch hour.

The manager was excited about the prospect of some live music, and he allowed me to sit on the espresso counter and perform. I played some flamenco, and the place quieted down except for one man who kept blowing his nose on a napkin. Two others began giggling like schoolboys but were silenced by angry glances from the rest of the crowd.

They whistled, clapped, stomped on the floor and rapped spoons on their tables for me. I told the manager he could pass a plate in my behalf and then keep all the money for himself if he would give my friend and me open menu for as much as we could eat. He agreed readily and went from table to table collecting while my friend came over and patted me on the back, his embarrassment forgotten.

It was my first experience at having a restaurateur go around and collect for me. I'd earned food for a friend. And I began to feel a little like Carlo Schmid's Maverick.

An old Arab, seated alone, invited us to join him. With his profound gaze, white beard and headdress, he had the look of a country metaphysician on the threshold of new discoveries. Adamantly, with high-pitched voice, he wanted to know for sure if I was American and how long I'd lived in my country.

"So you have lived there most of your life. Then you should know your country. Why then does your country remain friendly with Degaulle who suppresses our freedom here in Algeria?"

"That's an embarrassing question even the diplomatic authorities have to slip around with big words and vague theories," I answered.

"But why must it be embarrassing? Why the slipping around? Where is the America of 1776?"

"By breaking ties with France, America would be fighting your battle for you at great expense to herself," pointed out my French friend, indignantly buttering his muffin. "She is a big country, but she cannot fight the battles for everyone."

The old Arab folded his hands on his lap and gazed dreamily down at them. "Maybe not. But with or without America, the Arabs will be free."

My friend moaned in disgust but said nothing.

The road through to Constantine and Bone was without tacks, and we made the journey without mishap. My friend let me off near the port of Bone where I walked past the main dock in time to see a foaming mob of almost a hundred Arabs waving their arms and ranting. An Arab had challenged a young French soldier to a street fight and killed him. Police had just removed the dead soldier's body, and every face in the mob looked frightened. For the French soldiers would not take this lying down.

There was a French-owned cellar restaurant with brick walls where I was allowed to play. A large table of French sailors was particularly appreciative and contributed hugely when I passed a plate. Sailors have always been my best audience.

The happiest sailor, with his back to the brick wall, sat between a pair of tall wine bottles. He gleefully slurped minestrone soup from a table knife raked across his tongue, and then he pointed the knife at me.

"Aha, troubadour! Come eat with us."

They all cheered in unison as I accepted and sat with them.

The knife wielder's name was Peche. He reached into his pocket and produced a giant roll of bills. "You see, there is plenty money," he said warmly. He ordered me a sumptuous feast. "Why are you here in Algeria?"

"Because I have never been here before."

"Just that?" He stuck his teeth into a juicy piece of fried chicken, and the oil oozed onto his chin. "You must stay with us on board ship tonight. Plenty room."

"Where are you headed?" another sailor asked me.

"Tunisia, I guess."

"But how?"

"Hitchhike, of course."

"But that is impossible. There is an electric wire fence at the frontier, the Morice Line. None can go through it. There is no land travel allowed across the frontier to Tunisia."

The Americans in Algiers had told me the same thing, but I'd passed it off lightly as a bridge to be crossed when it was come to.

We spent a very happy evening in wassail, song and laughter, and then walked to the ship. We passed dark alleys and seaport fisheries that reeked of rotted sardines, and were approached by one of North Africa's thousands of independent black marketers who vend their illicit, ill-begotten wares in obscure alleyways by night.

Short, wiry and fleet of foot, he carried a basket of American military cigarettes. "You like American cigarettes? Ver' cheap! Changee money? You have dollars? You like pretty girl? School-teacher? Eh? Baksheesh!"

The sailors bought some cigarettes, and we walked on. But the ambitious little Arab wasn't finished with us. He stayed alongside us, offering everything from orchids to contraceptives at amazingly low prices. Then, seeing we were uninterested, he dug a plane ticket from his bosom.

"You go AWOL—go Tunisee?" He waved it in the air. "Here airplane ticket ver' cheap."

Peche stopped and looked at me with a smile. "Go Tunisee?" he chuckled, copying the dwarfish Arab's accent. He turned to the little fellow whose eyes were newly lit with hope. "How much?"

"Ten francs," beamed the coal-faced huckster, showing us the ticket which bore the official stamp of Cook's Travel Service and lacked the name of a passenger. It was like a blank check, save for the amount and destination—one way, Bone to Tunis, open date.

Peche handed him some bills, took the ticket and handed it to me. "Now you have no need to find a hole in the fence. You can fly over it and take it easy."

As we walked along the pier, we found a group of armed French soldiers excitedly

huddled over a map of the city. We listened to their discussion for a minute or two, and Peche looked deeply concerned.

"You know what happened today?" he asked me.

"You mean the street fight?"

He nodded. "These are all friends of the dead soldier. They will kill the Arab."

"A tooth for a tooth?"

With his finger, he drew a line across his throat and said nothing. The soldiers resolved upon their plans, split into several patrols and proceeded with their death mission. We went aboard ship and sat playing cards in the galley.

"It is the only way to handle these Arabs. We must be rough with them, or it is impossible to maintain control. Violence is the only language that speaks to them," Peche said. He slapped and killed a fly that was cleaning its wings on the table. "Killing that Arab will be like getting rid of this pest fly."

I went to sleep in a sailor's bunk, with visions of an Arab hanging by his neck and a sword sticking through him.

The ship untied and left for Algiers at daybreak. So I disembarked sleepy-eyed, without breakfast, and visited Mr. and Mrs. Nuncie, a cheerful American couple. They ran Bone's one bus company, had been among my audience the previous night, and had invited me to visit.

"Welcome," chirped Mrs. Muncie, delighted to see me though still in her bathrobe. "You're just in time for breakfast." She fixed a pot of tea while Mr. Muncie told me about the bombings.

"It's like living near the ocean and hearing the waves. They rock you to sleep, and one usually wakes you in the morning. Don't know what we'd do without them," he laughed. "I suppose we'd have to resort to an alarm clock."

"Did you hear about last night?" asked the blonde, petite Mrs. Nuncie. "A band of French soldiers killed six Arabs and injured a few others to avenge their dead comrade."

"Six! I wonder if the Arabs will figure, along with the soldiers, that six for one is a fair swap?"

"Well, I'd rather not venture my opinion," she mused.

"Why?"

She sank into a chair just as a plastic bomb explosion boomed from somewhere down the street. In response, she closed her eyes for a second, reopened them and sipped her tea. "We've lived here in Bone for twenty years and intend to stay on here for at least thirty more," she smiled sweetly.

Later in the day, they took me to the airport. Using Peche's ticket, I caught a flight across Algeria's eastern frontier to Tunis.

6

ATTACKED BY BEGGARS AND
RESCUED BY A YOUTHFUL SAGE

The plane flew very low over the sun-bleached ruins of Carthage. In plain view were the broken pillars and steps, the heavy walls of the House of Horses, the Frigidarium, and the Baths. Carthage was originally built, according to Virgil's epic poem, *The Aeneid*, by Princess Dido of Tyre in 800 BC. As I gazed down at the remains of her empire, I fantasized about her life, her fear of her brother Pygmalion, and the conditions she faced.

The Tunis airport, near these ruins, was unusually small for such a major city. I was still in another world with Princess Dido, thousands of years away in time, as I entered the customs area that brimmed with hawkers, officials and travelers. There were many curiosity seekers. Some were there only to enjoy watching incoming travelers get arrested when caught smuggling. Others, more opportunistic, stood around just to learn for themselves who was entering the country with what. At the sight of them I was quickly brought back to the here and now.

We passengers were lined up single file before the customs desk. A handsome family of Arabs stood directly in front of me. The wife wore a white robe, as did her three children, and she wore a white veil. She and her husband declared no merchandise for sale in their large bundle wrapped in a white bed sheet. The officer checked it, and it seemed to be all personal. But then, on a hunch, he dug a little deeper and found at least two dozen pairs of unworn shoes of various sizes, a large box of identical golden trinkets, and thirty or so leather-bound copies of the Koran—commercial goods. She quickly tried to bribe him. He felt insulted and called the police who arrested the whole family as the wife screamed piteously.

It wasn't the hysteria of her wailing that got to me so much as the piteousness. What would become of her lovely children now? Smuggling is a prison offense. Even the beggars and baggage handlers stopped their clamor and rendered a moment of sympathy.

Everyone was still in shock when I, next in line, was asked how much money I had. The truth had always protected me, so I was honest.

"Nine hundred dollars U.S. and 100 French francs," I whispered to him. (The outdoor cafes of Europe had been good to me.)

That was a lot of money in those days. He frowned at my dust-caked tennis shoes and old leather jacket, and demanded to see the cash. Perhaps I had a deal to smuggle dollars out of the country for a Tunisian, declaring money I didn't possess going into Tunisia so I could take that much out of the country later!

"Certainly," I said. "But is there a private room where we could do this?" We were surrounded by thieves, beggars, and those who make a living swindling hard currency from travelers.

He grew impatient. He'd just found one smuggler and here was another. This was his lucky day. "If you have the money, let me see it at once, right here, now. Otherwise you will be arrested for false declaration."

Reluctantly I pulled the wad of bills from my waterproof chest pouch, and the officer was both fascinated and surprised. "Let us count it," he said with a new air of respect.

He took the wad and organized the twenty-dollar bills into nine separate hundred-dollar piles that stretched across the entire counter. He seemed to enjoy his work, and we quickly gathered a small audience of knife-bearing street folk, black marketers and miscellaneous hucksters, all of whom began surveying me as a salivating deer hunter might size up a twelve-point buck.

Counting finished, the officer handed me the proper signed-and-stamped forms to keep with my money. Any exchanging into dinars could only be done at a bank, and these forms had to be properly filled in and counter-stamped with each transaction.

At least a hundred eyes watched hungrily as I carefully rein-serted the money into Mom's chest pouch and walked out into the warm and humid moonlit night to hitch a ride downtown. At least fifty people of all ages, sizes and descriptions followed me out the door, many of them desperately chanting to me.

"Saida, Charley. You come see friend. Meat a-cook ver' nice, ver' clean. Baksheesh, Charley, baksheesh, anna maskeen. You like something? Pretty girl? You like buy carpet? This way, this way."

They called at me from all sides. One very dirty, sniveling little shirtless boy plaintively wailed, "no mungaree, no mumma, no poppa, see, no shirt. I give you anything. Baksheesh."

They grew in confidence as they ran along beside, behind and in front of me, and I found it impossible to hitchhike. Passing autos only honked to clear the roadway. Word spread quickly that a rich American, with a chest pouch full of greenbacks, was on the roadside, and my fan club swelled to more than fifty very soon.

For the most part, beggars here won't physically molest a West-erner if he refuses to dole out a few coins. But these starving folk had actually seen or heard about my wad of bills. They had me alone with it and surrounded. The temptation was too strong. So as I skirted a lonely meadow, they began working as a team, like wolves, grabbing at my guitar case, reaching into my pockets and untucking my shirt.

I shouted at them and pushed them away as they approached, but this only made them more excited. Their violence increased until I was badly disheveled, besmudged and then brought to the ground by at least seven strong, shirtless teenage boys who climbed on top of me, anchored my limbs to the ground, tore open my col-lar and began fighting each other for my chest pouch.

Others crushed in from all sides, groping in vain, hoping to steal the pouch from the frantic bathless boys. None thought to lift the strap over my head from around my neck. Instead, in their adrenaline rush, they only pulled and twisted the pouch and strap—one desperate hand wrenching it from another, and yet another—until I began choking.

Strangely, I wasn't the least bit afraid. I felt as though these awful things were somehow happening to someone else—an entity other than me. Further, I was absolutely convinced the entity was all right and there would somehow be a happy resolution to this bad dream.

I was being badly pummeled, as well as choked, and lost consciousness for some fleeting seconds. But then I found myself gasping for air. I looked up at a smiling, swarthy, robed youth wearing a black fez and sturdy sandals. He held a large, mean-looking, gleaming cutlass, bigger than a butcher's meat cleaver. Single-handedly he'd terrorized the crowd by wielding this cutlass. They'd all fled, leaving the mangled pouch still loosely twisted around my neck—money and other contents still intact.

He was laughing. Then he clucked, with dry humor, "I could have let them kill you, cowboy, but I decided I wanted to meet you first. You are safe." He grabbed my arm and helped me regain my feet. For strapped to my back pack, I was a bit like a turtle turned upside down.

I surveyed the damage. My already scuffed guitar case was little the worse despite a few new scuffs and dents. There were some smarting, bleeding places on me, but there was nothing broken.

"Thank you," I said. "You have surely saved my life."

He warmly replied, "it was a pleasure, man. Those street boys are like animals—no better." He was about my own age but bathless and heavily bearded so that he looked a bit older—perhaps in his mid twenties. He was handsome enough to make a living as a model, were it not for his beard and a mean scar on his cheek.

He grinned as I stared at the scar. "I got in a knife fight," he said, proudly putting his finger on it. "I like getting in scraps." He showed me his chipped front tooth. "This happened in another fight. I speak English good, eh?" With a distinct cynical expression he added, "I read books at the U.S.I.S."

From this I gathered he'd had some experience with that fine bureaucratic division of the American Foreign Service but had some reservations about it.

I ignored it. "What were you doing way out here with this cutlass?"

"Aren't you glad? I just picked it up at the airfreight office—a gift to my old pop from his friend in Sfax. It came in handy just now. When I saw you leave the airport with that crowd around you, I figured it might."

I was filled with gratitude. "I'm very grateful."

Embarrased, he defended himself. "I guess you should be, brother."

He was civilized, and I liked him at once.

"Come, he said. I can show you the shortcut to town."

As we walked across a pasture and down a rutted back road to the outskirts of the Arab Quarter, I learned his name was Bahattin Ulukol. He was a Turkish-Tunisian student—a Humanities major at the local university.

"Where are you headed?" he inquired.

"To wherever I can play for my dinner and lodging. I'm a troubadour."

"That's cool. Why don't you come play for my old people? We've got some grub around the place you can eat. They don't speak English, but they dig art."

Bahattin's neighborhood was a giant sprawl of white, cement-walled courtyards. At some corners, atop the walls, were white cement domes that reflected the moonlight. Beneath these domes lived the people among odors of sewage and mule's underfoot.

We walked about a mile, along pebbled pathways and cobbled alleyways that passed through many Roman-style arches, to his house. His "old pop" was a well-to-do shopkeeper, and the Ulukols had their own ranch style multiplex around their own courtyard. It looked and smelled clean in this particular house. Bahattin had his own room with a bed, couch, wardrobe closet and desk, plus several rows of shelves about to collapse under the weight of so many American books.

The walls were made of perspiring cement. A hole in the domed kitchen roof served as chimney for the open wood fire where the family meals were barbecued.

We found the Ulukols seated in the courtyard to catch any cool breezes. The elder Ulukol was a man of formalities, morals, principles and experience. He smoked a strikingly beautiful hashish water pipe—an elaborate floor-standing apparatus. It filtered the smoke through coils of tubing that led to a handblown, stained-glass water tank half-filled with water that bubbled as he inhaled.

With the utmost courtesy, both elders stood to greet me. Bahattin explained where we'd met, and asked permission for me to stay the night. They smiled and nodded.

"Bahattin," I said, "please say to your folks I wish to tell them they have a very noble and courageous son, and that I thank my lucky stars that you happened along when you did."

He interpreted with a modest smile, adding details of the evening's drama.

The old man looked worried. In silence, he took several puffs from his wash bottle. I was fascinated by it. Even its mouthpiece was a study in quality craftsmanship. Then he said this was the first time he'd heard of such goings on at the airport, and asked if I would like him to inform the police.

I said I wasn't sure. In a kind of post shock, I began gazing at a spot that periodically appeared in front of me about a foot from my head.

"Perhaps that would be wise," he replied through Bahattin. It would mean many hours of filling out endless forms to no avail, for it would be a miracle if the guilty ones could ever be found and rounded up. And they were only poverty victims who acted in a mob situation where there was treasure for the grabbing. He advised that we sleep on it and think again in the morning.

Bahattin said this was an example of Eastern wisdom and left me to the gods of sleep.

The old man made an anonymously phoned report to the police the next day, describing the incident. And he requested that they patrol the airport and watch out for Western visitors with more care.

November on the Mediterranean Coast can be very warm. The new day brought a hot morning with the prospect of unbearable heat later in the day. But I was anxious to be headed on my way east. Bahattin shared with me his breakfast of barbecued beans and seasoned butterfat upon bread, and then decided to show me the town on my way to the eastbound highway. As we walked through a big market place near the British Embassy, a tangerine seller accosted us with a smile.

"You buy-a tangerine? Me got twenty child, all need shoes, tangerine real clean, take-a peel off, ver' sweet, good tangerine. Hey!" He walked alongside us for a block, and we didn't buy any. Then he stopped and swore at us in Arabic.

I was shocked, but Bahattin only smiled. "Split personality, these Tunisians. Nice when they're cheating you and their natural selves when there's no deal."

"How can you say that? You are Tunisian."

"Uh-uh," he said adamantly. "I'm half Turk. Don't forget."

The little street we then entered was lined with rug stalls displaying an array of brightly colored pseudo-oriental tapestry. One of them had a selection of fine sandals, and the merchant stood next to them appraising us. Just out of earshot, Bahattin briefed me on Arab-world buying strategy and then turned me loose on the merchant. "See how well you can bargain with him for a pair of sandals. Don't buy, and afterward I'll tell you what you did wrong."

So I entered the shop with Bahattin. I was impressed. For there were shiny copper vases and basins, also fine coffee tables, silks and jewelry. I quickly found the sandals.

The merchant came over, literally rubbing his hands together. "Yes, what you buy today, eh? Plenty good shoes. You want sandal?"

I picked out a pair. "I would like this pair. How much?"

"Oh, this one very nice sandal, but I make you a special price—only three dinar."

"But it is not that good. Look here. The thread is loose. No, I could not pay that much."

"Oh. This one has bad thread, but you could fix easy. I give it to you for two dinar. You buy now, cash."

I wiped my brow in disbelief. "Two dinar for this very poor, loosely threaded work? Preposterous. One dinar."

"But that is impossible. I lose money. My cost is 1.5 dinar, but I give it to you for that. You are a good boy. I don't need to make profit on you."

I walked toward the door. "Thank you, but it is too much."

"O.K., one dinar. O.K."

"Well, let's see," I said, counting some Algerian coins from my pocket in a cupped palm so as not to let on I had no Tunisian money. "Yes, that seems a fair price. You see, I am buying these for my grandfather. He loves sandals, but I am a poor man. Tsk. It seems I have only one fourth of a dinar. I guess I cannot afford the sandals after all. I'm sorry." Again, I turned to walk out.

"No, no, wait! I know how it is to have a grandfather. I myself am a grandfather. You take sandals for one fourth dinar." He was almost crying.

"Thank you," I said in amazement. "Let me think and come back. I didn't realize I had so little money. I need to think." Then we left him and walked on.

Bahattin was exultant. "You have talent," he said. "You got him down to his standard price—one fourth dinar. But now you need to learn how to handle people who approach you on the street."

He led me past the bazaar toward the restaurant section, coaching me as we walked. Soon we were forcefully accosted by an ambitious, impolite, offensive huckster with overbearing halitosis.

"You eat good here" he declared, pointing to his tiny, dismal and filthy restaurant. "You come eat my food. I fix you good meal, charge you only small money."

Bahattin looked at me questioningly. "Should we patronize the poor sufferer?"

The man's face perked up.

"I don't know, the place looks rather humble." I said.

"Yes," Bahattin agreed. "Look at the flies on the food, and smell the rotten meat."

"You're right. And with all that grease on the floor, my shoes would be ruined."

"It is known that these little restaurants are a bad omen."

"Indeed. Yesterday my fortune teller told me I would see a small restaurant with brown table tops, and that its owner would be unlucky—something about his license."

The huckster, who looked horrified at the fortune teller's prophecy, became further aghast at the remark about his license. It may well have been out of order.

"But gentlemen, ah . . ." He was speechless.

We kept walking, almost unable to contain our laughter. Finally, a safe half-block away, Bahattin broke down in hysterical laughs—his beard shaking.

But it was truly lunchtime, and we'd not eaten. I wanted to do some small nice thing for him. So I had him sit himself down in a nearby pleasant restaurant filled with very nice folks. Though my body was still bruised and sore, I was able to sit next to him and play for 10 minutes or so. The crowd applauded.

At my instruction, Bahattin passed a small waiter's tray among the audience for donations. He put on quite a show, thanking the donators by putting his hand over his heart and bowing like an Elizabethan courtier. "Merci, monsieur, gracias, senora, dankeshun," he declared, cavorting to everyone's delight as they added heartwarmingly copious funds to his tray. I told him to please buy our meal (which would've barely dented the generous windfall) and keep all the rest for himself.

As he was modestly accepting, we were approached by an imperturbable and privileged-looking, impeccably dressed Englishman with a handlebar moustache.

"Splendid show, chappies. Might I buy both your lunches?"

"Thank you, sir," we chorused.

He was a travel agent into the packaging of plush tours for large tourist groups as well as safaris for the London society set. "I just wanted to meet you and learn why you perform in restaurants. I say, it's all rather intriguing. So you're troubadours then?" He wanted all the details, and we willingly rendered them as we ate.

"And where are you headed next," he inquired of me.

Bahattin intervened and told me, "you should see Italy. It is a beautiful country."

I became silent in thought.

"Would you like to see Italy?" inquired the Englishman coaxingly, as though he might have an idea to offer.

"Well," I said, "it's close to Greece, and it's on my way east."

"Excellent," he responded in delight. "I want to help you in your troubadour mission, and I cannot think of a better way than getting you trans-Mediterranean on the next leg of your journey. Can you?"

"That would be wonderful, but how might I repay you?"

"You've already done that. I enjoyed your music immensely."

We went with him in his chauffeured Bentley to a nearby travel office. He arranged my complimentary plane ticket to Rome and confirmed his own reservation on a flight to Cairo for that very afternoon. It was all done in seconds.

"Good luck," the Englishman said, and he stepped away from us into his car before I had time to thank him properly.

Amazed, Bahattin and I stood on the steps of the travel office and watched his car disappear along the busy boulevard.

"There goes a true philanthropist," he observed. This man is efficient and kind. That is a rare find in Tunisia. Is this not also true in America?"

"It's true everywhere," I replied.

On my day of departure, we walked across the same field we'd crossed during my first hours in Tunis after he'd driven off the beggars. A farmer was plowing a section of the field with an ox-pulled plow. He waved at us, seeming not to mind our trespassing.

Bahattin gazed back at the farmer in deep reflection. "See how hard he works. Man is tossed in a sea of cycles in a deflating lifeboat with no rudder as he goes through life. He is caught in a see-saw of owing and paying—paying and owing. He is always borrowing and loaning—loaning and borrowing. This farmer bestows a boon upon his kernels of wheat by planting them. They reward him by giving him wheat and more kernels which he then replants and so on."

He smiled at me and continued, saying that there is no escape from the sea of cycles without the aid of a holy denizen of heaven who is himself escaped. It's logical that such denizens do reside simultaneously on earth and heaven. But they're rare. And they're hard to identify, for it requires an escaped one to recognize another who is escaped.

"You mean, it takes one to know one?"

"Exactly," he said.

"But how do you know there are escaped ones?"

"Because if there were not, the sea of cycles would be without end. And nothing so tied to mortal phenomena can be infinite."

He made sense, and I reveled in his wisdom.

The joy in this young philosopher, the smell of the sun on freshly turned earth, the sight of the pure blue sky and the prospect of travel should have made me happy. But I was about to part company with one who had, in only a short time, become a friend.

"If I could only get a passport, I would drop my studies and join you in a minute," he said. What you learn on your pilgrimage is more exciting than what I learn in the classroom."

I felt very honored.

With a sad heart, I went aboard the plane and took a window seat. Then I looked out to find Bahattin and wave once more. He'd climbed up on the roof of the passenger terminal. Standing there, he cut an imposing figure in his white robe and black fez cap. I'll always remember this debonair swashbuckling kid—trusty companion, youthful sage and pillar of courage. He became a white speck, still waving, as my plane soared away.

I felt very loved on that flight to Rome. Romance is incredibly nice of course, but I think the greatest compliment that can ever be received or bestowed is the gift of friendship.

7

JOINING A CIRCUS WITH THE HELP OF A MIDGET HORSE

Italy greeted me with a pleasant breezy afternoon, and the Italians presented a welcoming sense of cheer as they scrambled and mustered about. There was a free bus from the airport. It wasn't going to Rome, they said, but the people in it looked nice. So I thought I'd try my luck on it and climbed aboard. I wasn't necessarily in search of Rome—just good company.

It was a long ride, via back roads, through miles of sweet smelling citrus groves. We passed by a circus—a one ring big top. I've always loved circuses, and jumped from my seat requesting to be let off.

It wasn't yet show time. So I was allowed to meander at will among the lion cages, the high wire team in practice session, and some clowns who were juggling. I was completely taken by it all. This, according to the big sign out front, was "El Circo Del Ferdinando Togni."

I found a tent where elephants were kept together with a dozen midget horses. Understandably the elephants adore these tiny horses, which is why they're kept together. I too was beguiled by these midget horses. For with their gentleness and innocence, they reminded me of my truckload of sheep in Morocco.

Unafraid, one of the little horses—perhaps 28 inches tall, satiny white with flowing mane, reddish brown eyes and little gray hooves—approached me, and I began to scratch his head between his ears.

The animal trainer, a heavily set mirthful man, approvingly observed my rapport with the horse and offered me an orange which I accepted. The three of us held a kind of soul meeting then—the merry trainer sitting on a small barrel next to mine. He spoke to me with gestures, international words and smiles, and said his name was Sergio. I liked him and the horse so much I decided to play for them and chose a rhythmic exercise I'd written when I was twelve. Music always communicates better than gestures and words. Sergio proved easy to please. He grinned and chuckled.

The bold little horse stepped over to my guitar and began curiously inspecting it. I slowed my tempo and increased my accenting of the meter—even moving my body slightly in time to the music, sensing this horse would understand the music if I made the meter obvious enough. I was right. He caught on almost at once and began swaying his body in perfect time, copying me. Fascinated, I began moving my feet with the tempo to see if he might even do that. He watched my feet for a minute and then did that too! He began taking a step forward and a step backward with each beat of the music, his charming little face beaming!

I laughed and looked over at Sergio to find him equally amazed and delighted. He signaled that I should stay put, left me for some moments and returned with Mr. Togni—a warm and gracious man very excited about being alive. With twinkling eyes, Mr. Togni watched the little horse dancing. A crowd of performers and staff people quickly gathered to watch. The horse seemed to enjoy the attention. All the horses and elephants had names. This horse's name was Luigi.

Mr. Togni was very emotional and almost cried. It was a happy miracle, like discovering a pouch of diamonds under a loose brick in your hearth. He reached for my hand. "Young man, where did you come from?"

Warmly, with deep feeling, he invited me to dine with him and his lady in their trailer. His passion was such that I think we both would have cried had I not accepted. He allowed me to bathe for dinner in his own portable washroom beside his trailer home, and I had a fine pasta meal with him and his young lady.

"No one knew Luigi could dance." he told me as we ate. "The trader who sold him to me didn't know either, or he'd have said so

and charged me a fortune. He must have bought Luigi from someone whose animal keeper had recognized his specialness, loved
him for it and given him special training without telling anyone.
What a bonanza for us. A dancing midget horse is very rare. In
fact, I have never heard of another such midget horse. We owe you
a debt, young fellow. How would you like a job, starting tonight,
playing your guitar as a circus act with Luigi?"

We didn't really know anything about each other, but we were
both show people. And show people sense they know each other
somehow. I think it's the fact that we're sibling artists, with a common passion for art, that makes us a family.

"Let's try and see if it works," I suggested, my heart bubbling
with excitement. "I would love to spend a little time here with you,
though I'm a troubadour and must be on my way soon. Perhaps
Luigi could be trained to dance to a recording."

He had mixed feelings about that and quickly changed the subject. "We cannot offer you much to start. It would be just your
food, and your lodging on a cot in the elephant tent. Will that do?"

"That will do," I said, and Luigi and I were given a brief run-
through in the ring before the crowd was let in.

That evening, we had half a house—about 500 folks. Luigi and
I were preannounced in Italian by a flamboyant master of ceremonies and brought on with a fanfare played live by the small circus
band. I sat on my barrel before a microphone and played my composition while Luigi stood next to me and swayed. Then he moved
his feet and danced with delight, undisturbed by the sounds of
peanut and popcorn vending that became audible as the crowd
hushed in adoration of him. He was an absolute hit. His handsome happy face captured the crowd completely. They applauded
so solidly, it was clear he'd won their hearts and stolen the show.

Later that night, I was so excited for Luigi I could hardly get to
sleep on my cot in the tent with the elephants and midget horses.
But at last I fell asleep only to be quickly awakened by Luigi who'd
walked over to me. He was tickling my face with his nose, and
nickering. I think he was happy too, and he wanted to share his joy
with me. So I sat up, massaged him, hugged him and whispered to
him that he'd been truly marvelous. This pleased him very much.

We were an artistic success. But it had been Saturday night, and there was only half a house. On weeknights, there were only a couple hundred folks, sometimes even fewer. The circus was in financial trouble, and it made all the performers a little sad.

All was not lost though. For Luigi soon attracted the attention of the wife of Italy's wealthiest citrus farmer whose estate was nearby. She offered to buy Luigi, and Mr. Togni took the pair of us to her estate to perform.

I sat in the back of Mr. Togni's pickup truck, holding Luigi, as we drove along the tree- lined private road through her magnificent citrus orchard estate to the large circle driveway of her grand mansion. Luigi sniffed the delicious orchard fragrance with his ears bent forward, clearly enjoying it. The air smelled so good there!

We were conducted to a vast greenhouse lounge and spa where the tall, classically beautiful, elegant young brunette madame greeted us and cordially offered us drinks.

"I am most honored by your visit," she told me graciously, and we sat for awhile during which she and Mr. Togni chatted in Italian. Luigi trotted around exploring. He found and attended to some tender weed grass that was growing around the base of a small rock garden near the hot tub.

After some minutes, Mr. Togni directed me to play my little tune which I'd titled *Dancing Horse*. Luigi walked over to me and began dancing at once. Madame was ecstatic. For Luigi loved music so, and he exuded the excitement he felt on discovering the beat and expressing it with his movements.

Madame looked over at Mr. Togni to validate her joy with him and was surprised to find a look of sorrow on his usually benign face. He was miserable, for he'd become attached to Luigi and was remiss to sell him.

In sympathy, she lowered her eyes and became silent in somber thought for a minute. Luigi and I stopped performing, and I began scratching him between his ears.

Then she got an idea. Excitedly she proposed it. Assuming Luigi was able to dance independently of me playing, she would give Mr. Togni his exorbitant sale price and then leave the horse in the custody of the circus temporarily. Mr. Togni was elated, didn't quibble over terms and accepted at once.

What a fine, understanding lady she was. What an opportunity for the circus!

Mr. Togni was benign again. His weathered wrinkled face was bathed in smiles as we left. I too was very happy when he told me what had transpired in Italian between him and Madame. I was happy for him, but also for the circus performers. For they would now keep their jobs awhile longer while Luigi's reputation would have a chance to grow and, hopefully, begin to draw larger crowds.

I was happy and safe at the circus, but I had the world to see. There was no adventure in being happy and safe. I explained this to Mr. Togni. He understood and explained to me Madame's condition of purchase, whereupon we resolved to work with the circus electronics technician and make a recording of my *Dancing Horse*.

That afternoon I had some time alone in the ring with Luigi, and experimented with him by playing him a tune that was rhythmically subtler than *Dancing Horse*. He couldn't grasp the meter, but he danced anyway in his heartfelt effort to please me. His movements didn't match the tune. He clearly realized it wasn't working, for he wore a sheepish, almost guilty look, like a puppy dog who's made a mess on the carpet. I laughed, but was deeply touched by his gallant effort and played *Dancing Horse* again. He danced to it perfectly, so happy to be pleasing me. He enjoyed pleasing his friends.

The circus technician arrived with a tape recorder, and we taped *Dancing Horse*. I then left Luigi alone in the ring, and we played back the tape through the powerful loudspeaker system. Could he dance without me? Would he?

His career, and the future of the circus, depended on his being able to do it. We watched tensely. He seemed to feel alone and lost with no one to direct him—no one at his side whom he could please with his movements. He stood still in bewilderment.

Mr. Togni frowned.

I suggested we bring in Sergio who always conducted the midget horses in their group performance. "Maybe if he would just sit in the ring with Luigi . . ."

"All right then, if it must be," Mr. Togni said with reluctance. He would have preferred to have Luigi onstage by himself during his solo act, but it was not to be.

Sergio joined Luigi in the ring. We played the tape again, and Luigi looked at Sergio who began merrily swaying to the beat of the music. Then Luigi began to dance too, with confidence and delight. Sergio was a good and gentle man—the jolliest in the whole circus. Luigi was in good hands.

Mr. Togni sighed with relief and gratitude. Triumphantly, he announced, with a grand gesture, that he would bill Luigi as, "Luigi, the Dancing Horse," and feature him on his own color poster out front.

The next morning as I sadly patted Luigi on the head for the last time, Mr. Togni gave me sage advice to help ease my sorrow at leaving the circus. "As you think, so you live," he said. "Always think of the best. Don't think of a dirty little dive of a restaurant, or that will be your experience. Think of the best in town."

I was grateful. With an emotion-filled hug, Mr. Togni sent me, in the truck of one of his suppliers, to Via Veneto, the nicest street in Rome.

The days were growing shorter, and night fell before I found the heart of Via Veneto where the street cafes were the nicest I'd ever seen. The women wore expensive furs, and the men were dressed in silk suits—even tuxedos. There was little traffic noise here, so the sound of my guitar would be heard. This place was perfect.

Keenly excited at the prospect of discovering and being discovered, I sat down in one of the cafes and began playing. The peaceful vibration among the crowd was so welcoming, it drew from within me a most delicate sensitivity that empowered my fingers. My guitar responded with golden notes that didn't go unnoticed. For conversations quickly stopped. Heads turned, bending toward me in concentration.

After a some minutes, a short, stocky, youthful Italian paparazzo adjusted his camera and flash unit, rose from his table, and photographed me together with a handsome couple bent toward me. As the shutter clicked, there was a blinding flash. Before my eyes had recovered I was grabbed by the arm, pulled to my feet, rudely spun around, and pulled into a nearby alley by a powerful plainclothesman from the local police department. A second plainclothesman grabbed the paparazzo. As he too was being pulled into the alley, he immediately protested with such volume and vehemence his yelling got the attention of the entire café audience.

A dozen café patrons, who'd been listening to me, followed us into the alley and began splitting into groups representing two sides of a developing argument. The police said no street artist was allowed on Via Veneto, adding that I should be arrested for vagrancy and disturbing the peace. They further claimed the paparazzo had taken my picture, as I committed this crime, with intent to publish it in the newspapers, make me a hero for crashing class barriers, and encourage every beggar in Rome to do the same.

The paparazzo counterargued, waving his arms in grand gestures. He said his publishing the photo would reduce class antagonisms and not bring beggars to Via Veneto. For being an eccentric American tourist, I didn't represent the beggars. Publishing a photo of the Via Veneto crowd listening to a troubadour would help bridge the gap between the classes by publicizing common interests. Since when, he demanded, was there a law against troubadouring, one of Europe's oldest and most treasured cultural traditions?

Some of the patrons grouped off to the side and conducted their own debates. In one of these groups, the argument became so heated it broke into a fistfight that spread to another group. The sight of several men fighting drew dozens of new spectators, and Via

Veneto was quickly in a state of bedlam.

Those supporting the paparazzo began chorusing that the police were snobs.

Those supporting the police (among them the fiery, outspoken manager of the café) hysterically urged them to quell this peasant's revolt.

Two paddy wagons arrived. A squad of uniformed polizia surrounded both camps, threatening everyone with short wooden clubs. Most were driven away, but the paparazzo and myself, together with part of the crowd, were put into the wagons and driven miles across town to a shoddily kept precinct police building. We were herded single file up many flights of stairs to the top story—a three-room flat with a bare, dirty, unswept wooden floor.

While the plainclothesmen were reporting to the alarmed police captain what had transpired, the paparazzo sat down with me and explained why we'd been arrested, giving me the details of the street debates.

"Do you have any money?" he asked with grave concern.

"Why yes, a little."

Heartened, he said, "You might be required to show it in order to get us out of this. I've sworn you're not a bum, and we may have to prove it." He wrote down my name and some facts about my life as a troubadour.

"Have faith," he added compassionately. "I am in this as deeply as you. If you're convicted and held, I will be also. If you're set free, I will enjoy the same good fortune and be able to use the story. So I will fight for you."

An angry guard herded us over to the captain's desk. It was past quitting time, and they all wanted to go home.

"*Passporto*," groaned the tired old captain. White flecks of dandruff covered the shoulders of his ill-fitting black uniform that was badly in need of cleaning and pressing. Burying his face with his right hand, he stuck out his left hand for the document. It was placed in his palm by the inspector. The captain sighed a long sigh. For his day had been long, and now it was to be made longer.

Opening his eyes, he read my passport and the paparazzo's press card. Satisfied, he calmly announced that my only offense was vagrancy, and that I should be punished for that. The paparazzo, as he'd taken my picture with intent to publish it, should be relieved of his camera and held for malpractice against the public interest.

The paparazzo was incensed. He threw up his arms and shouted our defense with color and debonair flamboyance. "Against the public interest? You mean the interest of a few stuffed shirts!" No doubt citing freedom of the press, he threatened the captain with exposure unless he set us free. And with this, he pounded his fist down on the captain's desk with such force that it rattled and shook.

A pencil, and the captain's brimful cup of steaming coffee, were shaken off the table's edge and went plummeting to the floor. Much of the hot coffee scalded the captain's ankle. His leg rose in reflex reaction, causing his knee to hit the underside of the desk. In pain, and in a storm of fury, he rose to his feet, shaking his fist at the paparazzo, threatening to compound his charge with resisting arrest and attacking a police officer.

Two constables left to get mops, but really to get out of the captain's way.

I told the paparazzo he might try relaying that I too was a reporter—a "stringer" for the *Kansas City Star* with permission to send stories—not a vagrant.

Embellishing wildly, he told the captain I was almost the head of United Press International and Associated Press, and would spread this story all over America! I was able to understand much of what transpired, both through context and occasional Italian words that were similar to English or Spanish, and feared he might get us both into still deeper trouble with his exaggerations.

But amazingly, the captain turned defensive on hearing this new argument and actually began to cry. He said we both could go free if I could prove I wasn't a vagrant.

"Let us see your money," said the paparazzo, turning to me with confident eloquence.

I produced the handful of $20 bills from my pouch. He took the bills and waved them under the captain's nose. He actually reached out and shook them less than six inches from that tear stained face, saying I was an authentic eccentric—with money—who chose to play for his supper. He told the captain it was both legal and a God-given right to be eccentric in Italy. The captain stared back at him in silence, his tears flowing. The befuddled plainclothesmen stood speechlessly, blinking their eyes, and our case was won. We were escorted to the street.

The paparazzo took another photograph of me as we walked away from the police building.

"You should be a lawyer," I told him

"I studied law. Perhaps I will be someday," he grinned.

He was in a hurry and hailed a taxi in which he sped away. I walked down the street toward a park that had many tall illuminated fountains, and marveled to myself how wonderfully paradoxical our civilization was. Among the Dutch, one could be a street artist if he could prove he was a beggar. Whereas in Rome, you had to be rich!

In the middle of the park, among these beautiful fountains and surrounded by dozens of very tall, thin, sculptured fir trees, about a thousand souls were gathered to see and hear Neapolitan tenors vie in amateur talent competition to the accompaniment of three romantically strummed mandolins. Each singer airily sang, for five minutes or less, from a wooden platform, and was judged by a panel of experts and the applause of the crowd.

The singers and mandolinists were very talented. Entranced, I sat among the fir trees and watched. After a few minutes, a new singer came on who was marvelous. But his song was long, and he must've exceeded his five minutes. A twelve-foot cane appeared from behind the Stage Right curtain, hooked around his neck as he sang his final notes, and pulled him off the stage! The crowd horse-laughed and guffawed, and the next singer came on. He too was very talented, and I prayed for him that he would finish before his five minutes had elapsed. He did. The crowd loved him and applauded loudly.

Very excited, I walked to the rear of the stage and found the master of ceremonies.

"You play your guitar?" he asked.

I nodded.

"Ah, good. I am the manager. Anyone may enter this contest. You want to play?"

"OK."

He gave me ten minutes to prepare, warning I must keep my tune under five minutes or he would give me "the hook" (his 12-foot long cane)!

Two more singers performed while I prepared. Then the M.C. carried a chair to the microphone for me and introduced me as an American hitchhiker who'd just arrived in Rome with his knapsack on his back and would now perform.

As I walked on and sat in the chair before the microphone, there was some chattering among the crowd. I sat smiling for about ten seconds and politely waited for silence. The crowd responded, and I played them a tune I remembered had lasted exactly 4:20 when they timed it during production of the radio show in Oslo. It was *Arabias,* an adaptation of my own that mingled my original ideas with adaptations of catchy old gypsy flamenco airs guaranteed to inspire a crowd.

The microphone was sensitive. The powerful amplifiers and huge loudspeakers distributed the sound perfectly, and even my most tender notes carried to the farthest reaches of the park. Thousands of hands clapped in acceptance of the Spanish style music. There were shouts for an encore. But the five minutes had elapsed, and I left the stage just in time.

The M.C. was pleased. "The next singer does not mind waiting five more minutes. Please give them an encore, I think." So I walked on again, and the intensity of the applause doubled. The panel of judges was smiling.

I won first prize—a job performing without pay at the very large and magnificent Ristorante Corsetti located among city's outskirts near the construction sites for the upcoming Rome Olympics.

"You did a good job," the M.C. said warmly as we drove along in his car to the ristorante. "You will be happy here. It is very nice, and you will be treated well."

He understated the grandeur. Ristorante Corsetti was a massive, newly built Greco- Roman building with rows of white columns at the entrance to which we ascended by climbing a long flight of carpeted, white stone steps that glittered with mica and other reflective minerals. Even the late Emperor Julius Caesar would've been proud to eat here. It was a large restaurant. But as it was broken up into small uniquely decorated sections, it was an intimate place wherever you sat in it.

I was introduced to the busy manager who wasted no time with me. He simply said, "you play for the people and we give you dinner. O.K?"

I agreed and went around exploring. In the main room there was a large stage where a full orchestra played. Among the side rooms another artist was already performing on a small stage—a tall bushy-haired German with a goatee.

In his mid twenties, he wore smartly tailored Bavarian lederhosen. He sat on a low chair, his knees pointing up like those of a praying mantis. Methodically and forcefully—with little nuance or understanding—he strummed his guitar with a plastic pick and looked blankly at the columns behind the audience. As he performed the American folksong, *Tom Dooley*, his mouth opened wide with each word he sang in his strong accent:

> Hung down yaw het Tomb Doo-ley,
> Hung down yaw het und clry . . .

He was far from being an authentic American folksinger, but the audience cherished him. They applauded merrily as he unfolded his 250-pound, nearly seven-foot frame and walked from table to table collecting tips.

We were introduced in the kitchen afterwards.

"Pleased to meet you. I am Johann," he blared in his gruff resonant voice. He grabbed my hand and, in friendly enthusiasm, wrung it to the threshold of unbearable pain.

We found each other amusing and took turns performing half-hour sets. I found him shrewd as he was gruff. He showed me how to get tips.

"You grind a few coins in your hand like this," he demonstrated, "and you go to a table, pretend they've given you the coins and thank them profusely—and a little too loudly. Then the others will get the idea."

This was necessary because the management didn't pay and said they'd throw him out if he passed a plate. But the restaurant was a place to perform that offered protection from the police. "The fuzz in Rome are tough," he said.

"Tell me about it." I replied.

I stayed awhile, sleeping at first on the boards of the big stage under the grand piano in my sleeping bag. The cute Italian girl who played that piano took me sightseeing on her motor scooter by day. And by night I learned, like Johann, to say loudly to a startled couple at a table, "thank you, how kind of you." Not that I wanted the money. But the personal contact with me, as they put coins in my hand, gave folks a natural opportunity to speak with me. So I would get invitations to sit and chat with various couples.

One such couple—charming, musically aware, cultured young Italian newlyweds—invited me to sit with them and have my dinner. "So you are a traveler? Well, so are we," said the husband whose name was Marco, a Sicilian croupier from Monte Carlo. They were embarking on honeymoon tour of Italy's East Coast. Marco was an artistic man of vision and initiative. While hearing me play he'd had a vision.

"I know of a place for you to play that would be perfect for you." he said, his face aglow. "How would you like to play at a castle by the ocean?" He creatively described the magnificent Castello di Miramare by the sea near Trieste. He said he would take me there in his car, and I consented to go with him and his lady.

We motored along a narrow country road past purple vineyards and quaint farms. Wrinkled old women hobbled along the roadside, bent over under the weight of their large bundles of sticks they carried home to be used for stove fuel. We passed beautiful valleys dotted with old sculptured buildings, houses, huts of clay, and well preserved feudal castles. Many of the castles were perched, with their still inhabited cobblestone villages, atop small mesas. Clinging to the steep sides of these mesas were the velvet carpets of purple grapevines gently caressed by golden sun rays.

There was a special Saturday evening concert to be held in the courtyard of Miramare Castle. Marco knew the sponsors and arranged that I perform as guest artist. I was honored to be part of such a distinguished program of chamber music played by some of Italy's finest classical musicians. I played a mini concert of my compositions for about 20 minutes. As I played for the select audience of classical music cognoscenti in this heavenly place, it felt as though I was performing during a former life.

Built during the 1850s for Archduke Maximilian, the castle stands right on the picturesque rocky coast with the surf lapping at its granite foundation. Not unlike those growing in Carmel where I grew up, the Castello's weathered old trees bestowed a benign enchantment—a mysterious gravity that inspired everyone. I was given a clear photograph of the castle, which I've kept and cherished all these years.

The castle stands right on the picturesque rocky coast.

Afterwards Marco and his lady made me their honored guest, taking care of all my needs and putting me up in luxury hotel suites adjacent to their own as we traveled southward along the coast. After many stops at some of Italy's prettiest places, we arroved at Prindisi, the end of our journey together.

His full name, and that of his lady, are lost to me over time, but I've a special place for them in my heart. We parted company near the docks, at my request, in early evening.

"Might you need a little money to help you on your way?" he offered with tenderness.

I was moved by the love in him. He was a fine gentleman, this croupier. A gentleman is one who, while doing you a favor, behaves as though you're doing a favor for him. This is the way it had been with Marco. I declined by telling him his offer meant more to me than money, embraced him and his lady, and watched them drive away.

My plan was to find a ship headed east, and I didn't have to look very far. There were several ships moored there. Less than an hour of meandering led me to the Lydia. She was very old but freshly painted and generally renovated—an attractive vessel of about five thousand tons. Her portholes were mostly lit up, as it was dusk. An apron-wearing mess cook stood at one of the side openings, pouring out a cauldron of dirty dishwater.

He smiled and greeted me in Greek, then Italian followed by other languages, until he found I responded best to English. A backpacker down at Prindisi's docks could be any one of a hundred nationalities unless you happened to know the origin of his Kelty pack.

"You play the guitar?" he inquired with a nod at my battered case.

I felt the buzz an angler feels when getting a nibble on his line. "Sure, but my hands are too cold. Is there a place inside where a man can warm his hands?"

That worked.

"Come aboard. I have hot coffee." He led me along a half-clean hallway to the crew's mess where there was a hot stove and a table.

He brought out a complete hot dinner for me. As I ate we talked of many things. But he kept referring to my guitar. "Flamenco, ah, that is very popular now in Greece. There is a quiet taberna near my home in Athens where a flamenco guitarist plays each night. Can you play the soleares?"

I finished eating, warmed and cleaned my hands, and played him a soleares. He was a keen aficionado and listened with lust as several men arrived. Word spread quickly, and soon I had a standing-room-only audience of crew members in tee shirts and jockey underwear. They listened in pin-drop silence. My best audiences have always been sailors. Their time at sea makes them book readers, thinkers and observers.

"Are you going to Greece?" asked the cook.

"Yes, if I can find a way to play for my passage. I'm a trouba-dour. So I don't buy tickets with money—only with music."

This elicited a murmur of conversation among the crew. "This ship is going to Greece tomorrow," one of them explained. "We are trying to figure out how we can get you on."

A controversy ensued among them. There was an empty cabin, and there were lots of potatoes. But also there were regulations designed to prevent this kind of free passage to vagabonds. Finally they agreed I should talk to the captain after the crew's first officer had paved the way.

"We are a Greek ship—half cargo and half passenger," said the cook. We're headed for Corfu, Ithaca, Patras and Athens. But tonight you must sleep in the empty cabin next to mine. Tomor-row you will go to the captain," he directed.

The captain was in his seventies—an old sea salt with twinkly eyes—one seemingly of contented disposition. I found him bent over his charts on the bridge as seagulls heralded the early morning arrival of pregnant fishing boats. He held a string of yellowish-brown "worry beads" in his hands, and manipulated them constantly.

"So you are the young man who gave the galley concert last night. I have heard much about you," he croaked in a gravelly voice. You wish to come with us to Greece? Why then do you not buy a ticket?"

While I explained about the troubadour traditions, he rattled his beads and pensively stroked his chin.

"Um, well, if you promise to entertain in the First Class Lounge every night of the voyage, like you did for the crew last night, per-haps I can arrange it for you."

I was delighted as a kid at Christmas. "Thank you, sir. I would be most grateful."

I was given a room in the crew's quarters and was to receive three meals a day. I cannot describe how good it feels to win, with your music, the status of belonging instead of being a tourist aboard ship. What a privilege to be invited from the heart—in return for something personal that came from your heart—despite a daunting array of ingeniously thought out marine, insurance and ship's agency regulations designed to prevent this very kind of thing from going on. These regulations shouldn't be, but we've created a strange world for ourselves.

The last of the cargo and passengers were brought aboard, and we cruised with the early evening tide away from the colorfully setting sun. Like a great revolving kaleidoscope, the sunset changed, minute by minute, from one breathtaking, sky-consuming pattern to another. I sat happily hypnotized on the aft deck and watched the display. The sea was calm, and we made smooth progress toward the Isles of the Odyssey.

At dinner a hot bowl of split pea soup, with a thick slice of melting butter floating on it, was placed in front of me by the cook. Burley, weathered crewmen sat with me, drinking from their soup bowls.

"Greece will now have another guitarist," smiled the cook. "You will be happy in Greece, playing in the tabernas, and the young wenches will flock to invite you to bed!"

To my embarrassment, this drew an array of horse laughs from the crewmen. One of them produced a case of beer, and within minutes they were singing bawdy Greek ballads, spilling almost as much beer as they drank. I left them to go tune my guitar and prepare for my concert upstairs.

The First Class Lounge was paneled in old, dark-stained oak that creaked and groaned at its mitered joints as the ship rocked. Placed around the various coffee tables were dozens of overstuffed, extra-large easy chairs—all upholstered in white and filled with dream-vacationing young couples.

I sat on the one high table and began to play. The young folks responded with enthusiasm, so I gave a full concert. The old captain, seated on the far side of the lounge, rattled his worry beads to the beat of the music. Especially fond of three-quarter time, he enjoyed complete empathy at a soul level.

Crunching his beads with one hand, he would wave the other as though conducting and make a "tsk, tsk" sound with his tongue and front teeth, accenting the first two beats of each measure. For variation he would change the sound to "thh, thh" while his face got a faraway spacey look, and his entire body became engrossed in keeping time.

Young folks seated near him found him amusing. He noted this but didn't seem to mind, for he was beyond the age of self-consciousness. During applause, he would clap very slowly, louder than anyone else, and continue after everyone else had finished. All would wait until the captain had finished, whereupon I would proceed with a smile, happy that he was apparently pleased with the entertainment he'd booked on the ship.

The morning of the second day was warm and sunny. I ventured forward to the ship's bow where I stood gazing at the various islands we passed, wondering which might be the isle of the Golden Fleece or those of the Cyclops or Sirens.

A willowy young blonde brought her deck cot to a private sunny spot just far enough beneath the cantilevered bridge to be out of sight of the young officers thereon. Not seeing me, she removed the top half of her bikini and began sunning herself.

Her fair body glistened in the sun. Round and voluptuous—the essence of perfection—she was a delight to the eye, and I was only 22. So I slowly walked over in hopes she might tell me who she was and if she was traveling alone.

"Ahem, uh . . ."

"Oh!" She hastily drew a towel over her bosom and eyed me with reproach.

I apologized. "Sorry to disturb you, but you caught me off guard out here."

She replied with a look that might be reserved for viewing a nest of cockroaches. "Good morning. You have chosen a bad time to introduce yourself."

I sat down at the foot of her deck cot, as there was no other place to sit. She withdrew her feet as though I might be leprous.

"Look. I just noticed you were alone and came to say hello. Excuse me for living." I shrugged my shoulders and rose to leave.

"Wait! I didn't mean to be quite that way." Her eyes began to flutter coyly. "I enjoyed your music last night, but you must admit you found me rather uncovered."

We talked of her life. She was a traveling English journalist and called herself Zoe. She rambled on about stories she'd written to raise money and continue traveling. There was a short love story for a pulp magazine; then an eye-witness account of a Mafia demonstration she'd sold. And the money was so good she could travel first class. She was sophisticated, educated and wise, and she'd risen above much pain for one so young.

She took in the warm breeze with serenity. And with that towel draped around her bust, she seemed a prize mermaid of Neptune's harem. So I began to lose track of her tale, becoming more aware of her beauty and warm presence. Her blue eyes were frank and penetrating.

Abruptly she stopped her narrative. "You're not listening."

"Yes, yes, so you sent it to the Paris bureau of the *Herald Tribune*. Then what?"

"No, that was the first story. You're not a good listener," she scolded in her crisp Queen's English accent.

"Um, maybe not. What will you do when you get to Athens?"

Thus we talked most of the day away. Each morning we met there. We met again each evening, after my concert, at a private place near the aft deck where we sat behind a lifeboat watching moonbeams dapple the water. She would kiss me with the same openness and frankness that was in her eyes and lean her head on my shoulder. We were a pair of artist philosophers, and that entire Mediterranean Sea was ours, together with all its islands. Even the whole world—the entire universe—belonged only to us.

She said she could learn some tasty songs, whereupon we could do some shows and be troubadours together. She could live by the troubadour code too. I loved the sound of her voice. The sound of it excited me, no matter what she said.

I told her that there would be blizzards and sub-zero temperatures in the upcoming Winter. "Could you sleep with me in a sleeping bag wrapped in polyethylene on a powdery snow bank at the side of a road?"

Her eyes looked straight into mine with an earnestness that scared me. "I would always follow you if you chose to do that."

"But I wouldn't put you through it. I'd buy us a room and lose my troubadour status."

"But I could pay with my half of the money if it came to that."

"Nope. You have to be a troubadour to travel with one. Let me think about this, OK?"

Later that night, as I sat alone on deck and mulled over the prospect of making Zoe wait until I finished my troubadour travels, an old Elizabethan proverb taunted me. "If you do not when you may, you shall not when you will." It was tearing me apart. There was so much pain attached to being young and in love.

My thoughts were interrupted by the rattling of worry beads.

"Arhumph," said the captain clearing his throat.

"My, you're out late, sir," I said.

"It is always late. It is always early. But I like the wee hours for thinking." He smiled openly.

"What sort of things do you think about so late at night?"

He sighed and leaned on a railing. "I regard the stars, check the ship's course and review the weather when there's a new officer in charge. And I think about my wife and things I've missed because I have lived at sea." He punctuated this with a slight rattle of the worry beads he held behind him.

I immediately drew a parallel between that and my present problem.

"Ah, so you are about to decide between freedom and a woman," he mused with a grin. It was the knowing smile of one who saw clearly that my problem was hardly as unique as I fancied. "That is always a difficult quandary. I myself tried to have both at the same time, but it was impossible. I married young, even though I knew I wanted to be at sea. And over the years, I've supported my lady while she has flitted about with other men. I'd have been better off to have hired a mistress in each port. Young man, you are about to fall into the same trap. I take it you will always be a troubadour?"

"If not in body, then always in spirit."

"Hmm, then allow me to discourage you from taking on this girl. Women are troublesome cattle. After a few rough seas, she'll balk on you. She'll come down with illness, exhaustion or pregnancy at some inopportune place, and what will you do? Will you leave her or do the right thing and give up your freedom?

"You are young still and in a position to have both—the only requirement being that you must wait and have one before the other.

You are still in the pilot's seat. You can always have freedom first and a woman later, but you can never have them in reverse order."

"Yes, but love too comes only once," I told him.

"Nonsense. Since my marriage, I have found a dozen women in a dozen ports whom I'd rather have for a wife than my present disloyal one," he told me with a touch of remorse, looking away from me out through the mist to the black horizon.

I gaped at him in surprise, but he kept looking away from me straight out into the night, not seeming to care a whit that he'd shocked me. "You seem dumfounded at this revelation of such a personal nature, but I tell you all this out of my concern for you. Choose your woman with care."

Such was his outlook. Scorned, rebuffed and exploited by one whom he'd loved and trusted, he roamed the sea with his worry beads, contemplating his predicament.

He reminded me that regretfully I must leave the ship when we arrived at Patras in the morning. My berth was reserved by extra crew that was coming aboard, and numerous regulations and practical considerations barred me from camping on the ship or moving in with Zoe. I thanked him humbly for his hospitality and advice, told him I'd had a really good time and went below, leaving him to contemplate the stars.

I tossed and turned, unable to sleep. It would be harder to obtain the pleasures of guest friendship if I had a partner with me. It would be much more difficult for two people to live by the troubadour code—nearly impossible. For potential hosts who've room enough for one guest rarely have space and resources for a pair of them. But still I thought Zoe to be exciting.

Zoe didn't know where she would stay in Athens until she got there but gave me the address of a friend who would know. As I disembarked in Patras, neither of us thought we were parting for more than 48 hours, and I went straight to the roadway that led to Athens.

8

BLIZZARDS, HARDSHIP, AND
PERVERSION BY GUNPOINT

Athens was near and yet far away, because I was a long time finding rides that were slow and short. But after some days I arrived late at night and was bewitched by the Old World charm of the bohemian sector known as the Plaka. Shafts of light illuminated narrow cobblestone streets from the half-opened doorways of happy tabernas where merrymaking Greeks drank arrack, a white precipitous liqueur of amazing potency.

Passionately they sang melodious traditional folksongs. Old men sat on the street corners baking chestnuts on portable open fires, their kerosene lanterns casting a weird light upon the parched nuts. Tantalizing odors of the baking process drifted along the streets.

Two smiling boys began walking alonside me—bold little fellows. "'Otel?" said one, leaning his head on his palm.

"No hotel—no money," I replied good-naturedly.

They eagerly whispered to each other in Greek and then spoke again. "Come," said the first boy. "I know a place for you sleep. You alone?"

"Yes, alone." I trusted them, as they didn't seem to have a scam going.

They led me through the city and up a steep hill to a long, winding path that led further upward. "How far your home?"

"California? Oh, it's about 12,000 kilometers from here."

They clucked their tongues. "Twelve thousand? Very far."

Thus we chatted and climbed. They told me they'd learned English in school and planned to visit America one day. For the moment, they lived in a nearby tenement with their families.

We arrived at a clearing and a high wire fence. "Where are we going?" I asked.

"To the Acropoli," they said, casually pointing ahead of us. There indeed was the Acropolis, its pillars reflecting the light of the strong silvery moon. "You sleep there." Then they made me promise to tell no one the secret they were about to show me.

Intrigued, I promised them.

We followed the high wire fence for a hundred yards or so until they found the small hole in the fence they were looking for. Why is there not a hole in a fence anywhere in the world some small boy doesn't know about?

The spot looked intact from a distance, but there was a neat slice in the chain link wire. One needed only to raise the flap and crawl through. Inside we found the ground between the trees to be hard and covered with sharp pebbles. There was no soft ground where I could put my sleeping bag.

So we went right into the Acropolis and sat between the pillars. Fascinated by the acoustics, I decided to play some notes on my guitar and listen to them bounce off the ancient columns. The boys smiled and giggled in delight. Then they watched me unfold my 9x5-foot polyethylene sack and put my sleeping bag, knapsack, guitar and myself into it, whereupon they said good night and left. Though tired, I stayed awake as long as I could and listened, in the eerie moonlight, for the ghosts of Socrates, Plato and Aristotle.

I awoke and got out through the hole very early, so as not to be discovered, and went to the address Zoe had given me. It was the office of a news correspondent friend of hers. He told me she'd stayed only a day in Athens. Her mother had written to her, via him, that her father was dying and wanted to see her. Her parents worked at the British Consulate in Calcutta. She'd booked passage on Air India and left only the previous day. He handed me a note she'd hurriedly written for him to give me.

Though hurried, it was a long letter. I took it out to the street and sat down on a park bench with it.

She said I reminded her of Voltaire's Candide, but that no one is really free. For we all have attachments of one kind or another.

She wanted very much to be free one day and to be with me then. What a lovely person she was! My sadness at not finding her was tempered by her declaration that she wanted to be with me. I needed only get to her.

I decided to continue troubadouring eastward around the world. I would aim my journey so as to pass through Calcutta and find Zoe again, and this time fate would be more kindly disposed to us.

I hitchhiked on the back of a motorcycle up through the mountain wilderness of Macedonia. Southern Greece abounds in sun during Winter, and the charm of these mountains is unsurpassed. From the tops of steep cliffs, one can see a hundred miles over mighty crags, colorful windswept gorges and lush meadows. There was a fresh mountain breeze. I was alone and free. Happiness flooded through me at this realization. I knew Zoe would be delighted by these mountains and pretended she was with me.

When we reached Salonika around midnight, the streets, though neon lit, were empty. The only activity was that of bars and brothels, and it was cold. Salonika feels the Winter, while Athens remains bathed in sun.

I found a warm whorehouse, the Mimosa, where a striptease act was in progress. The whore mumma was in charge of the "door," as they say in the nightclub business, and she took money from all who entered. She spoke no English. But I pointed to my guitar and made strumming gestures, and she summoned her bouncer who spoke with me.

"You want to play your guitar here and charge no money?" he asked incredulously.

"Yep. All I want is a meal and a bed for the night."

He confirmed this to the whore mumma. A winsome middle-aged woman, she exuded the warmth of one who has lived and loved. She led me to the dressing room where I washed up and prepared to perform. Sharing the room with me, changing costume between acts, were two sensuous and ravishingly attractive girls who didn't find my presence the least bit disturbing. They went about their work calmly chattering. And when it was my turn to go onstage, they wished me luck with bright smiles.

The audience was predominantly male. Considering that I was sandwiched between two strip acts, the fact that I received a little

half-hearted applause was something to be celebrated. A hot veg-
etable and noodle dinner was served in the dressing room. The
whore mumma was pleased and brought me sandwiches and fruit
which I put away in my pack. That food was destined to keep me
alive in the days that followed.

A well-dressed young Greek gentleman entered the dressing
room. He spoke no English but conveyed through one of the girls—
and by his behavior—that he admired me and wished I spend what
remained of the night as a guest in his flat. He seemed artistic and
sensitive with delicate feelings. The girls were all booked. So I had
no other place to go and didn't wish to offend the man. Further, one
of the girls told me the whore mumma had sent him in order to
resolve the second half of her bargain. So I accepted.

His apartment building was very near. Sharing no common
language, we walked to it in silence and passed through the front
garden with its many fine, life-size sculptures of nude men and
women. His one-room flat had only one double bed. There was
no couch. Something about the situation didn't feel right. I used
gestures to indicate there was no place for me to sleep, and I
would leave. But he wouldn't hear of it. He gestured adamantly
that I should lie down with him on his bed. As there was much
compassion, even a smile in his manner, I felt reassured. So I
unrolled my sleeping bag on top of his bedspread and climbed
into it.

He stretched out between the sheets on his side of the bed,
reached under his pillow and pulled out a .38 caliber revolver.
He cocked it, pointed it right at my head between my eyes and
puckered his lips a few times. Bewildered, I first focused on the
lead-tipped cartridges inside the cylinder chambers. The gun was
loaded. Then I focused on his face again. He was gazing at me with
a deep and sincere yearning for love. He had a grossly heavy dark
beard. And his thick lips, which he kept puckering at me, seemed
like two slices of rotten liver.

For an instant I began to feel nauseated. But then I was rescued
by a profound conviction that filled my thought. He *was* the delicate and sensitive child of God I'd originally seen him to be. He
was extremely intelligent and sensible. I traced my conviction to
Father Charleton's counsel and my upbringing in the Christian

faith. And as my heart went out to this love-hungry Greek, I automatically trusted implicitly that he wouldn't hurt me. Trust genuinely in the love and wisdom of your adversary, and he becomes an ally. It's really true. Trust is an invisible protective shield.

Confidently, slowly, I put my feet on the floor and peeled off my sleeping bag. He watched, still pointing the pistol at me as I rolled up the bag, put it into its canvas case and strapped it to my pack frame. I dressed calmly, picked up my gear, walked to the door, opened it without looking back at him and exited. I suppose he could've shot me in the doorway and then told the police I'd attacked or tried to steal from him. But he was a gentleman. And with my attitude, I'd told him I thought him so.

Once out in the street, I kept walking all night in order to stay calm and keep warm.

It began snowing at dawn as I stood beside the road that led to the Turkish frontier. Cars seemed in a hurry to get where they were going before the snow got really bad. So none stopped for me. Inches of snow quickly fell. Passing vehicles began churning it into slush, projecting much of it onto my trousers as they passed.

For a week I slept out in blizzards and sub-zero temperatures, hiking and hitchhiking through snow drifts. I was kept barely functioning by occasional friendly townspeople in the small villages along the way who allowed me to sit and sleep near their wood stoves. A troubadour's life isn't always a perfumed walk, and this was one of those times when it wasn't.

During my second week out from Athens, windy blasts propelled the snowflakes at about 40 miles an hour. For protection against the weather, I wore almost every article of clothing in my pack. There was a set of long underwear. On top of this, I wore two pairs of trousers, two shirts, a medium leather jacket, a pair of cotton-lined mittens, three pairs of socks, a pair of low-form white canvass tennis shoes, and Mr. Oziel's raincoat—certainly not proper protection for a blizzard in Macedonia.

During my two hours of waiting on the roadside south of Alexandropoli, I was passed by only two cars. Chains clanked as wheels sank into powder. Windshield wipers were useless. A driver saw what he hoped was the roadway through tiny, hand-chipped peepholes in the ice.

But presently a rural bus, so packed with humanity its windows were steamed from the inside, spun its chain-laden wheels and whined into view. It zig-zagged from one side of the road to the other, as traction was tenuous. But the driver saw me, stopped and opened the bus door. My jaw was frozen, so I couldn't speak to explain about the troubadour principles. But I managed to say, "no drachmae," and simply trudged on.

The friendly driver would have none of this. He left his seat, hopped out and waded through the snow alongside me, insisting I ride for free. Once his bus is full of paying customers, a Greek bus driver can apparently take on hitchhikers at his own discretion.

There was a welcome warmth inside, thanks to the mass of humanity and animals. Three tightly packed crates of live chickens filled the rear seat, and their bewhiskered owner lay atop them fast asleep. The chickens squawked frantically for want of space and ventilation. He must have been very tired indeed to sleep through all that. Every seat was taken, as were most laps, with children or pets. A pair of big Labrador retrievers compounded the discomfort as they jumped and fidgeted, barking their rebukes with every lurch of the bus.

But it was nicer here than outside. I stood in the aisle, holding onto the backs of seats for support as filthy snow water washed over my frozen feet and warmed them.

Still hours west of Alexandropoli, we stopped amid a flat plain to pick up a lone hunter who wore a thick parka, mittens and Eskimo-like headgear. He carried a long shotgun in one hand and three half-dead ducks by their necks in the other. As he entered, he proudly raised his catch high in the air so all could see it and congratulate him.

He stood in the aisle facing me as we drove onward, observing my soaked cotton trousers with friendly concern. Then one of the Labrador retrievers began sniffing and nibbling at one of his ducks. He pulled his ducks out of the dog's reach. The dog was persistant though, so he cuffed the animal gently with the butt of his rifle.

The dog squealed, growled and bared his teeth in defiance. His owner, a strong, leathery old hill woman, rose from her seat and clouted the hunter with her handbag in a bolt of vengeful fury.

Some strong words were exchanged before she hit him again—this time in the solar plexus—and sent him reeling.

He stepped back to avoid falling, kicking me in the shin, and the two of us collapsed with our full weight upon the rear seat where our combined force broke open one of the chicken crates. A dozen terrified cackling fowls broke out. Scattering a blizzard of lost feathers, they spanked us with their wings as they hopped around to escape the pair of elated dogs who danced and barked in pursuit.

Confusion reigned for a half-hour while the passengers debated whether this old hill woman, whom they agreed was most certainly a she-devil, should be made to ride on the roof. The bearded chicken owner was in a rage at being attacked, awakened and damaged. He demanded the hunter and I pay for his lost chickens and ruined crate. He got nowhere with us. So he tried threatening the old woman who spat viciously right into his eye.

Finally the good bus driver recaptured the chickens himself with our help. There were some tools aboard with which he skillfully repaired the crate, calming everyone with diplomacy and cheer. Such a fine man!

I left the bus at Alexandropoli, still favoring a throbbing shin bone, and underwent more days of relentless blizzard all the way to Orestias. It was only three more kilometers to the Turkish frontier. And what was to be found there?

More blizzard.

9

ROBBED BY TURKISH TRUCKERS

Just east of the frontier, a 1935 Dodge sedan, with many holes in its floorboards, stopped for me. It was a kind old goat rancher and his two sons. As we drove along they gave me a huge block of golden-brown goat cheese and half a loaf of homemade bread. I'd eaten all my food supply from the Mimosa and was very hungry. But I wasn't sure the cheese was something to be eaten, for I'd never seen goat cheese. So I munched at the wholesome bread and gazed in wonderment at the cheese.

The old goatherd smiled a semi-toothless smile at this. He still had about half his teeth, and some of these were crowned in gleaming gold. He was almost bald, and his white-whiskered face was weather-beaten with deep rivulets. And like his sons, he wore rough homemade clothes of thick cotton rags.

He laughed and pointed to the cheese. Then he put his fingers to his mouth and licked his chops, indicating it was something very tasty to be eaten. Cautiously I broke off a small piece and tried it while the old man studied me. I was amazed that it tasted delicious, like caramel candy but much more wholesome.

Seeing I liked it, he laughed with such deep pleasure I felt honored to be in his company.

Soon we scaled a high cliff that commanded a view of the great city of Istanbul. It was an inspiring sight with its mosques, spires, temples and domes. As I was admiring it, we came to a crossroad and stopped.

"Istanbul!" he said, pointing to the city with pride. He got out, pointed to his car and to the road that led further up the mountain toward his goat pasture, indicating that he was going up. If I wished to descend into Istanbul, we would part company here. So I packed away my bread and cheese, and they left me at the crossroad.

A tired delivery truck stopped, and its kind driver took me down the hill into the city where I walked around exploring. There was much artwork in the buildings, churches and statues, connecting me to the romantic aura and glamour of old Constantinople and the Turkish Empire. But my feet soon got tired, and it was getting late. I realized I was covered in dirt and in no condition to perform anywhere. I needed a rest and cleanup.

Mr. Togni's advice rang in my head, "as you think, so you live. Always think of the best in town, and that will be your bill of fare," he'd said. Just at that moment, I happened upon the venerable Istanbul Hilton Hotel. It was a luxury building, with several gaudily uniformed doormen and a school of Rolls Royces and Mercedes limousines out front.

I entered the lobby unchallenged and told the receptionist I wished an interview with the general manager. ("The worst they can do is say no," my step pop Jack used to tell me as I grew up.) He got the manager for me on the lobby phone, and I must have said the right things because he invited me upstairs to his living quarters for an interview.

He received me wearing a flowing robe, relaxing on the plush couch of his expensively decorated kitchen suite surrounded by his many rare objects d'art. A cultured oriental gentleman from Singapore who spoke many languages, he was friendly from the start and seemed fascinated with my story of playing personally for Pablo Picasso, the current blizzards, the whore mumma and the goatherd. I showed him my hunk of goat cheese, offered him some and he tried it.

"Why this is the finest goat cheese I've ever tasted," he said, truly amazed.

Encouraged, I proposed to play for the hotel guests in trade for room and board, and he allowed me to use his washroom to clean and warm my hands that I might play for him.

After listening attentively, and with much enthusiasm, he said, "We have a nightly dinner show in the penthouse showroom where you would be the perfect opening act. What do you have to wear during your performance?"

I told him I had a pair of dress boots, a wash-and-wear pair of trousers and a wash-and- wear shirt.

"Just a street shirt? That won't do. You need something with a touch of flair." He went to his closet and found me a colorfully polka dotted Cavalier shirt with blouse-like sleeves. "Wear this," he said, "and you may please keep the shirt." He smiled cheerfully. "It's the shirt of a troubadour."

He summoned his night manager to arrange everything, and I was shown to a beautiful, air-conditioned, carpeted, two-bedroom suite. There were two king-size beds, a kitchen, a dining area, a conference room, and a sitting room furnished with poshly upholstered high-back chairs of hand carved oak. There was a big basket of fresh fruit on the conference room table. All the standard rooms were occupied by attendees of a very large convention that week. So the only vacant room was this expensive suite.

I didn't know what to do with so many luxuries. I just roamed around, tried some of the fruit, lay down on one of the big beds and smiled at the ceiling. Then I went in and bathed in the double tub. It felt like I was dreaming.

The penthouse supper club showroom was glamorous and well run. I opened the show for a belly dancer who wore bells on her wrists and ankles. While I felt she was nowhere near the great Sonya, she was every inch a pro and had good presence. Though vastly different, we blended well together and I stayed on for almost a week, living like a king. Then, fully recovered from my long exposure to hunger and blizzard, I became restless as a pent up wind. I was a troubadour with a goal and explained this to my cultured friend from Singapore who'd attended my performances each evening. He readily understood, and with much wanderlust I walked out onto the endless roadway eastward.

I reached the Bosporus and beautiful Marmara seacoast where I found a friendly trucker and his lackey. In Turkey the trucker only navigates and drives. His lackey, or cleaner, has to kick the tires now and again, check the oil and keep the truck immaculately clean inside and out.

About 200 miles southeast of Istanbul, way up in the hills beyond Adapazari, the road became muddy. A torrent of rain and hail made the going even more difficult, so we stopped at a lonely mountain coffee house. It was a tiny point of light in this wilderness—a happy sight to the rain-soaked traveler.

A few trucks were parked out front. Inside it was lit only by lanterns and candles. There were four, large, bare-wooden tables filled with coffee-drinking truckers. In the very center of the room, between the tables, was a shiny round copper tank about six feet in diameter. Heated from beneath by a bed of hot coal, the tank was outfitted with elaborate plumbing that provided multiple offerings including steam, hot water, heat, hot milk, hot cider, tea, Turkish coffee, café au lait and cappuccino, just to mention a few.

Many fine tapestries adorned the walls, complimenting exotic mural paintings—all illumined by the glow of at least a hundred overhead candles mounted in wrought iron chandeliers. It was a theater made to order, and I couldn't resist playing some flamenco.

An old shepherd with a very long white beard, and an endless white moustache that blended and poured gracefully into it, sat alone with his hot teapot at the one small private table in the far corner. His robe was dirty and old. He held his large six-foot staff rooted upright upon the floor with one hand while he drank his tea with the other. This man was surely a mystic. As I played, he gazed at me—not from inside his head as most men do, but from another galaxy. He seemed happy, wherever he was from, and his face haunts me to this very day.

My trucker told everyone I was an American guitarist, and I continued playing while everyone listened. I was given a fine meal and some Turkish coffee. While eating, I looked around for even one female among the crowd. But there weren't any. One saw few women in such public places. The women stayed home. That was the way.

As we ate, our lackey must have mentioned the discomfiture of being jammed into our truck cab with not only me but my guitar and pack. For a sour-looking driver and his even sourer, swarthy-faced, evil-eyed lackey offered to take my guitar to the next trucker's rendezvous—a town called Eskisehir. I politely refused, but our lackey pleaded with me. So I let them have my pack.

The evil-eyed one roughly planted my pack into their cab. With a sinking feeling, I watched them drive off into the snowy night. Our lackey checked our tire chains, and we followed. The road narrowed as we passed over high mountains, slid dangerously near the edges of precipitous cliffs, and minced through inadequate detours where roadwork had been arrested by the storms.

In four hours we covered the seventy miles to Eskisihir and stopped at the all-night café where we'd agreed to meet the other truck. Neither that driver or his evil-eyed lackey was there. We waited in vain. My driver apologized and left me, saying to be patient and wait. Such bad luck. I waited with sunken heart for a half-hour, watching the steady flow of truckers and drunks deposit slush upon the café floor with their boots.

A pale, dirt-smeared, very tired boy came in trying to sell his tray of sweet cakes. He wore an oil-stained beggar's coat far too big for him. He tripped over the hem and fell, scattering his wares onto the filthy floor. He hurt his knee in the process and began to cry. To my amazement, the men laughed at him and left him to pick himself up. He swallowed his tears, gathered up the contaminated sweet cakes and tried to sell them.

He tried to sell me a sweet roll. The truckers had left me some bread and cheese. So I pushed the food toward the end of my table that was nearest him and gestured that he should sit and eat. After brief hesitation, he rendered an expressive, heartwarming smile so charming I'll never forget. He sat and wolfed the food like a starving animal. Then he found a used napkin and removed the grit from his cakes. With rather amusing mime and gesture, he explained he was in business. He'd bought those cakes from a baker. He was about nine—my age when I'd become a child actor at Carmel's Golden Bough Theater.

He rose to leave with his tray. I went with him, figuring he'd be making the rounds of the cafes and might lead me to an audience for my music. Also I thought it possible the other truckers might've misunderstood my driver and gone to another café.

At the next café I found the evil-eyed lackey. He was auctioning all the possessions in my pack. He'd laid them out on a table, and some men were looking them over. One was admiring my new polka dot shirt. Another was actually bidding on my flashlight. I'd arrived none too soon.

I was in disbelief but stayed calm, picked up my emptied pack and began putting my things into it. The lackey began swearing at me, mustering a commendable display of self-righteous indignation. He could have worked up the startled crowd of bidders. So I let myself get angry and grabbed him, swinging him into a row of stacked chairs that tumbled on him as he fell. Then I stood over him, waiting to hit him when he got to his feet. But the falling chairs, and perhaps his conscience, had pummeled him enough. He cowered and ran out, unable to look at anyone. I went back to collecting and packing my things, the boy helping.

When I was all repacked, he went around among the men with youthful moxie and panache, hawking and selling all his sweet cakes while I watched him in delight. He definitely had the makings of an actor. He led me to another café and connected me with a trucker friend who was headed south to Ankara.

A modern city, Ankara is the capitol of Turkey. It looked bleak and dreary when I arrived. Gusts of bitter-cold, wintry wind forced hands into pockets, and few ventured onto the streets. There was such a grayness and lack of mystique, I felt I might as well be in Culver City, USA. For along Attaturk Boulevard it looked just the same. There were even modern busses and smog. And industrial soot tickled your nose.

But this was the city of embassies and consulates where I could get visas for Syria, Jordan and Lebanon before proceeding. My passport pages being already filled with previous visas and immigration stamps, I would first need to visit the U.S. Consulate about attaching an accordion of new pages with the official Department of State seal. The American Embassy /Consulate building was in an area of town heavily occupied by American Air Force personnel and their families.

In the huge embassy lobby stood a cheerful 15-foot Christmas tree decorated with twinkly colored lights and gleaming tinsel—my first hint of yuletide in this Muslim country. It was Christmas Eve. A merry staff party was in progress. As she stamped a new accordion of pages into my passport, the consulate secretary nodded at my guitar case and invited me to play.

"The ambassador had been scheduled to give us a Christmas Eve address, but he's detained at the airport," she explained. "Would you fill in for him with your music?"

Such faith, for none there knew of me!

So I sat in front of the tall Christmas tree, and everyone gathered to listen. I played *Silent Night*, and some other Christmas carols, and a happy sense of communion set in. We were surrounded by millions of Muslims who considered Christmas a blasphemous event celebrated only by infidels. This strengthened rather than dampened our spirit, and the closeness between us was so thick you could almost reach out and touch it.

A U.S. Airforce officer happened to be among the crowd. In parade dress uniform, he came over to introduce himself. "Welcome to Ankara. I'm Colonel Chaveau. Do you think we could get you to play at some of our service clubs over the holiday?"

He was a gentleman of strength and goodness, and he invited me to his home to share the blessed day with his family. I told him I was going to Calcutta to meet with my exciting lady friend. And later that night, I played *Silent Night* again for the Chaveau family while we sat around their tree.

The colonel's eleven-year-old son asked something about Jesus. The good colonel answered him lovingly. He compared some of Jesus' teachings with those of the great Muslim saints who taught us that the gift of human birth, together with any experiences in the human form—whether good or bad—was a blessing so wonderful it was beyond our power to appreciate it. "Therefore," he said, "we should be grateful for anything that befalls us."

He spent many hours getting my visas from the Syrian, Jordanese and Lebanese consulates, and many more hours taking me around to several military service clubs where I performed over the next couple of days. And as this marvelous man put me on the road to Beirut, he reminded me that folks should be grateful for whatever befalls them.

"What a nice thought," I said.

10

RON & MEL, BRITISH ROCK-AND-ROLLERS
WHO CAUSED THE TWIST TO BE BANNED

The Lebanese consul in Ankara had refused me a visa until I'd procured one for Syria. The Syrian legation would issue their visa only if I had a Lebanese visa. But after several frustrating trips back and forth with me, Colonel Chaveau had finally prevailed and gotten them. Now I had both visas, and the Turkish frontier officer examined them.

"You will be going to Lebanon by land via Syria? All right. Do you have any Turkish coins?"

"About fifteen lira."

He looked excited. "Aha! You will be arrested if you try to take the coins into Syria. It is illegal. But as you are a nice man, I will help you and buy the coins for two Syrian pounds."

"But they're worth three times that in any bank."

He pursed his thick lips. "I will not bargain with you. Either you sell them to me at that rate, or I will report you to the Syrian police."

I was flabbergasted. "Supposing I just throw them into the bushes."

"Yes, then you would be safe from arrest but two pounds the poorer."

He had me over a barrel, so I made the trade on his terms. He was so delighted, he didn't even bother to make the usual search of my gear.

Just across the gate, playing checkers in front of their own customs shack, sat the Syrian customs-immigration team. They made me wait until they finished their game. The defeated immigration officer was noticeably disgruntled as he took me into his shed to be examined.

"Excuse me," I said. "Is it illegal to possess Turkish coins in Syria?"

He looked at me in surprise, scratched his ungroomed head and grinned a knowing grin. I'd cheered him with my question. "Of course not. Do you have any?" He quickly stamped my visa before I could answer.

"I had fifteen lira, but I sold them."

That Turk had been shrewd. On a sheer bluff, he'd robbed me as part of his unofficial money-changing program. The Syrian knew—his attitude gave him away. He might even have been pulling the same scam with northbound travelers in cooperation with the Turk. When I asked him if I might make a quick trip across the gate to settle something with the Turk, he replied, "that is impossible. I have stamped your visa, and it is good for only one entry into Syria. If you cross the gate, I must first stamp you out of Syria, and you may not reenter without first returning to Ankara and getting a new visa."

What a racket they had going! In this way he and the Turk protected each other. I was incensed and upset. But soon a traveling salesman, driving a fast comfortable car, came by and took me all the way to Beirut.

He was pleasant company, and I quickly got past my anger toward the frontier officials. South of the Dagliari Mountains, the weather was warm. And here in Beirut, on the Mediterranean Coast, the climate was excitingly balmy.

Sophisticated and attractive women walked the streets wearing the latest fashions. Among the modern high rise buildings, street trams, sidewalks and wide avenues with modern cars, there were head-dressed Arabs driving bullock carts and horse-drawn gasoline trucks. Both cultures met here with nonchalance. Revolutionary terrorist coups d' etat took place from time to time. This was a duty-free port city. A free-enterprise, survival-of-the-foxiest environment prevailed.

In modern bookstores the latest copies of *TIME* and *Newsweek* could be purchased, minus any pages that happened to mention the word "Israel." All such pages were always torn out by the vendors in accordance with the national taste. Rand McNally's detailed maps of the Middle East were also available in many shops. But on each copy, the narrow strip called "Israel" had been carefully blotted out with a black felt pen. Thus the Red Sea flooded over to the West Coast of Jordan, handing the children of Israel the same fate suffered by Pharaoh's host on the day of deliverance.

Not far from the Place Des Canons, I began exploring an avenue that tantalized with its shady palms and colorful theatres. And it was here that a long, black, chauffeured Cadillac gently pulled alongside me and stopped.

"Young man, would you like a lift?" offered the French-accented, pleasant voice of the impeccably dressed, elderly man of benevolent countenance who sat in the rear seat.

"Many thanks, but I've no particular destination other than to see this town as the breeze directs."

"All right," he said. "Come with me, and I'll show you the sights." He spoke so warmly I climbed in with him.

"My name is Nicolas Bustros. I am the federal minister of protocol. You must be very tired with that load on your back. What? You say it weighs only 25 pounds? Well it looks heavier than that."

The chauffeur drove us through the business district. Then we passed the waterfront where sat a score of ships with their bellies being loaded and unloaded—always a sign of brisk economy. "I think you will find us a thriving, prosperous little country," he said. "Unlike most Asian countries, we have established a hard currency good anywhere in the world. Many of our industrious men go abroad, make money, and bring it back here for investment. We inherited this trick from the Phoenicians who were our ancestors."

He looked at his watch. "But now it is time for lunch. And, as you are a troubadour, would you take lunch with me in my home? I want you to meet my youngest son who is very little older than yourself. He is twenty-three, and you are, ah . . ."

"Twenty-two, sir."

"Ah, twenty-two—a perfect age to be. I had suspected you to be younger than that. There is just enough wisdom at twenty-two to be happy and still enough youth to be vigorous." He loaded his tobacco pipe, chewed the mouthpiece ruminatively and speculated, "my, but you are a brave young man to have ventured so far from home alone in this manner. It must have taken a lot of courage."

"I don't think so, for I have very little courage. But I've learned that folks everywhere have hearts of gold, that home is wherever I am, and that love is everywhere."

"But surely now," he wondered in a kind of feigned puzzlement, "you cannot truthfully say that you have come all this way without having met foul play on occasion."

"Granted. But foul play is soon forgotten in the wake of good things."

"Indeed. That is most interesting." He blew a puff of smoke at the roof and contemplated. Our arrival at his mansion found us in deep discussion of optimism, morality and mystery.

An impressive row of thirty-foot pillars fronted the big stone house. Within hung the largest collection of valuable paintings I'd ever seen owned by one man. On the ground floor alone, there were enough of them to fill an art gallery. Décor was French Arabic.

A large household staff served us at a spacious, polished 17th-century table, the food steaming beneath hoods of sterling silver. It was French gourmet with a touch of Lebanese. Bustros' son Claude was smooth at the edges, and he shone with the confidence of modern westernized youth. Nicolas introduced us as we sat to eat.

"Claude owns and operates a nightclub in which he has invested his own savings," the minister explained. "Perhaps you might be interested in staying awhile in Beirut and performing on his floorshow. I take it you play in nightclubs?"

"Sometimes," I replied with a grin. I always love it when offered a chance to play. "What sort of show do you put on?"

Claude began to talk for himself. "Rock 'n roll, daddy," he said, smiling back at me. "Now that my pop here has banned the twist, we just rock."

Astonished, I looked at Nicolas. "So you're the famous man who banned the twist! I read about it. It's in the wire services, all over the world."

He smiled modestly. "My ban is good only in Lebanon. My authority extends no farther than that."

"But why? Why did you do it?"

Nicolas exchanged a concerned glance with his son and explained, "well, one of Beirut's top nightclubs has been featuring a pair of young Englishmen who sing rock and roll, playing their guitars and doing the twist. The young female public has taken to these twin boys with such affection as to create an immoral atmosphere that attracts even the general public, not only pulling down the morals of the entire city but causing other nightclubs, including Claude's, to languish with insufficient trade . . ."

"We do all right," Claude interrupted. "But these two cutesy-faced Brits pop refers to, Ron & Mel, play to SRO audiences at the Kit Kat just down the street from my club. They've created an ugly vibe in town that encourages club-goers to come over and trash my place. They behave like animals."

Nicolas continued, "We all thought that banning the twisting in their act would solve the problem. But the twist was hard to legally define in the law."

So Ron and Mel had simply changed the character of their wrigglings and writhings to meet code, and the Government ban had become a bellows to the flames of vice. Nicolas was a deeply religious man, and I could see he was genuinely in despair for his nation over this thing.

I attempted to comfort him. "I don't play rock music myself—only my own kind of guitar inventions and some flamenco."

Claude looked disappointed. "We need a rocker."

"Yep," I submitted. "One must fight fire with fire—rock with rock."

"That's it."

The elder Bustros cleared his throat modestly and spoke to his son. "But perhaps you could compete by starting a fad with this young American artist."

Claude retorted with a son-to-father gaze that told of complete impatience with what he perceived to be the old man's lack of music business awareness.

Nicolas shrugged, duly chastised, dipped his fingers into his finger bowl and dried them with his napkin. He looked at me. "I've observed your interest in my art collection. That masterpiece directly ahead of you is an original by Paul Cézanne. And those beyond the next entranceway are recent works by Pablo Picasso."

"Oh," I said. "I would be most interested in them now that I have played for him and met him."

"So you have met Pablo?" His eyes began to shine.

I told him about that night in Aix-en-Provence. He seemed to relish the story and asked if I'd like to play for him out on the terrace during coffee. So I sat with him and Claude on the terrace and played them a baroque sonata I'd composed. Nicolas was the more interested of the two. He shared with me a common passion for art and music, and I found much love in him. He took me on a tour of his home—a palace with long, echoing masonry corridors lined with priceless paintings. The feeling he'd created there was so beautiful I nearly wept.

But I had the world to see. As we shook hands, Nicolas ordered his chauffeur to take me anywhere I desired in Beirut. I chose the bazaar at the Souk Sur Sock with its color and excitement.

At this busy marketplace, carpet sellers staggered and pushed their way among the teeming crowds, carrying gaudy Persian rugs stacked high on their shoulders. These fine satiny carpets blended handwoven orange, chartreuse and red patterns. And the sellers chanted their attributes as they carried them along. If you showed the slightest interest in his carpets, a seller would remove them from his shoulder and stack them on the ground to be inspected.

Purple, silver-brocade bathrobes of satin were sold for almost nothing. They blew in the breeze as they hung in front of small, cubicle, tent-like shops that reminded me of amusement booths at an American county fair. Black scarves, silver trinkets, bronze vases, platters, candelabrums and hand-tooled moccasins all sat out in the open air, the better to reflect sunlight and tempt the buyer.

An Arab merchant was pulling an overladen reluctant donkey. The animal's bleating helped drown out the oppressive flow of Arabic singing on the countless, tinny-sounding transistor radios in the shops. To one accustomed to chromatic scale and specific tempo, Arabic singing often sounds like a mosquito buzzing at the ear—a rasping sound that puts no end of strain on the singer's vocal cords, causing one's own throat to require a swallow in sympathy.

"Hey, Charlie!" called a shopkeeper. "Come in here. I have secret to tell you. You want slippe with blonde tonight? Pretty dancing girl, nice young boy?"

"Whisky, Johnny?" cried a street vendor.

"Changee dollar? You have dollar, want to sell?" screeched a money changer—an emaciated old man, squatted like a spider in his three-foot-square booth, surrounded with samplings of every currency in the world that he bought and sold. Being a free port, Beirut had no restriction on currency exchange.

"Hashish, Billy, you need hashish? Good hash, ver' cheap," sang a sulkish-looking boy as he ran alongside me. One had to be as impolite as they were and completely ignore them.

At the entrance to one of the larger booths, a youthful Arab sat on the ground in a shady spot. He plucked at a very old, strange-looking, three-string, mandolin-like instrument of ancient design, concentrating on his notes—his mind far, far away from the noisy world where he sat. I paused to hear his tune. Suddenly seeing me, he jumped to his feet in surprise.

"Hey, you wanna buy rug? Good carpet from Baghdad? Huh? Huh?"

"Baghdad? Hmm, if you have one that flies, I'll buy it."

"Very good, sir. Uh, flies?"

"Nothing. I was just kidding." I looked at his carpets. One of them bore a hand- embroidered caravan of camels. It was truly a masterpiece. Deeply colored threads were painstakingly hand-woven to give photo-like detail, and each of the men's faces in the scene had distinct individuality of mood and feature. "This one is beautiful," I said.

"Aha," exploded the youth. "It flies if you put it on an airplane. So it flies. You can have it for only twenty pounds."

"Yes. But as it doesn't fly on its own, there would be the plane fare. That would cost still more. However you speak good English. Maybe you can help me."

He bowed.

"I'm a guitarist looking for a place to play so I can get a carpet one day. Where in Beirut might a guitarist play?"

A strong dark-skinned youth, he thoughtfully rubbed the acne on his adolescent chin.

"Maybe the Kit Kat. It is my favorite nightclub. The Casino has the most money and nice curtains, but it has too much shouting and drinking."

He told me how to find the Kit Kat. Then he descended on another potential buyer before I'd walked twenty feet.

The Kit Kat was nestled among a row of similar clubs down at the sea front. The bay lapped against a high barnacled wall that served as part of the club's foundation. There were palm trees and buzzing neon lights adding to the playland atmosphere.

Plastered on the Kit Kat's big front doors were grainy, life-size action photos of two identical sideburned, baby-faced young men. They were performing in sparkling Ivy League sport jackets, continental slacks and white suede oxfords. One of them had a guitar strapped over his shoulder. His tongue hung out as he bowed his knees inward. The other held a hand mike, rocking with his back on the floor and feet in the air. Underneath read the caption, "See and hear the sensational Ron & Mel, exclusively at the Kit Kat."

So this was the source of Bustros' worries! Well if they couldn't be banned or beaten, maybe they could be joined.

As it was late afternoon, there were no customers. The light of day revealed a drab foyer having seen grander days. The droopy-eyed cashier would tell me nothing of the manager or his whereabouts.

But there was a prodigiously muscular matron in green, tight-fitting satin standing nearby. "You weesh to see Raja?" Her thickly French-accented resonant voice sounded like a cat purring. "He is in hees room at zee Old Colonial Hotel in zee alley across zee street behind zee Normandy Hotel."

She surveyed my guitar case and smiled. "Tell heem Yvette sent you. I am Yvette. Good luck." She walked away with queenly posture, the muscles rippling in her broad shoulders.

Raja, a half-cast Arab, sat behind an old desk that was heaped with a disheveled array of dusty papers. He was mostly bald. His body looked like an upside down V due to a hopeless melon belly and lack of use. His eyes were bloodshot, and a sour disposition made him appear pinched and unhappy. I told him my story and said I was a troubadour.

"Well, so you're broke and you've gotta play for your dinner, eh?" he remarked with a cynical bitterness, having not understood, believed or cared about my tale. To him I was a commodity to be sold for capital gain. And as his capital outlay would be limited to some leftover goulash and an unused, ill-wanted room in the Old Colonial, his profit would be practically 100% of my yet unproven worth.

"No, I'm not broke. But I'd like to play because I'm a troubadour."

"Troubadour? O.K. Go down to the kitchen and they'll fix you some goulash."

Just as I was leaving, a thin, red-haired, petulant, unhealthy-looking young man of Nordic appearance entered. Raja's face brightened a little on seeing him. "This is Kurt, one of my employees from Norway," he said, introducing us.

"Glad to meet you," I said. "What do you do here?"

He snickered without smiling and shrugged. "Just hang around and make people happy."

"Kurt is my bouncer," Raja said.

Kurt sneered at that, and Raja laughed.

I went out wondering how such a skinny kid could be much of a bouncer.

The Kit Kat's floor show was ostentatious. It employed about a hundred artists, musicians, dancers and stage hands from all corners of the world. The performers wore dazzling costumes, makeup, and lots of confidence. The staging was elaborate, and the sound was loud.

All hundred of the artisans lived rent-free in the run-down Old Colonial. And they ate cost-free together, like a big family, in the Old Colonial's dining room. Raja owned both the Kit Kat and the Old Colonial.

Dinner eaten, the artisans straggled out the door, down the dirty alley and across the boulevard to their comfortless dressing rooms at the Kit Kat where they painted themselves for the early nine p.m. show. There were flaming-sword dancers, jugglers, singers, skaters, mono-cyclists and magicians, comedians, comic mimes, fiddlers and belly dancers.

Among these was my friend Yvette, the French contortionist. The band played Tchaikovsky's *Nutcracker Suite* to bring her onstage. She entered with a few ballet steps, wearing a bikini that revealed her washboard stomach muscles, massive biceps and rock-hard bust, all of which drew a murmur of awe from the audience. Then the musicians became silent, and I played improvisations while she did her double-jointed body positions so impossible-looking they drew gasps from the crowd.

After her exit, I played a three-minute solo, dressed in my polka dot Cavalier shirt and performing boots.

Then the anchor feature came on—the act folks had really come to see. The band began to rock and roll, blowing all the dust from those huge loudspeakers. The crowd came alive with screams and cheers. Ron and Mel jogged onto the stage with their guitars strapped over their shoulders and sang a breathy cockney version of Elvis Presley's hit,

You ain' nu-in' buh-a houndog
Cuh-ryin all-a tye-aye-aye-aye-ime!

One of them immediately reclined on the stage floor—writhing on his back with one fist over his eyes, as though bawling, and the other hand holding his mike. The other twin wiggled his knees in front of his own mike stand and strummed his guitar,

You ain' evah cau-uh rabbah
An' you ain' no fuh-ren o' mi-aye-aye-aye-ine!

Then, with phenomenal energy, as they stood together facing the crowd, they mimed ecstasy and jerked their groins rear to front. And their young lady fans—both married and single—drowned out the music with delighted screams.

Ron and Mel continued with a whining, nasal version of something spawned by the Everly Brothers, and concluded by getting all to clap and sing along with their twelve- minute "finale" version of, "*When The Saints Go Marching In.*"

The crowd invariably would shout and stomp, refusing to let them leave the stage. So they would continue—giving of themselves with such deep feeling that everyone felt they were world-class rockers. And I do believe they were. Given a good record company and proper management, I believe they'd have conquered the world.

The late show began at 1:00 a.m. every morning. We retired at last by 5.00 a.m., if we were lucky, and rose for the day between and two and three in the afternoon.

Bleary-eyed, hung over and smelling of decayed flesh, the performers would crankily shift themselves to the cheerless dining room for coffee or Bloody Mary. They kept the window closed and shuttered.

My first "morning," I couldn't bear to sit with them. I left, still hungry, just in time to meet Ron and Mel walking down the hall on their way to a restaurant, and they invited me along as their guest. They'd watched me play from the wings and wanted to learn about my music.

They were exact twins, pleasant-mannered, serious-minded, and alike in every detail down to a tiny freckle on the tip of each of their upturned noses.

"We were pretty ba' little boys," Mel (I'm pretty sure it was him) explained. "At fourteen, we joined a gang and became Teddy boys when we lived in the West End uh London. We were in wi' a rough bunch. So when we turned eighteen, Pop made us join the British Merchant Marine.

"For years we sailed, working hard on merchant ships, chipping paint and wiping grease. But we had a jolly good time of it. One night we tied up in Beirut. We took our guitars, came ashore to serenade some girls and have a wild nigh'of it, and found ourselves at the Kit Kat. Raja heard us singing and offered to use his government connections to free us of the ship. He gaw' us resident permits, kept us for free, gaw' us money and wardrobe, taw us to perform professionally and gaw us in show business."

"He gaw us on t.v.," Ron added, "and we gaw famous in Beirut. Then someone in the government agitated 'gainst us, and they made a law against our twisting. Someone up there didn't like us, and I suppose they figured we'd qui' after that. But we just modified things a bit and carried on, and, believe it or not, our crowds gaw three times bigguh."

I was excited for them and said, "It was only Nicolas Bustros who banned you. He was worried about the morals of his nation's young female progeny. But he's a nice guy, really."

"Nicolas who?" They were fascinated.

"Bustros, the Lebanese Minister of Protocol. He invited me to lunch yesterday and told me everything. He has nothing to hide. He says the town's young folks began behaving wildly when you two started doing your twist show. He was just acting to try and preserve civility in his nation. I really like him. You would too."

They both seemed very gratified to know exactly who it was who'd banned them and exactly why. No one had told them.

Mel grinned. So did Ron. Then Mel's grin broke wide open to an expansive smile. Glowingly, he said, "I gaw nuh-in' 'gainst 'im. He di' us a faivuh!"

We all had a good laugh over that. Then Mel said, "Our only problem now is that Raja is ge-in to be a bother."

"How do you mean?"

"Blimy, mate, didn't you know? He's queer as a sevenpence!"

"And that gigolo, Kurt," Ron snapped, "he's a paid panda!"

"A what?"

"His fancy boy!"

"Oh."

"Raja's been geh-in more and more friendly. It's pretty sick. But there's a club owner in Amman that's been taw-in with us. After New Year's Eve—the night our contract expires—we're leaving for Amman," Ron said with a serious look at his brother.

"No," said Mel, "we should stay another fortnight and geh' a contract first. It's beh-uh business."

"Men like Raja, if he's what you say he is, are known to make their advances by gunpoint," I cautioned. And I told them about the young Greek I'd met at the Mimosa.

Ron looked scared. "C'mon, Mel, let's leave this fuh-in place."

Mel was the stronger and more positive of the two. "Face it, he's not guh-uh do that."

"How do you know?"

"He wouldn't dare. We're his stars."

"And we're his first love too—he keeps our pictures near his bed!"

They argued thus, but Ron won, temporarily at least, with my help. We decided Raja's empire was an unnatural, unwholesome, decadent world of zombies, and that we would soon leave.

Some days passed, and New Year's Eve arrived. Beirut was alive and jumping with streamers, confetti, pointed paper hats, kazoos and live music. Hundreds of strangers formed a human chain and danced the bunny rabbit down the middle of the Place Des Francais.

The Kit Kat was so crowded there was no standing room left. Champagne spilled and oozed from the tablecloths as the band blared. Few paid much attention to our show.

Even Ron and Mel couldn't hold the crowd. But they'd been given a case of French champagne by Raja, and they invited me and some sensuous young ladies to their upstairs dressing room to help them drink it.

While we celebrated, there was a coup d' etat. During the worst of the gunfire—about 3:30 a.m.—Mel stepped out onto the dressing room balcony. Raising his champagne glass in a mock salute he shouted with dry sarcasm, "happy new year, chaps," to some terrorists who were patrolling the street below. He stepped back inside just in time to dodge a piece of brick someone threw at him, and laughed lustily. Raised by the switchblade in London's "worst end," he was afraid of nothing.

New Year's Eve is a novel and perfect time for a coup. But this one failed in spite of it. For a handful of heroic government troops had been alert enough to rescue the president from assassination, penetrate the intrigue and foil the entire terrorist plot—all between midnight and four a.m.—while the populace swam in champagne.

The very first day of 1962 found government soldiers still in the streets, mopping up what was left of the scattered coup force. Not a single soul was above suspicion. Mel had given me a stamped international aerogram with which to send word to Mom and Jack, but a soldier refused to let me take it, my pack or guitar, into the post office without a thorough search.

Directly behind me in line, awaiting his turn to be searched, was an American, Chuck Webraight. He recognized me. With much excitement, he said, "I saw you playing at the Kit Kat the other night! The girl I was with liked you very much and . . ."

Another soldier came over and began frisking him. He held his hands in the air and continued talking. "Look. Give me your aerogram, and I'll mail it for you while you guard your gear. They'll never let you take all that stuff inside. Wait here for me, and I'll take you to lunch. O.K.?"

A friend in need is welcome indeed.

He was a freelance pilot who made a living flying his own plane. As we ate in a fine Arabic restaurant staffed by shapely, veiled waitresses, he entertainingly described how he flew bizarre folks to forbidden places. He even carried certain cargo that could not come to official attention.

"Do you ever fly to Egypt?" I inquired.

"Why? Do you plan a visit to Nasser's paradise?"

"Of course. One cannot say he's toured the world without having seen the Nile and the pyramids."

So he took me to meet his friend, Buck Ewing, who piloted the private plane of the Trans Arabian Pipeline Company—an American firm known as Tapline.

Ewing was a tall, likeable, clean-cut young American with a perfect set of bleached white teeth. After a short conversation in his office, he sent me to his friend, Dr. Norman W. Boustany.

He scratched Dr. Boustany's name and address on a note pad and handed it to me. "Here. We never fly to Egypt, but this man's billionaire brother Emile used to go there. Norman will steer you right, or I miss my guess. When we at Tapline want something done, we go to him. He's got a heart of gold."

Webraight left in order to keep an early afternoon appointment, and I stood alone in the street with Ewing's piece of paper. "Rue Commodore, Itani Building," it said. The Itani building was only minutes away where I found a neat, bronze plaque immersed in concrete bearing the inscription, Norman W. Boustani, M.D. The receptionist, a friendly and attractive Englishwoman, ushered me in to see him.

He was a happy man, happy to meet me, happy about the weather, and happy that all things happen for the best. "You are a troubadour then? That's wonderful. I love guitar music. Please play me something."

He wheeled his desk chair from behind his desk so that he might sit closer to me. In his forties, he chuckled in delight when I played. Then he produced his own guitar from behind the waste basket.

"See what you think of this guitar," he said, handing it to me.

The tone was deep and mellow. "It's a very good classical guitar." Do you play?"

"No. I bought it the other day and have been planning to find a teacher. Do you teach?"

"A little. Show me what you can do," I replied, handing it back to him.

Luckily there were few patients that afternoon, as it was a holiday. So we wove a lengthy lesson between his appointments. He was a quick study—talented as well—and showed much pleasure at his rapid progress. His happiness was contagious, and I was delighted with him. He allowed me to stay and watch as he worked with his patients. I think he cured them more with his loving manner than with the medicines he prescribed. For as they left, they invariably looked a shade healthier than when they'd entered.

"You must come home and have dinner with my family and me," he said, fumbling in his desk drawer for a key. "And as for a place to sleep, you must stay here on the studio bed in my clinic. There are blankets, sheets, towels, a shower and . . . oh, here's my spare key to the front door. Now you can come and go as you wish at any hour."

A man who trusted as this man was surely a man to be trusted. So when, as we drove to his home, he overwhelmed me with, "I will attend to getting you a complimentary sea voyage round trip to Egypt," I knew his promise was as good as a ticket in hand. And it was.

11

BEING FORCED INTO SMUGGLING IN EGYPT

Dr. Boustany put me on a small freighter that carried about a hundred passengers, and I sailed with them to Port Said where we were all taken, one small boatload at a time, to the customs house. We were greeted by a small crew of officers and the usual array of black market scouts, shysters, and hustlers disguised as chauffeurs, baggage handlers and tourist advisors. Just as in Tunis, they stood around analyzing us for what we might be worth to them. On seeing them, I was reminded with horror of my near-death adventure with their brethren at Tunis customs.

So when presented with a lengthy financial information form, printed on such low- budget pulp paper that it tore at the touch of a pen, I decided against impressing the Egyptian authorities with my wad of greenbacks. I filled out the form, and the officer read it.

"So. You have one Lebanese pound and five American dollars. That is all?" He poised his pen to make the signature of acceptance.

"Yes."

He raised his nose, lowered his eyes and critically examined my battered guitar case and well worn leather jacket. He'd seen many such young men who'd tuned out—wife deserters, shiftless beatniks and ne'er-do-wells. He countersigned the paper, and I was free to go.

At first I felt very guilty, having under-declared, but then took heart from the knowledge that I would now be able to leave the customs house in safety. My experiences with frontier officials elsewhere had caused me not only to lose respect for them, but to become wary of their dishonesty, greed and insensitivity. I saw them only as dangerous men, and forgot I was a guest in this country which, if good enough to be visited, is certainly good enough to have its questions answered honestly. And I was destined to be taught this lesson.

A new asphalt road skirted the Nile Delta, a flat and drab landscape, all the way to Cairo—a city of vast distances and unfathomable hordes of the aimless set who seemed to have nothing to do and nowhere to go. Those few who had an itinerary but couldn't fit into the already crowded busses, simply hung on to the fenders, windows, bumpers and outside stairs. The bus drivers sped around corners with little regard for centrifugal force and its effect on their freeloading passengers.

It was permitted to ride thus by the bus company. And it was reluctantly conceded by them that if a passenger wished to so risk his life riding on the exterior, he need not pay the fare. So there were always a few budget-conscious adventurers astride the headlamps and fenders, even those few times when there were seats available inside. In addition to the monetary advantage, they enjoyed the freedom of hopping on and off at will without regard for the established bus stops. And they avoided exposure to the asphyxiation and germ-spreading suffered by the paying passengers.

Still there was a good reason to ride inside. For the tightly packed standee passengers made it so difficult for the poor buffeted fare collector to make his rounds, one's chances were fifty-fifty that he wouldn't have to pay anyway.

Barefoot bathless children flocked after a Westerner by the score soliciting baksheesh, shoeshine work, offering their bodies and begging for trinkets, buttons or pocket combs. The same restaurant meal could be bought for anywhere from two to eighty piastras. Near where one paid two piastras, black beggars rolled out of alleys—their eyes pleading and voices whimpering in supplication for alms, but deep down cursing all for not being so unfortunate as they.

Those with more ambition collected around Cairo's Nile Hilton hotel to prey on the rich tourists. Once established there, beggars had to fight off other beggars from less lucrative sites. With the gift of English speech and a respectable suit of clothes, a man could hang around the hotel exits, brazenly offer himself as a tour guide, and gather groups of tourists for tours of the pyramids and the sphinx.

So the Nile Hilton was very well "worked," but I decided to give it a try anyway.

The manager was of Germanic extraction, middle-aged and half bald—so typical of those who manage top flight hotels around the world—and graciously granted me an interview in his immaculate office.

"Thank you," he said. "But unfortunately we don't have a floor-show. You cannot be of any assistance to us."

I was anxious to bathe and relax in clean comfort again, having been cramped on a small ship at sea with minimal facilities and then suffering the dirt of the Nile Delta and the slums of Cairo and Port Said.

"How about some live music in the bar?" I suggested.

He got excited. "But of course. I had not thought of that. You are a musician then?"

"I play a little."

"Good."

He summoned a bell hop, and I was escorted to a complimentary room overlooking the Nile. I was to receive free meals—as much as I could eat—three complimentary stamped international aerograms, and 15 Egyptian pounds if I would stay for a week. The hotel was like a pharaoh's palace with its wide, sprawling, brass-banistered circular stairway. Among the gargantuan stone pillars, and beneath possibly the world's biggest chandelier that glittered with gold leaf and multifaceted crystal, there were giant exotic plants and grand entrances to majestic ballrooms. I was very excited, for I would have to perform only in the evening and would have six days to explore in and among the pyramids.

I was never given an audition, but the hotel's interior decorator was assigned to pass on my wardrobe. "Polka dots on your shirt will not do," he shuddered, grimacing at my Cavalier shirt from the Istanbul Hilton. He sent the hotel tailor to my room to take measurements and make me a similar shirt out of the finest black gabardine, with orange stripes, at company expense. I still wear that shirt sometimes, even after 50 years.

The turbaned dining room waiters were dressed in flowing robes of orange, yellow cloth belts and silver accoutrements.

Sitting down for dinner early, so as to be ready to play by 8 p.m., I was awed by their matchless flair and eclat as they went about their work. Most of the tables were still vacant, and the room was quiet.

Just after I sat down, the night manager burst into the room and breathlessly announced to the headwaiter that His Excellency, the United States Ambassador, was on his way for dinner and would arrive any minute. And minutes later, the very overweight American Ambassador to Egypt did indeed make a noisy entrance with his raucous party of six.

"Where's all your American tourists?" he roared to the head-waiter who'd rushed over to show him a table.

"We threw them all out, in order to better serve you, sir," the Egyptian happily countered in fluent English, with wit, poise and polish, ignoring His Excellency's grammar.

"Good. Glad to hear it." The ambassador bowed, hemmed and hawed awkwardly, and sat himself down. Seconds later, he dropped his silver napkin platter and upset the salt dish, spilling salt onto the tablecloth.

The waiter rushed over to remedy the table. "Even ambassadors are human, sir," he smiled, brushing the salt off the table onto a tray with his own napkin.

The embarrassed diplomat flushed red, cleared his throat and, thank goodness, remained silent. A blonde-haired young man and his lady friend, who'd watched all this from their table near mine, stifled their laughter and couldn't stop giggling throughout dinner.

At eight I sat in the Safari Bar and began to play. I expected folks to keep chatting and drown me out. But instead they quieted down and became an informal concert audience. Surprised, I began playing my heart out for them.

The blond young man and his lady came in, found a seat as close to me as they could, and began concentrating on my sonata. They both smiled copiously at me, applauding louder than anyone, and invited me to sit with them as I took a break.

"Bravo," he said in a dense Russian accent. "You play well."

"Thank you. Well, you certainly do laugh a lot when you eat."

"Oh, but didn't you see? The American Ambassador is a pig."

I was shocked. Furthermore I'd never met a Russian before in my entire life. So I just stared at him for some seconds before responding, "I guess he's human, like the waiter said."

He apparently recognized my nationality by my accent. It took him by surprise, and he almost choked on his ice cube. "You are American! Pardon me. Pardon me, please. I am very sorry. I didn't realize . . . I mean I assumed you were European because you play so quietly with such feeling."

"Thank you. It's OK. And my ancestors were indeed European."

I could see he was chagrined at his indiscretion, but he would just have to live with it. Nothing I could say would make him feel any better. I decided he might like to talk about himself and inquired, "Who are you?"

He introduced himself and his beautiful lady friend. (She was Egyptian, understood no English, but smiled nonstop.) "I work at the Russian Embassy. We do not come here to the Hilton. For this is an American enterprise, and we are not feeling at home here. But tonight I thought we would try it just this one time."

"Do you like it?"

"It is very modern. There is a lot of room. Would you like a drink?"

"Thanks, but I don't touch alcohol."

He looked surprised. "But you must be unusual. I have heard that Americans drink much."

I told him millions of Americans don't drink and invited him to visit America and see for himself.

"That would be impossible. We Russians may not travel in America. Even Mr. Khrushchev was confined to New York when he visited."

"Is it not the same for Americans who wish to visit Russia?"

He nodded soberly. "Yes, it is the cold war."

There was a moment of silence. Then he smiled and said, "But you and I are meeting here in Cairo. That is good. I am very happy to meet you. I have never met an American before. And your music is so sensitive. It is not like rock music."

"And I've never met a Russian before." I shrugged and we both laughed, enjoying the moment very much.

He knew a camel driver with a stable near the pyramids, and kindly offered to take me on a camel tour the next day. We adjourned, and I watched him lead his lady down the grand staircase.

The following morning he returned to pick me up, and we went by camelback among the pyramids, learning of their scientific wonders. The camel driver said stray cats and other small animals have been known to get lost among the vast labyrinths inside a pyramid and starve. Their bodies are eventually found, sometimes after many years. In some cases, depending on their location within the pyramid, the long-dead corpses are still in lifelike condition. Modern science has no answers to many of the mysteries there.

I stayed on for a week and got footsore viewing the mummies and artifacts at various museums. Then a pair of German students from the hotel took me in their Volkswagen Beetle to Alexandria—ancient port on the Mediterranean and home of untold international intrigues, scandals, thieves, smugglers, and illegal under-the-table transfers of contraband between the world's billionaires.

It was a busy, crowded Saturday night, and every small tavern had its musicians playing. Celebrative gaiety was at its peak. Beggars, chanting their laments and curses from the running boards of parked horse-drawn coaches, were powerless to penetrate the noisy flood of happy songfests and good cheer.

The city was shaped like a long snake, skirting the crescent bay so that wherever your location you were near the sea. So it was a short walk to the port. Here I found it ghostly quiet and noticed the full moon that had been blotted out by the neon lights in town.

Aimlessly I walked along the pier, enjoying the privacy of having to myself the shimmering moon, the quiet night in this wonderfully strange place, and the sound of my own footsteps on the thick wooden planks. There was a rolling mist. Fishing nets and coils of rope lay scattered here and there.

I happened upon a Russian cargo ship with "Albatross" printed on her massive towering bow in Russian letters. I stopped to admire her fresh coat of paint. She emitted little sound but the mellow squeaking of her metal hull against the rubber tire casings attached to the pier.

"Ayah, do you play that guitar?" called a bold, friendly voice from within a nest of crates that were stacked near the ship.

I turned to find a shabbily dressed black Egyptian in his late teens. He emerged and walked over—a bright handsome lad of medium height. Without a word, he began tenderly fondling my guitar case.

"Ayah, may I see it?" He smiled, and the contrast between his teeth and black face was startling.

I placed the case on one of the crates and opened it. The guitar's inlayed mother-of-pearl mosaic glittered in the moonlight. He beheld it with the passion of a jewelry connoisseur viewing a great diamond. "It is beautiful. Do you play it?"

I shrugged. "Of course. Every day."

"You do?" He smiled challengingly. "Would you show me?"

I was a troubadour, and here was an audience. So we sat facing each other on a pair of crates, and I played. He flashed his white teeth again in a broad smile. "Ayah, so nice. Is this a flamenco or classical guitar?"

"It's both—a rare breed from Madrid known as guitarra universal, made by the Gonzales family."

He studied the guitar further. "Judging from the construction style, it is 19th century. And the strings. They are of French nylon?"

"You know guitars!"

"I am interested in them, yes. Have you ever seen another guitar like yours? I would like to have one just like this one. Could another one be found?"

This kid was a bit forward, but I was impressed with his confidence and knowledge. And he was likeable. "It would be hard," I replied. "I've been to the finest luthiers in New York, Paris, Vienna, London and Munich, found none like it and none that I like as much as this one."

We talked guitars, and I played a bit more by way of demonstrating this and that. Soon we had an audience of Russian sailors lined up along the railing of the Albatross.

"My name is Magid," said the boy. He smiled up at our audience. Then he looked at me eagerly and nodded toward them. "I know these Russians. I could get us supper aboard. But I know how you Americans feel about the Russians."

So he was full of initiative and sophisticated too!

"Our governments, yes," I said. "But I hope there are no problems between the people."

"Ayah. Then I will see what can be done." He confidently mounted the gangplank, quickly negotiated and returned to take me aboard.

We supped in the wardroom where I gave a concert for the ship's officers. Many of them spoke English. One officer requested

I play a traditional aire he'd always loved, the famous romanza, dating back to the 12th century, that became the musical theme for a modern classic film, *Blood and Sand*. I began by telling them a story about it first.

"It was written, as far as we know, by a southern court troubadour. During the Dark Ages, when all music other than liturgical was banned, this one tune from the troubadour era somehow survived. It pirouetted down through the centuries to Amadeus Mozart's time. Mozart heard it played by a traveling gypsy in a Salzburg café one night. Mozart was moved to tears by it. He declared to his friend sitting with him that he would trade all his concertos to have written it. I call my version *Tune The Gypsy Played*, in honor of that traveling gypsy."

Those who understood English quickly translated the story for their comrades, and I played the old aire. The tune has a noble soul living in it. That evening, this noble soul spoke to us about its memories of astral gold—of its joy, sorrow, bliss and tears. No one applauded when I finished. We just sat in silence.

I looked over at Magid. He was grinning ear to ear.

At length, the galley steward broke the stillness by working the lids and creaky cupboard doors of the elegant oak-wood buffet in search of drinks for everyone.

A 2nd Engineer, about my own age, wanted to know why I was roaming the globe in so lazy a fashion. "Are you not wasting your life?" he asked with candor. "Should you not be giving professional concerts in theatres?"

I thanked him for his compliment and told him I didn't know that answer. But I did know that we're given life to experience joy, and that I found joy in seeing far off lands and performing music for the folks who live there. Being a troubadour is a giving kind of life with many rewards. For the folks I play for are kind to me, and they lend me their wisdom which brings me happiness.

I explained that when you play a professional concert, folks come to the theatre to hear you and then go home, leaving you alone in your dressing room with your money and your doubts as to what they felt when you played. But when one plays for his supper, he is taken home by his audience. He learns of their thoughts and feelings, and how they look upon the world.

"Instead of just one family in this world, I have many families." I concluded.

"But what happens when you grow old?"

"I will be so rich in fond memories as to warm my heart forever."

"But you cannot feed your stomach with memories."

"My needs will be simple. Old men don't eat much. And one cannot measure his wealth by how much money he has, so much as by what he has relative to his desires."

He liked that, and asked me what I wanted most from life.

"To have my music be twice as beautiful so I could love twice as much with it."

He seemed to like that too, and another officer pursued me with questions about the hazards, misadventures and methods of my daily life. I explained how simple my life was, whereupon he began asking how long it might take to learn to play the guitar well enough to set out on his own. He was genuinely intrigued.

"America has its Peace Corps. Russia could have troubadours," he declared, proposing a vodka toast to the idea. The toast was heartily made, and they invited me to go with them to Istanbul.

"Thank you, but I've already just been there. And it's very cold there now."

"As you wish. We return to Alexandria in two weeks. If you change your mind, look us up then."

As they would be sailing with the morning tide at 4:00 a.m., I opted to leave them. The officers stood in a handshaking row, and I was privileged to bid each a formal handshaking farewell as young Magid stood by, his white teeth showing in a radiant smile.

As we left the ship he didn't seem to want to part company, having become a little attached. "I know a place where you can sleep for the night," he said. And he took me to the office of his friend, the port commissioner, a cheerful, well fed, short man who wore his uniform with pride. His was a good soul, from the look on his face.

"Do not worry," he said, as Magid introduced us. "We have a clean bed in the rear office for you. I know how it is to be travel-ing." He examined my scuffed guitar case, and emotion covered his face. "Ah, I see you are an artist—a cellist. But what great artist has not suffered lean times? Your time will come, my boy. Your suffering will come through in your music one day as it did for the great Casals."

"But I'm not suffering, sir. I'm having the time of my life. I hope that's all right."

"Ah, you are gallant too. But let us hear a sweet passage from your cello. Do not bother putting rosin on the bow just for me."

He was so excited to hear music from a live vagabond, he didn't mind at all when he discovered it was only a guitar. The three of us sat, and I began playing a medley of classical studies I'd written.

Only a few minutes into the medley, we were interrupted by a hoarse, panicky voice—that of a man utterly distressed. It came from just outside the door. We stood, and in came a pair of port police dragging a struggling, briefly dressed Chinese coolie. Young and strongly built, he was a bundle of nerves. His eyes were glazed with horror as he shouted hysterically, glancing back and forth between his captors and the commissioner.

Another dock worker entered, better dressed and relatively calm, and he began telling the commissioner a story. Periodically the coolie protested and the guards shook him until he stopped. When the story was finished, one policeman produced a tiny box that had been found on the coolie. It contained two large uncut diamonds.

The alarmed commissioner gazed at the coolie in shocked silence. The handcuffed coolie responded with the look of a man begging for his life. He made a choked effort to smile, as if trying to say, look, we're regular guys so let's be friends. If the commissioner was moved by this, he didn't show it. He ordered the coolie be made to sit on the floor in the corner behind his desk while he took particulars from the calm informant. Forms were pulled out of drawers, the official interview was begun, and guitar music was totally forgotten.

Magid took me aside and explained. The informant dock worker had caught the coolie in the act of smuggling the diamonds from a ship and was turning him in for commission.

"If you report a crime in our country, you receive ten percent of the value of all confiscated, stolen or smuggled items. Every Egyptian is therefore a freelance policeman working on commission, making life dangerous and hard for criminals."

I was astonished. "Then this informant is filing for his ten percent?"

Magid gazed enviously at the informant. "Of course. And it will be a big sum—enough for him to retire. Those diamonds are worth a lot."

"What will happen to the coolie?"

"If convicted, he'll be sent to prison for a long time and probably die there. And the government will keep the diamonds." He paused a moment in sad reflection and added, "the government needs the diamonds, so he will be convicted. The government always confiscates and keeps."

I gazed at him in astonishment as he continued. "This coolie was only a bribed delivery boy for a big syndicate who won't ever be caught. But the informers are clever professional men, and Alexandria is crawling with them. They even join criminals to gather evidence before turning them in. Do not ever break the law in Alexandria, for you have no chance."

For one so young, Magid had seen and learned a lot, living and working down at the docks. As it was getting late, he gave me his address and went home. I bedded down in the back room of the commissioner's office, feeling the insecurity anyone might feel on learning he's among a society of dedicated spies, bounty hunters and detectives.

The morning being bright and sunny, I went exploring and came upon one of Egypt's last vestiges of European colonial aristocracy, the posh Alexandria Sporting Club. It was on vast and beautiful acreage. Chauffeurs waited with their master's Rolls Royces in the parking lot, while their masters trotted out for exercise or spectator entertainment in one of the stadiums. The club boasted a major horse-racing stadium, a tennis stadium, rolling lawns, groves of trees for strolls, jogs and picnics, a nightclub, restaurant, bar, gymnasium building, billiards tournament room, and a modern, air-conditioned executive office building.

I've always loved playing tennis. So with Mr. Togni's words, "always think of the best in town," echoing in my head, I approached the executive office building and went in. I was given an interview with the club secretary and offered to give a concert in trade for a two-week membership.

He listened with interest to my travel tales, and asked if he and his staff might hear me play. So I happily tuned my guitar while he summoned several of his staff, and I played them a baroque piece.

He was enthusiastic and chatted in Egyptian with his staff. They all agreed, and he turned to me. "Could you tell your story, just like you did for me, and play at the teenage dance this Friday?"

"That will do fine."

A staff member came in and handed him a paper which he read to me.

"You have an interesting resume in Egypt, young man. I see that you arrived at Port Said on the ninth, aboard the Greek ship, *Medea*, clearing customs at 9:52 a.m., stayed at the Nile Hilton in Cairo from which you mailed three letters on January 14th, and made contact with an official at the Russian Embassy. Then you stayed four hours at the National Art Gallery on the 16th, spent last night in the commissioner's office at gate 64 of the city dock, and you are, at the moment, in good standing with the government."

I was more than a little amazed.

"Do not be concerned. It is a matter of precaution we take with new visitors, however delighted we are to have them as guests."

"But I had no idea I was being shadowed. Is this done with all visitors?"

He nodded. "All foreigners are watched closely in Egypt." And with that, he introduced me to his assistant, Mr. Said Fahmy, chairman of the tennis committee. Mr. Fahmy took me to the tennis stadium locker room, outfitted me with tennis racquet and apparel, and assigned me a spacious locker in which to keep it all.

He was also the club tennis champion, and he spent the afternoon playing a match with me on the stadium court as six ball boys attended to us. The sounds of our feet sliding on the clay court, our racquets hitting the ball, and the applause of the audience we gathered, echoed crisply throughout the stadium. Then his friend from the audience, Dr. Ahmed Abdou, took me home as houseguest for awhile.

Mr. Fahmy generously gave me much of his time in the days that followed. One evening after tennis, he played hooky from his wife and family and took me to a street full of cafes and bohemian coffee houses. His gentle face had sparkled when I'd told him how a troubadour does things, and he wanted to watch me work.

He was clean-shaven and wore a respectable overcoat that reinforced his air of authority and importance. He paved the way for me by getting the managers of the cafes to let me perform. Alexandrians were generous. They filled my plates with piles of paper money and invited me to eat with them. They fed Mr. Fahmy too. He was delighted to accept all the meals offered him, and we ate and drank until our bellies would hold no more.

But there appeared an unsmiling, hard-looking, robed Arab who sat near us in one of the small coffee houses. He gravely watched as I collected money. So intently did he stare that I became fidgety and was glad when Mr. Fahmy suggested we leave for another place to play—on the other side of town.

"This is the finest nightclub in all of Alexandria," he said, as we walked into a fabulous Greek establishment called the Le Glon. He arranged with the manager that I perform on their floor show as opening act for their popular songstress, Emilia, after which I would pass a plate.

I opened with a flamenco malaguena that quieted the noisy audience. Maintaining pin-drop silence throughout my performance, they demanded an encore. Mr. Fahmy had a large tray waiting, and I passed it. In two minutes it was brimming with paper notes, many for fifty piastras and a pound. As I rounded a corner table near the streetside window, I caught the face of the unsmiling Arab again.

He'd followed us all across town. His cheeks reflected the streetlight glare, and he looked hard and bitter as he beheld my large booty. He stared me straight in the eye with a poisonous gaze before slipping away into a nearby shadow, leaving me to worry and wonder about him.

Emilia then sang. Her tunes were sweet and Greek, as was she, and she was accompanied by her band of musicians who played mazurka, mandolin, and various string and woodwind instruments. So lilting, passionate and charming were her voice, manner, classic Greek appearance and silky movements, that everyone was enchanted.

The audience kept her onstage for a half-hour of encores. Her voice warbled, purred, and seemed to be that of a Greek goddess as she sang the beautiful *Athena* with awe-inspiring power and grace. Such a big voice from such a petite little body! It was dramatic. She was scarcely 21 and living alone in Alexandria, according to the manager and his wife at whose table I sat. Mr. Fahmy had gone home, leaving me in the charge of this prosperous, potbellied, elderly Greek manager who'd promised him I could sleep out the night on the barroom settee.

Emilia sat with us right after her performance. Still high with her heartwarming reception, she giddily jabbered with the manager and guzzled a whisky cordial. Then her eyes met mine in silent exchange of compliments.

"Good show," I said.

"Thank you. And you also did well. Are you in Alexandria long?" Her voice and manner were excessively warm.

"Oh, somewhere between a day and a year. Troubadours never know."

"Are you married?"

Her forwardness made me laugh, and I decided to amuse her. "Yes, I have six wives," I replied agreeably. (One doesn't always know why he says things.)

"That must be very costly."

"Not at all. In fact they support me as I travel around. One is a secretary, another a painter, and so on."

She giggled. "I don't believe you. In Europe, men are allowed only one wife."

"As you wish." I shrugged and laughed again. "Are you married?"

"Oh, no. I'm still looking, and my standards are high."

She was an honest girl and meant everything she said. We spent the wee hours listening to her band playing sugary Greek folk tunes as we drank a variety of beverages. The setting of this club was so very Greek, I forgot I was in Africa. Even in exotic Alexandria there are nightclub settings with foreign themes, reflecting the ever present human desire to be somewhere else.

At closing time I found the settee in the bar and began putting its cushions on the thickly carpeted floor where I planned to sleep. Emilia watched in disbelief. "You cannot sleep here," she admonished with compassion. She replaced the cushions on the settee, chuckling as she put the last one in place. "You must stay the night in my apartment, or I will buy you a hotel room. Which shall it be?"

"It would doubtless be cheaper and more interesting if I stayed with you."

So it was settled, and we left together.

She was related to the wind, as was I, and we found ourselves in one another. Time melted when we were together. I admired her artistry and sophistication. She'd headlined at fine clubs since her early teens, and was a veteran cabaret artist at 21.

I stayed with her for several days but kept playing tennis with Mr. Fahmy. And I performed at the Friday night sporting club dance. Then it happened that one night I went to play in the lounge of the Hotel Windsor—one of Alexandria's finest—and met Captain Dumble.

I sat on a barstool, played for about ten minutes for the small crowd of a dozen or so, and a drunk woman got up and passed a plate for me. Just as she was putting the money on my guitar case, a man sitting between two cute French girls on the corner couch bawled out to me, "Hey, California, come on over and have a drink."

This was Dumble—a handsome, youngish, suave, American gentleman of the world, whose merchant ship was moored at the dock.

Sitting officiously on a straight-backed wooden chair, facing him and the girls, was the double-chinned, paunch-bellied, serious-minded Mr. Georgelis, the ship's owner.

I sat on the portion of the corner couch that faced both men. One of the girls reached over and caressed the back of my neck.

Dumble—skipper of Mr. Georgelis' ship—tried to interest me in a whisky soda. When I politely turned that down, he stood up to attract the waiter's attention and yelled, "orange juice on the rocks for the troubadour." He sat down again, kissed both ladies, and turned to me.

"Where are you headed? East, by any chance?"

"Yes, sir. I plan to hitch a ride across the Arabian Desert, thence to India and Thailand."

Mr. Georgelis gasped. Dumble put his tongue into his cheek. "You're going to hike across the desert?"

"Well, there are camel caravans, sand trucks and such."

Dumble laughed a long explosive laugh. "Sure, but you don't need roads, hotels, food, civilization and such nonsense—just the wide open dunes." He laughed again and devoured the neck of the girl on his right—much to the jealousy of the other—while Mr. Georgelis watched him with the attitude of a spectator at a chess tournament.

"The Arabian Desert is thousands of miles of nothing," Dumble laughed.

"Nothing, that is, except the occasional cannibal tribe along the Trucial Coast," added the knowledgeable Mr. Georgelis—his double chin wobbling like a serving of Jell-O as he spoke.

"You mean there is simply nothing?"

"Nothing."

"There's got to be something. What about the American oil camps?"

Georgelis shook his head. "They won't help you unless you're an employee. And the camps are hundreds of miles apart. In between them, while attempting to get from one camp to the next, you'd be consumed by the sun, sand and vultures. There's nothing there to see or do that would be of interest to us infidels. The Saudi Embassy understands all this, so they don't even issue tourist visas to Americans and Europeans."

The girl on Dumble's left raised her skirt above her knees to bewitch him. He hollered an exclamation, kissed her knee, and she tittered.

"You'll be kidnapped by Bedouins, robbed, castrated, and sold to a sheik as a slave or a eunuch," said Dumble. It's happened to many who've attempted the crossing. It's all kept quiet, of course, to keep good relations with the Arabs. We need their oil more than the lives of the few idiots who venture into the dunes on their own."

"But I must cross the desert. It's the only way to get east. The Iraqi border is closed to all traffic due to recent military coups, and Turkey is under four feet of snow with more coming."

Dumble exchanged smiles with Georgelis. "Then you must go by sea."

"Would you take a troubadour aboard?"

Dumble smiled and lit a cigarette. "Yes, if the troubadour wouldn't mind being a wiper for a while."

"What's a wiper? Is it hard work?"

He and Georgelis exchanged smiles again. "I need a wiper," he answered. "We're headed east to San Francisco, via Saigon. Union regulations may prevent me from dropping you in Saigon, so I might have to take you all the way to Frisco. You've had enough traveling anyway, haven't you? The wage is $426. You'll get a free trip to Frisco, $426, plus seaman's papers that will entitle you to work your way on any ship."

(He neglected to tell me a wiper's job is the lowest, meanest and most wretched on the ship, especially when going through an equatorial region like Saigon. For the wiper works in the hottest parts of the engine room, getting himself coated with oil and grease in temperatures of 120 degrees and 99 percent humidity. I didn't know any of this at the time, but Dumble's attitude seemed suspicious enough.)

Georgelis' attention focused on my plate of paper piastras. "How much money have you there?" he gleefully asked, as though it were his. Together we counted it, and it came to several pounds.

"You want dollars for all your Egyptian money?" Dumble offered.

"Sure."

He nodded to Mr. Georgelis who produced a thick wad of American dollars. I gave him all my Egyptian pounds, and he gave me their full worth at the official Bank of Egypt rate.

"Well, what say you to my offer?" Dumble asked.

I wanted to think about it overnight, so Dumble proposed I stay at the Windsor as their guest and that we adjourn until morning.

I slept until noon, having sapped my energy the previous day playing eight sets of tennis and spending a late night. Dumble spent the morning at the American Consulate obtaining my seaman's papers without my knowledge. I lunched with him, and he took me to the consulate.

The vice consul was a clean-cut, mild-mannered, firmly dispassionate sort—the kind often chosen for his position. His cultivated serenity conveyed that he had God and the entire United States of America on his side.

"It's my understanding that you wish to sign on with Captain Dumble's crew," he said to me.

"I've said that I might sign on."

"Well, we've sent to the Coast Guard for clearance on you, and it came only a few minutes ago."

"Then I may sign on?"

He nodded.

"Whaddya say?" inquired Dumble.

I took a deep breath and committed. "I think I want to keep traveling on my own. God gave me this whole world to live in, and I've inspected only half of it."

Dumble rolled his eyes. "Good God, the fellow has choked on the dust of North Africa and frozen in Asia for a year, and still he hasn't had a enough!" He faced me. "You know, I figured you a pretty good risk last night. What happened?"

"I told you, I needed to think overnight."

Dumble looked helplessly at the vice consul who then told me I was missing a fine chance for gainful employment and a safe passage home.

I replied that I wouldn't be here in Egypt right now if all I wanted was a job and safe passage home.

Dumble tried a new tack. "That Egyptian money we changed for you last night. Did anyone see you earning it?"

The vice consul stiffened.

"I suppose so."

Dumble raised his eyebrow. "Boy, then I'm glad I'm not in your shoes. This town is loaded with spies. And speaking of shoes, you better hide those greenbacks in your shoe, because your chances of getting them out through customs are zero now that you've made a public spectacle of yourself earning it in a soft-currency nation!"

Shocked, I asked the vice consul if this was true.

He looked worried for me. "I'm afraid it might be."

Now it dawned on me. The unsmiling Arab had seen me earning money. So that was his game. He was a spy. Ten percent of my earnings were as good as his!

I turned to the vice consul again. "If I'm searched on leaving the country, will they confiscate any money undeclared upon entry?"

"Indeed they will." he said.

"There's more than a thousand dollars undeclared."

He beheld me with profound sympathy and told me that under Egyptian law my money belonged to Egypt the moment I signed the paper under-declaring. Further, American citizens are imprisoned for such breaches of customs regulations, and Egyptian prisons are not up to Western standards.

"They're vile," Dumble added. "There are rats, roaches and lice, not to mention the lousy food, if any. If you were a member of my crew, we could get you and your money out safely enough. On your own, you have no chance."

I gazed through the window at the sky, shaking my head in disbelief, but said nothing.

Dumble rose to leave. "I've got to go get some work done. If you decide to sign on, call me at the ship." He shook hands with us both and left.

The vice consul sat down and beheld me with compassion. "Yes, I am afraid your unsmiling Arab has earned himself a hundred of your dollars. The rest belongs to Egypt."

"What if I give it to you to send to my friend Dr. Boustany in Beirut?"

"I'm not permitted to use our diplomatic pouch to help you disobey the law. And if you attempt to mail it yourself, your package will be inspected. So I'm afraid you'll just have to learn a very expensive lesson. I'm sorry."

Shaking my hand, he wished me luck with my problem as I left in a state of depression.

I wandered around the city in this very unhappy state and came upon what was known as the Street of Old Bathrooms. There was a poorly kept little park where I sat down and contemplated.

I'd failed to be as good as a sheep. I'd not forgiven and forgotten the indiscreet customs officer, the beggars in Tunis, the lying, thieving, money-changer officials at the Turkish-Syrian frontier, the French Immigration officer who stole my ticket, and the extortionist Rabat police. I'd accepted and remembered negative attributes for these government officials, leading me to presume the worst, and then to under-declare when I got to Port Said. I was no better than those jackals.

A raggedy Arab appeared in the middle of the park, raised the front of his robe and, without inhibition, began to urinate.

He seemed a reviling spectacle, but women and children nearby took no notice. The Arab smiled, waved at us all and walked on. I decided he was repulsive and belligerent, but I envied him. He was less decadent than me. He was free to wander the street without worry. I, on the other hand, was a corrupt liar about to be raked through the judicial system at the word of an informer, and maybe do time in some Egyptian dungeon.

After some hours, this sulking in self damnation proving fruitless, I returned to the Le Glon to open once again for Emilia and spend with her my last night in Egypt as a free man. My ship was leaving for Beirut in the morning. I still had the 2nd half of Dr. Boustany's round-trip ticket, but that would be of little use now.

The gaiety of the evening did little to raise my fallen morale. When we reached her apartment, Emilia demanded to know the cause.

"You act like the sky has fallen," she said. "Tell me what has happened, no matter how terrible, because I can help."

And maybe she could at that, with her nimble and active mind. Her love was very strong. Something in her cheer caused me to realize I'd been seeing the corruption only skin deep. I needed to look further and see the love all those corrupt officials needed to give and receive—to see the perfection of their creator reflected in them. I knew that if I could only do this without attachment to any outcome, I would feel and experience harmony. With this new thought in mind, I told Emilia of the day's events.

She chuckled. "I've done that, only I told them I had more money, not less than I really had, so I could leave with more than I'd brought in. All the Greek cabaret artists do that. But this does not help you, does it. Let me see . . ."

With the instinct of a veteran smuggler, she divided my money into two half-inch bundles, wrapped them with brown gift-box tissue paper and brown cloth tape. Then, expertly, with her amazingly petite hands and agile small-bone wrist, she managed to cloth-tape the bundles inside the guitar on the underside of the front plate, beyond the 2nd rib where no ordinary adult human hand could reach.

I shook the guitar as hard as I dared, and the tape held fast. It would require coathanger wire and lots of gradual undoing to get it out later. If customs were to use a spoon mirror in their search, they would find the bundles so neatly wrapped as to appear to be large cleats—possibly part of the construction of the instrument. We judged that if they found the money now they deserved to keep it.

I arrived at the loading dock 45 minutes ahead of boarding time to join the long line of passengers applying for exit clearance, telling myself this was all just paranoia. But at the customs desk, they had a star next to my name on their list. The officer phoned for a special agent who took me stepping through a maze of suitcases, crates, bundles and cackling fowls to a back room with no furniture save a bare wooden table. He summoned another officer. The two of them locked the room's only exit and confronted me. They were big and tall men, and they meant business.

I was ordered to undress and remove everything from my pack. The men were cold and businesslike, and I responded by behaving as they did. Zealously, these bright professionals examined packframe tubing, coat lining, socks, and heels of boots. One of them examined my scalp for a toupee. Then he checked my guitar case lining. His associate double checked him on everything. I'd never even thought of sewing the money inside the velvet lining of the guitar case and found myself admiring their experience, skill and professionalism. They tried to open my can of shaving cream, and I convinced them by sacrificing a little lather.

Finally one of them requested I loosen the guitar strings! That's when the shock of it all really hit me. I felt my brain turn a bit numb, and butterflies took over in my stomach. But with a poker face, I quietly turned the tuning knobs until the strings were loose enough to permit a hand to enter the sound hole. He pulled a fountain pen flashlight from his pocket and peered in. But the ribs blocked his view, and he had no mirrors. Would he go get a spoon mirror of the kind that dentists use?

I began to feel like there was a cold sweat on my forehead. He put down the flashlight, put his hand in and felt around. But his hand was, as I'd hoped, as big as mine. This annoyed him, for he certainly realized the possibility of something taped further in. The other officer tried. His hands were smaller, but no match for Emilia's. They looked at my hands. Assuming I couldn't get any farther in than they could, they said I may tune up the guitar again and put things away.

"Whatever were you looking for, gentlemen?" I asked.

"It is nothing. Just routine," one of them said as he stamped my clearance paper.

I made a silent vow never to lie again.

The ship left on schedule. As we sailed eastward toward Lebanon, I wondered if I should risk the Arabian Desert. Captain Dumble had been wrong about my getting out of Egypt with the money. But could he be wrong twice? What of his dark prophecies about Saudi Arabia?

12

SAND, SUN, AND SKY IN THE ARABIAN DESERT WITH CHAMPAGNE SMUGGLERS

While I'd been away in Egypt, Dr. Boustany had obtained my Saudi Arabian visa. It hadn't been easy, for the Saudis were not issuing tourism visas. But they knew and loved the kind doctor, as did most everyone in Beirut. And as he'd enlisted Tapline Inc. to help me with a letter of sponsorship, the embassy had made an exception in my case.

His brother Fuade was a music buff and had state-of-the-art recording equipment set up in his living room. The night before I left for Arabia, he held a dinner party/recording session for us all in his home so there would exist in the world a high-quality, private recording of my work.

"There are no roads, hotels or other facilities for you in Arabia," Dr. Boustany warned me during dinner. "That's why there are no tourist visas. In their letter, Tapline has said they'll give you minimal survival assistance only if you arrive at their encampments out in the desert. Basically you'll be on your own out there," he said, deeply worried.

But I'd resolved to cast my fate to whatever winds life by the troubadour code might bring. So he arranged a ride for me on a gasoline truck to the Arabian frontier town of Turaif, via Damascus and the parched wilderness of Jordan.

It was an old truck, and the driver spoke no English. But he was a veteran trucker and a solid, kind man. We passed through a region of sun-fired clay dust that billowed and whirled about and beneath us as we bumped along an ancient road, pocked with bumps and ruts, that descended the hills of Damascus and led to the deserts of Jordan. This road was so old I wondered if it was among those taken by Saint Paul two thousand years ago.

The bumps were so severe I had to hold the guitar on my lap or it would surely have been damaged. I reduced the pain of the bumps by gazing dreamily at the sun's reflected glare upon a seedless earth, allowing myself to drift into a semi altered state.

The driver had brought lots of food which he shared with me at his trucking company's log cabin high in the hills south of Damascus. We were visited by severe frost during the night, and I awoke with throat so sore I could utter nothing. But as we entered Jordan, the heat became so intense my throat recovered.

We passed through Jordan and came to the final Jordanese checkpoint before the Saudi frontier—a pair of camel hide tents decorated with colored ropes and silvery trinkets. Between the tents was a corral containing a few camels. It seems we were the only folks to come along that day, so the colorfully dressed customs-immigration official stepped out to invite us for tea in the main tent. A shiny cutlass was secured inside his black cloth belt. He wore a brown skirt and black patent leather boots. His headdress was white, flowing, and trimmed with a braid of black rope.

There were three others dressed just like him inside where comfort was established with many layers of colorful carpets, silk pillows on which one sat, and a sense of good fellowship. It smelled of frankincense, musk and new saddle leather. Bright tapestries adorned the canvass walls. None of the men spoke English. So I listened to Arabic- spoken social chatter as we sipped tea for an hour or so before getting around to papers, passports, and our long trip to Saudi customs-immigration in Turaiff.

Less than a mile down the road, my driver suddenly turned off the asphalt onto loose sand as though perhaps he'd lost control. But instead of righting himself, he drove farther from the road, see-sawing up and down the dunes.

I gazed at him, wondering if perhaps he'd lost his mind. Seeing me in distress, he thought a moment and then laughed, pointing to his head.

So our path was in his head! There was no road to Turaif. Okay, I thought. But as we passed dune after dune, far beyond sight of the road, everything looked the same. We could've been traveling in circles. Aside from the occasional bleached skull of a long-dead sheep, human or camel, there were no landmarks.

My observations were interrupted by the appearance of a small dark spot rapidly gaining on us from the rear. My driver noticed it too. With a gleeful laugh, he floored his gas pedal, and we skipped across the sand at a dangerous speed for a gasoline truck.

But the friendly race was a mismatch from the start. The spot quickly overtook us, and I could see the gleaming cutlass of our friend the customs officer. His white flowing headdress rippled in the wind as his trusty camel whisked him effortlessly across the dunes at a gallop.

My driver had forgotten to pick up his permit, having left it beneath his tea glass. I remembered having seen it there. But not knowing what it was, I'd not mentioned it.

We took out the Primus stove, boiled some water, and had another social hour with him before resuming our seemingly aimless journey through this no-man's land.

Hours passed without any sign of a road, tire mark, or even a cactus. "Nothing," Mr. Georgeliss had said. Well, he was right about that.

But as dusk descended we saw a red beacon blinking and headed toward it. Land ho! With neither sextant nor compass, my driver had calculated our course so accurately as to bring us to within sight of that beacon. The human brain is wonderful. Desert people are born with navigation tools inside their heads.

The Turaiff American oil camp was entirely surrounded by a 12-foot cyclone fence crowned with three strands of barbed wire. At the guarded entrance, a hand-operated drawbridge served as a gate. My driver let me off there and went off to the nearby Arab village, or souk as the Arabs say.

Within the fence lived Kenneth Parr, an American oil engineer I'd met in Beirut. He'd offered me his home, a shower, and a glass of ginger ale if I ever made it out to his desert castle. I called him from the guardhouse phone at the drawbridge.

He could hardly believe it. "You made it way out here on your own? Stay right there. I'm on my way to get you."

He took me to a party that night, where I rendered a half-hour mini concert. The camp superintendent was there and invited me to play for the school children the next day.

But morning brought a haughty, robed, Muslim customs officer to Parr's office with orders to confiscate my guitar. Someone had reported it. No live music was allowed in Arabia.

Kenneth gently explained to me some hard reality. "Muslim priests control Arabia. Today you must visit the Arab Quarter and go through Saudi customs and immigration—something you couldn't attend to last night because they were closed. Try to pretend your guitar is a hobby horse or something. Live music is considered immoral here. All musical instruments are banned by the priests. Radio and hi fi, yes. But do-it-yourself music is forbidden."

He sent me off with the haughty Arab who led me outside the gate to the large undecorated customs building. There were many trucks and truckers—my driver of the previous days among them.

A friendly shepherd, clothed in a blanket and sandals, was smoking a hashish pipe in the waiting area. While awaiting my turn to be inspected, I sat on the cement floor with him to try a puff at his invitation. The blue smoke gave me a mild dizzy headache, so I stopped after one or two puffs. But we sat together and smiled over the antics of both the truckers and the officers when undeclared carpets, new sandals, new clothing items, gold, necklaces and similarly embarrassing items were discovered. Usually the affairs were settled with a negotiated bribe.

There were boxes of oranges for the citizens of Riyadh, bundles of musty cotton, and crates of machinery among the sacks of flour, grain and wilted produce. Officials, dressed just like the Bedouin travelers, ran about with smudged pads and pencils keeping records of it all as best they could.

It took about an hour to clear each truck, due to the many illegal items and lengthy haggling over the extent of the offenses and amount of the bribes.

But I was at last taken to an inner office for my interview with the chief inspector. A local traveler doesn't normally merit an interview with the chief. But as I was a "Europee" headed across the desert on my own, it was apparently a matter requiring some sophistication and delicacy.

The chief sat behind an old crate that served as his desk. He picked some mucous from his nose and rubbed it onto his filthy robe. Then he roughly mauled my passport, wiping upon it any remaining residue.

"I see that you have a visa, but this is all very strange. What is your business in Arabia?"

"I'm on my way around the world."

"Yes, but what will you do in Arabia? Are you a Tapline man?"

All Europeans were Tapline men, so I nodded. "I'm visiting the American oil camps here."

Despite his grossness he was a sharp old fox. "Yes, but are you a Tapline man? Are you officially employed by Tapline?"

"No, sir."

Four trainee officers quietly entered the room and seated themselves, apparently to study me and learn from the proceedings.

The chief frowned and made a token search of my back pack. Then he focused on my guitar. "Open that suitcase," he ordered rudely, with rising emotion.

I opened it, and he beheld the valuable-looking instrument with elation. I'd been a mystery to him, for Europeans never visited his country except to take oil. But now he'd discovered my motive. "So. You will bring this instrument into Arabia and sell it for a quick profit on the black market."

"I'm a troubadour" I countered, offended. "I would never sell or part with my guitar. It's an inseparable companion, like my right arm."

"Troubadour? What is this word? Well, it is no matter. You may not enter Arabia with your guitar."

"But sir, I'm helpless without it. A troubadour is one who plays directly for his food before art lovers and kings. Without my guitar, I cannot eat."

"You have no money?"

"Of course, but . . ."

"Well then. You can send your guitar by mail to the next country on your itinerary. That is the only thing you can do."

"But this is a very old and precious instrument, and mailing it is very risky."

He frowned impatiently. "The last man who argued with me about his instrument was a very sorry man indeed. I ordered his merchandise chopped for fuel wood." He had the authority out there to do just that, and eyed me with a sadistic hope I might argue again so he could issue the fatal order.

I shrugged and sat in an old chair to think. He huffily left, giving me an hour to decide.

This left me alone with these younger officers who appeared mellow and friendly. Some were as young as me. Being young, they might be "liberals" and feel rebellious toward the religious order that outlawed music, I thought to myself. I'd learned, in my 22 years, that urgencies were best dealt with by not rushing them. Somehow, in the coming hour, this apparent granite wall of a problem would crumble if I could manage to let go of it.

I just sat and stared at my guitar, not looking at the officers but speaking to them mentally with an inner conviction that they were extremely bright, in sympathy with me, and—like four angels that wandered in—might somehow reflect the wisdom needed to deal with this contingency. I was going to be taken care of. I don't know how I knew this. It was just one of those rare inner hopes that sometimes builds and becomes so strong as to generate what actually happens next.

The youngest officer broke the silence and spoke to me in good English. "I have heard guitar records, but have never seen one played. Music is illegal in public places, but this is not a public place. You may please play here if you wish," he invited softly. There was eagerness and hunger in his tone.

I smiled in disbelief. He had to be kidding! "You've never seen a guitar played?"

He shook his head in modest embarrassment. He was being real.

I looked at the three others. They shrugged and shook their heads too.

I'd seen enough strangeness here already, so I believed them. And what better way to spend my last hour with my guitar than to be playing it. I was going to be fine. I just knew it!

As I took the guitar into my lap, the youngest officer rushed over to close the office door.

I began with a sad, soulful farruca. Another officer got out several hashish joints from his robe pocket and shared them with the others. Hashish was, of course, perfectly legal in Arabia. I found it rather odd. For I was used to California where music was legal but hashish was not. They lit up and puffed on the joints as they listened—delight all over their faces.

I played a second piece, and a third as they watched appreciatively.

Then the youngest officer had an idea. "Why don't you have one of your American friends at Tapline sign a paper guaranteeing you will not sell your guitar in Arabia or play it in public places. Then, if our chief has this paper, he might let the guitar enter the country."

(May the goddess of love forever bless that young man!)

When the chief officer returned I suggested the idea, and he said if I could get a Tapline official to sign such a paper—an actual affidavit—he would himself be protected. He gave me a green light to go try.

I'd known Kenneth Parr for only a few hours. But he was warm, extremely calm and trusting. He knew of my dedication to music and understood it. But would he put his relationship with the Arab government on the line and guarantee me to them?

He was up to his ears in urgent business when I returned. Pale from a life spent working in control rooms and offices, he was personally responsible to see that the oil flowed out of Arabia 24/7 at an awesome number of pounds per square inch through a 32-inch pipe that stretched across thousands of miles. The wheels of nations depended on his decisions and actions every minute.

But he dropped everything and had me summoned into his office so we could discuss my little problem.

He leaned back in his chair and actually twiddled this thumbs.

No wonder he can be so calm, I thought to myself. He can tune out the pressure.

He smiled. "I bet you've never before met with so much resistance to a troubadour as the forbiddance of your guitar."

I nodded. His smile told me volumes. He was kind, caring, and deciding to help me.

He summoned the camp superintendent and an Arab on his staff who'd been Western-educated at special Tapline schools—a corporate attorney well versed in Saudi law.

My situation was discussed and weighed. They concluded that if it were properly written, Parr could sign such an affidavit without jeopardizing Tapline. He would only be risking his own neck with the Arabs, were I to flake away and sell my guitar or get arrested for playing it in a place where the general public is invited and admitted.

"Then I'll sign it," Parr said without hesitating. He ordered his attorney to draw up the paper in Arabic and make three copies to be signed by the customs chief, me and himself. He would keep one. The chief would keep the second, and I would carry the third with my passport. It was my special, non transferable permit to possess the guitar. I would need to have it countersigned by each territorial customs office along my travel route—particularly by the office that checked me out of the country on my day of departure from Arabia—certifying that I still had the guitar.

Elated, I returned to customs with the affidavits. The chief read and liked them. He signed and stamped them with the official seal of his office. He kept one, clipped one to my passport and gave me the third to return to Mr. Parr.

He shook my hand as I left. Now that he could see I had a good friend among the Americans, he accepted me himself. Congenially, warmly, he coached me. "It must be signed by all the customs checkpoints you come to, and then mailed to Mr. Parr who must see that I receive it," he instructed. "Furthermore, you must not be seen playing your instrument in a public place, or both you and Mr. Parr will be arrested. I do hope this does not happen."

"It won't," I assured him.

And once again I walked the face of the earth free of problems, feeling radiantly happy. I'd perceived those four young officers as intelligent, helpful friends. So these were the young officers who spoke back to me.

"It's the man you perceive in the man you speak to who speaks back to you," Mom's last words of advice as she and Jack put me out on Highway 40, rang repeatedly in my head. That was good advice.

I stayed an extra day in Turaif and gave that performance for the school kids. A private place, the school was modern, well-equipped, and staffed by housewives with teaching credentials. The scholastic standard there was unusually high—the students unusually bright and friendly. As I played to this quiet, intelligent, appreciative audience, I found myself wishing I'd been lucky enough to attend such a school and to have had those kids for my classmates.

Mr. Parr and his wife were a joy as they warmly hosted me in their fine desert home. Then he found me another gasoline trucker headed southeast to Badannah, about 100 miles deeper into the desert. Leaving the great pipeline to run itself for a few minutes, he came with me to the truck and inspected it to be sure I'd be safe.

"Remember, I didn't sign that paper just as a favor to you alone," he said. "I expect you to caress those nylon strings for our compatriots in Badannah with my best wishes." He winked and added, "maybe a few Bedouins, too."

Badannah was a short journey of only a day, during which we came within sight of some desert folk who lived, breathed and moved among the ageless, ever-drifting dunes in their everlasting search for water.

The American camp there was superintended by a Mr. Arnold, equally as kind as Mr. Parr. As word had preceded me via inter-camp communications, Mr. Arnold had me taxied from the gate directly to a luxurious private room with refrigerator and hot shower. A full evening concert was arranged for me that night for the entire Badannah oil camp community of about 150, and it was held at what they called the "Civic Auditorium." His Highness, the local shaikh, also attended with an entourage. The small hall was packed. They passed a cigar box after my show and presented it to me stuffed with American and Arabian cash.

An American pipeline technician gave me a tour of the camp and nearby souk. He was a tall, beefy young Georgian, Big Jim, whose friendly laugh filled all space.

"I suppose you've noticed there are only a few dozen Americans among the population of 150 here," he drawled. "That's because Tapline and Aramco, the Arabian American Oil Company, have a policy. We train the Arabs to take over the high-skill positions. As soon as they master the technology and prove themselves capable, we put them on the job and remove the American.

"Eventually the Arabs will be owning and running the whole show. Tapline figures this is about the best way to help a backward country enter the coming technical age. In this way they won't be left high and dry down the line when the oil's all gone."

I was proud to find, during the ensuing weeks, that Americans did indeed have this policy in place throughout Arabia. I believe it's the most effective kind of foreign aid.

We inspected both the electronic control room and the engine room that propelled the oil along the pipeline. Then we toured some of the luxurious homes of the American personnel. Almost every home had a big copper tank in one of the bathrooms, just as they'd had in Turaif.

"What about these tanks? Whatever are they for?" I asked Big Jim.

"A body's got to have a little booze now and then," he said. "Most everyone here is a self-made moonshiner. What we drink at our nightly cocktail parties is mostly third run moonshine on the rocks—140 proof or so."

"But, like guitars, it's prohibited. How do you get away with it?"

"Yep. Prohibition is alive and well here in Arabia. But we confine our drinking to the base, so the government ignores it."

I was startled to learn this, and stared at him. "Always confined?"

A small laugh escaped his lips. "Oh, a little drips out now and again. Sometimes it gets discovered, and there's some static. Then we have to do something to make peace with the Muslim priests and get them to remove their war paint for another spell."

He could see I was very interested, so he gave me a color photo he'd taken of one of the bathroom stills. I've kept it to this day.

We drove in his Mercedes, equipped with special balloon sand tires, to the nearby Arab "souk." There were ruins of old structures standing alongside new buildings of the same camel's dung composition. The

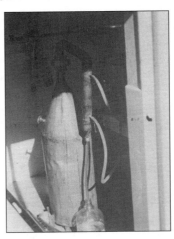

"Oh, a little drips out now and again."

main street was vastly wide and paved with sand and pebbles. An aloof policeman stood in the center directing traffic, though there was none. Ours was certainly the first car to pass by that day, and he treated us as though there were fifty more behind and in front of us. Though dressed in regular Bedouin clothes, he proudly wore a red band around his arm, a symbol of authority.

A jackass stood sniffing at a large pebble. Beyond him, down the street, a half-hearted outdoor marketing of sheep, wool and supplies was in progress. None yelled, walked or worked harder than absolutely necessary. For this was the month of Ramadan when all Muslims fast during the day and feast only at night. This leaves the day uncontaminated by worldly lusts or human hypothesis. One becomes open to spiritual pursuit, bowing toward Mecca and gaining Allah's favor, even traveling to Mecca on foot, gaining favor with each step.

The streets were clean. Being a provincial village, Badannah wasn't crowded. There was a single, well-pruned tree, lovingly planted and watered, in the town center.

Women in black robes and black veils walked about in groups, quietly chatting.

Men and boys were dressed in traditional robes combined with Western-style coats. Some wore stiff and bulky overcoats made of old carpets for protection against the sand storms.

While desert nights are fiercely cold, the days can be hot. So for further protection against temperature extremes, ultra-violet rays and blowing sand, men's heads were often hooded in raggedy Turkish towels or fragments of old tablecloth.

If we loitered long in one spot, we'd be followed by groups of boys and destitute men who wanted baksheesh. But these were good-natured suburban folks. So when we didn't dole out coins, they remained friendly anyway. Here in this village everyone had water. If hungry they could go see the Americans and possibly even get a job if they chose to associate with heathen Christians.

The penalty for malicious murder in Arabia was beheading by the sword of an executioner in the public square. And punishment for the third conviction of thievery was amputation of the thieving hand under the same public conditions. As we passed the public square, we saw two such amputated hands, with advanced rigor mortis and decay, mounted on two separate pikes nailed onto the eve of a building. It was an effective reminder to would-be thieves.

The town cemetery was on a lonely unmarked dune just south of the souk. Hun-

These stones offered little protection.

dreds of corpses lay scarcely ten feet apart in shallow graves covered with only a few shovel loads of sand held in place, to some extent, by a sprinkling of small stones placed on top. These stones offered little protection from the fierce desert winds that often denuded the corpses and scattered the bones and skulls for many miles.

Big Jim was a good host. He found me a truck headed east to Rafha, where once again I gave a concert for an entire Tapline community in return for a meal and a bed.

The morning after, I checked in with the Rafha customs house to have my affidavit countersigned. Here I met an industrious, fine-looking crew of Arabs driving three decrepit trucks. They were on their way to Quaysuma, about 150 miles to the southeast, and decided to take me along when I explained I could provide them with a private dinner concert.

These were gentle-looking men, very friendly and well supplied with provisions. One truck had a load of old threadbare tire casings. The other two were empty of cargo but carried many provisions. As we headed out into the endless sea of sand, I had to trust yet again that my drivers knew where they were going.

Soon we came to a desolate stretch of harder sand that was covered with sharp pebbles. All the tires on all three of our trucks were threadbare, and we began getting blowouts. We got so many it took us more than two days to make the 150 miles to Quaysuma.

Each time one occurred, my childlike driver would look over at me with a grin and make a hissing sound, mimicking the tire. Then he would hop out and make us some tea while the repair proceeded.

These Arabs had plenty of patching equipment and were good at patching. Their weakness lay only in getting the wheels on and off. The blowouts generally occurred on the inner tires of the double wheels, so there was much manipulation of bolts and lugs that were stripped from misuse and overuse.

Our tire wrench was slightly too big for the lugs. So even if the lugs weren't stripped on the inside, they were soon stripped smooth and round on the outside. I didn't really worry until I noticed that when my driver couldn't get a lug on or off, he would become angry and pound on it with a heavy steel hammer until the devil in it had been driven out. But there was no need to worry, for the plan worked somehow. And over the years since then, I've been told by more than one brilliant technical engineer that a piece of machinery responds to its operator's attitude.

We saw no migrating desert folk other than one very poor Bedouin clan whom we met at dusk of the second day. We'd only just stopped to fix a flat tire, having gone a record 45 minutes or so without a puncture.

They emerged from a canyon between a pair of dunes, and would have passed into the oblivion of another had they not seen us and come to get some water. They came toward us—all twenty of them, perhaps twenty-five including the children and infants. Their wealth included a pair of mangy camels and a flock of six underfed sheep.

Between our three trucks we had sufficient water to drown a hundred people. So we gave these nomads enough to fill their camel skin water bags, and they decided to join us for tea while our tire got repaired by the cleaner and his two helpers who rode in back of one of the trucks.

Then we sat around a Primus stove with some jars of unappetizing, pickled privy parts of camel and lamb offered to everyone present by my generous driver. As was customary, the men ate first.

The women sat in silence watching them eat. Clothed in black burlap, these women were unveiled and weirdly beautiful. Some had beauty spots and tattoos. Their soulful, charcoal-darkened eyes reflected awesome humility and spiritual awareness. Glittering trinkets hung from their penetrated nostrils and earlobes, and they wore shiny bracelets and anklets. Their jewelry, as well as their livestock, was a mark of their wealth. There was comparatively little jewelry among this small tribe, and none of it was genuine silver or gold. But I remembered Big Jim's having mentioned that it's Bedouin custom to advertise your family's wealth by decorating the women in this fashion and then selling the jewelry from their noses, ears and wrists as money is needed for food and clothing.

One very winsome young mother sat playing with her infant who responded gleefully despite the bleak desert life to which it had recently been assigned. Its sex remained a mystery though, until she raised it into the air and kissed it on the penis.

I steadfastly declined to eat anything, although one of the Bedouins kept imploring that I try his casserole of oats mixed with the blood of a recently sacrificed sheep. My refusal to eat was causing some embarrassment. But then I drank some tea, and everyone felt better.

One of the tribesmen was mentally retarded—perhaps a madman. Incessantly he would roll his yellowed glassy eyes around, make clucking sounds like a hen, beat his bony chest, shudder from head to foot, and then relax and laugh to himself about some private joke known only to him. He too ate little or nothing, but no one paid him any heed.

Though he and I traded a smile. For we quickly discovered, from each other's gaze, that we enjoyed a mutual kinship with the wind.

I'd no sooner begun thinking this would certainly be a unique audience—and definitely private, as there was no one out there but us for at least fifty miles in any direction—when my driver nodded toward my guitar in the truck, grinned and made a strumming gesture.

So I hauled out the guitar and began playing flamenco. Everyone stopped talking and listened intently. Perhaps because it was night time, these particular individuals allowed the sins of food and music despite Ramadan.

The halfwit stopped beating his chest when I played my sad farruca. As he listened, the music seemed to take him far away to a place for which he passionately yearned.

Their understanding of flamenco and its meters was impressive. Two of the women began clapping to the alegria and bulerias with the eclat of grenadine gypsies. I'm puzzled to this day about this and their lack of veils.

These brave desert folk spent the night among us, and I felt very honored to be among them.

It took us only five hours to make the final fifty or so miles to Quaysuma the next day, for we'd long ago passed the region of sharp pebbles and made excellent time. My driver delivered me to the front gate of the American oil company there.

Dramatically, we came down with yet another flat tire right at the gate. My driver laughed good-naturedly and set about fixing it, while the gateman pouted unhappily. His gate was blocked by these unofficial vagrant vehicles whose only reason for being there was to deliver an unofficial, uninvited American vagabond.

If the folks at Badannah and Rafa had been kind, those at Quaysuma were just the opposite. The gateman allowed me to walk in, though I knew no names of anyone to call and request admittance. I was grateful, for I'd had nothing to eat for more than 60 hours and was salted and peppered with sand and dirt. But his favor yielded no fruit.

For when I entered the recreation hall about mid day, I met the camp manager—an American southerner who called me a hippie. "Hippies aren't welcome here," he said sourly. "We don't take kindly to leeches."

His anger rose with every phrase as he continued, "We're not running a hotel here. And even if we were, we wouldn't go around giving our rooms away to tramps. Don't you ever bathe?" Who gave you permission to come through the gate anyway? Look here. I'm the camp superintendent, and I'm telling you to get out. We don't like leeches."

His rage brought redness to his neck and face. This made him quite literally a southern redneck, and his breath smelled of alcohol. The men near him looked a little smashed too, and I was horrified.

It's unwritten Bedouin law that anyone who wanders in from the desert to your camp be given guest friendship and hospitality for three days, after which it's up to the guest to insist on departing and leave. I made an exception here. I stayed three minutes and left.

I visited the local Quaysuma Province Customs Office as required. As I was the only Westerner to pass through on his own in many years, I was invited to tea in the home of the chief officer, a kind old man who was extremely warm to me. He was as curious about me as I was about him.

Inside, it was cool, dark and well insulated. The walls, made of whitewashed camel's dung, were several feet thick. Delicious and nourishing refreshments were served with extreme care and attention by a staff of veiled young women. Ravenous, I proceeded to devour all the biscuits. This seemed to entertain him, and he ordered that more be brought. It was destined to be my last solid food for over a week.

The floor was covered with about ten thick Arabian carpets, stacked one upon another, and we sat on satin pillows stuffed with eiderdown feathers. Arabian tapestry of the finest character adorned the walls. The room where we sat was lighted by a very small window that faced the private courtyard. And there was an elegant hanging oil lamp that burned incense.

"So you are making your way all alone with your knapsack across this fair country of mine?" he inquired cordially and poured me some tea. "And have you been playing your guitar for your fellow Americans?"

I nodded.

"Good. I am sure they have been enjoying your visit here. I must be sure to caution you however. You are not to play for anyone outside the American camps. As you may already have been warned, it is an offense to the Arab people to make music of any kind in their presence. It violates our religion, and it is therefore against the law."

If he only knew! He was so kind, I wanted to tell him about the Bedouin vagabonds I'd met in the desert only fifty miles north, and of their heartwarming reception of my music at that private performance. But I thought better of it.

Instead I showed him my affidavit, and he verified on it that I still possessed the guitar. Then he produced a huge, very old log book that was buried in the stack of rugs. It was more than three feet across when opened, and about 30 inches high. He proceeded to copy my passport particulars into it, using a flamboyant feather-quill pen that he dipped into an ink bottle. He wrote slowly in fine Arabic calligraphy.

As he worked, three of his wives passed through on their way out to Quaysuma's one lonely street. He nodded at them as they bowed and went out—probably to get more biscuits. Their veils and long black robes hid their forms. But they moved like young women, and they were pillars of courtesy and grace.

When they'd left, he asked me if I was familiar with the name of Richard Halliburton whose name appeared near mine on the page. I didn't know, and he enlightened me about this famous adventurer who'd passed through this province and come to register.

I questioned him a little about himself. He didn't mind at all, and told me about his life, wives and habits.

He asked me how I liked Arabia. I replied that I was enjoying the simplicity of just sand, sun and sky to roam in—that I enjoyed the desert dawns because they were so orange and rosy-fingered.

He liked that. And he kept me talking, munching biscuits and drinking tea, until a subordinate officer entered with news that a merchant camel caravan, headed southeast, had arrived at the checkpoint out front.

We rose and went to greet them—a group of dust covered, raggedy Bedouins in crudely improvised semi western clothing—a man and six boys with eighteen camels.

The chief clearly knew the leader of the expedition and summoned him to meet me. He was tall, strong, bearded and

Quaysuma's one lonely street.

tough—this caravan driver. His name was Ibrahim. Smuggling was his trade. All the officers knew and liked him and looked forward to his arrivals. For his usual cargo contained illicit hooch, and he was generous with his bribes.

Searching his camels, the chief found mostly cases of champagne. But there were bottles of other precious spirits. Ibrahim picked out a fine bottle of the French bubbly and handed it to my host to keep under his coat. The chief obliged with a nice smile and kept inspecting. The rest of the cargo, including fine cloth and tapestry, was acceptable except for occasional further bottles of spirits. Discovering these, the chief feigned irritation and was calmed with yet another bottle—this one Scotch whisky—which he tucked under his wide cloth belt with the champagne bottle. All wore smiles again.

The chief poised his pen to sign the Manifest, as Ibrahim watched hungrily. But then the chief had one more request. He pointed his pen in my direction, saying he would sign this Manifest without further ado provided the expedition take along yonder American friend and produce him in good condition at Nariha, eight days journey to the southeast.

As this wouldn't be too far out of his way, Ibrahim eagerly and hastily agreed, and the Manifest was signed.

I liked the look of this Ibrahim and went to get my gear while a camel was cleared for me to ride. Unlike the elderly, docile, resigned camel I'd ridden in Cairo, this was a lively, one-hump, grayish-white and muscle-bound beast who had ideas of his own. He'd been working hard lately. And though somewhat tired, he decided to let it be known he didn't entirely approve of humans riding on his backside.

Threateningly, he turned on me with a shriek and snapped his fearsome yellow teeth near my shoulder, all of which he could have devoured easily. But I'd worked with horses in my younger days growing up in Carmel. I stood my ground and looked him in the eye while Ibrahim secured my guitar and pack to the back of his saddle. That helped. But this very tall camel wouldn't get to his knees and allow me onto his back until Ibrahim angrily jerked on his hemp rope hackamore.

I climbed on with a shrinking heart. My fate was now in the hands of this unfriendly beast and these smugglers out in the middle of a vast lonely desert half way around the world. What would become of me now?

Left alone with me on his back, the camel stood motionless, snorting and regarding me distastefully out of the corner of his jaundiced eye. But at least he was calmer. And as the caravan pulled away from the customs station, he moved with it. I shakily turned my head and waved a hasty farewell to my kind chief. He waved back smiling.

We cleared all signs of civilization in minutes. And save for the belly-stirring motion fully appreciated only by one who's ridden a camel, I immediately began to enjoy being a member of this caravan. Soon we entered a region of softer sand and higher dunes.

An afternoon wind began making ripples in these velvety dunes—ripples that moved much like those created by a stone thrown into a lake. As sunset approached, the sand took on a golden hue. I began enjoying a game with my eyes, crossing them slightly so as to alter my vision, and the landscape appeared from the dune tops as vast moving ripples of gold dust that stretched for a thousand miles in all directions.

Immersing myself in this vision, I became aware that our caravan was microscopic—like invisible specks of windblown dust—here in this vast universe of sand, sun and sky. I found the lost and helpless feeling born of this realization to be exciting, and was already beginning to discover the power and majesty of the Arabian Desert where things never change—where one finds the past and future within the here and now.

My camel soon got used to me—or merely resigned. He walked with steady rhythm up one side of a dune, down the other side and up the next, without faltering a single step. His feet made a soft pleasant sound as they caressed the sand. The up and down movement was not fast and jerky like that of a horse, but slow, long and swooping like an elevator. My stomach got used to it very soon, and I found it enjoyable.

As this beast was going to be my companion for awhile, I took the private liberty of calling him Cannonblitz. Cannon because of his violent personality when aroused, and blitz because it sounded good at the time. He was destined to carry me on his back for eight days while we covered several hundred miles of wild windy desert. And during that time, we were to become friends.

It was nearly dusk before Ibrahim found a place where we could put ourselves for the night—a deep depression flanked on all sides by four tall dunes. The animals were unloaded and tied into a circle near our small, sheer cloth tent that was quickly erected.

I now had the chance to meet my human companions for the first time. If they were to prove undesirable, it was a bit late to do much about it. Ibrahim was pleasant as ever and ordered the others around with kind firmness. Not that he had to tell them much. Though boys and teenagers, his crew of six was far from tender. They behaved like older men who knew what to do, and how and when to do it.

A Primus stove was set up and tea prepared. We sat in a circle and had tea while I watched them chat. One of them looked more like an American Indian than an Arab. He was thickly built like Chief Ironhorse. Not as sociable as the others, he kept his head bent down as though moping on some dark thing.

The most talkative was a thin and wiry lad. He set the pace for mood and conversation, never running out of things to say though his association with this bunch had been long and everything they'd experienced they'd experienced together. The others seemed entertained by him, occasionally laughing at what he said.

Using charades, he began communicating with me. He was Khaled, and headed home from somewhere. He learned I was American, recently a student, and hiking all around the world playing music. He told the others who wanted to hear me play.

They seemed a fine lot of youths. I uncased the guitar and began playing a ballade. All listened in silence. I played a little flamenco. I could see that they preferred this. Then I played some calypso. They liked this best of all, and even Ironhorse smiled. Fortunately Arabs like Western music better than Westerners like theirs. They clearly liked rhythm more than melody, and Khaled said the words, "calypso, Radio Jeddah," gesturing that I should please play more of that. I gathered he'd heard calypso on the radio and liked it. So I played more calypso to which he did a hilarious dance.

Dinner was brought out by a kid whose face was covered in peach fuzz. Cheerful, he too was eager to attempt speaking with me. They all liked him and considered him a fine cook. He prepared a dish of off-white paste into which everyone dipped with dirty fingers. It looked like mashed rice mixed with used motor oil, and it smelled like a rotting tractor engine. I didn't like the look or smell of it and declined to eat any.

Next were pickled gizzards and privy parts of desert livestock fixed similarly to those of the truck drivers. Again I declined.

For dessert, there were sheep's eyeballs stewed in brown oil. The eyes were uncut and undamaged, as though surgically removed from their skulls with care. These eyeballs stared at us—even from within their filthy glass jar—and my companions ate them whole, chewing on them with deep pleasure.

The fact that I declined to eat began causing comment and concern, so I poured myself another glass of tea which contained some sugar. Ibrahim defended me with a shrug. It sounded as though he might be telling them Europees have different eating habits—that perhaps they didn't eat at all during the month of Ramadan. Whatever he said, it made them think a bit. And they stopped trying to force a gourmet's choice eyeball on me.

We were all travel-weary. And as conversation by charades is a bit exhausting, we abandoned it immediately after dinner and retired. I spread my polyethylene ground cloth just outside their tent and prepared to bed down there. Ibrahim inspected the warmth and quality of my eiderdown sleeping bag, fingered the material, marveled at its design, and said goodnight in Arabic.

They had only a few light blankets between them, but they kept each other warm inside the tent. I was grateful to be out in the fresh air, cold as it was, and went to sleep counting stars. Every star in the universe was out in full radiance, presenting a display of infinity so three dimensional as to include me as I lay there. I was so drawn into it, I felt I was at one with all things—that my soul was at one with all souls in the universe.

Several times during the night, I heard them talking and arguing in the tent and wished they could see the stars from in there. Then, like me, they'd have been so awed by the great harmony of the universe, any and all argument would have been out of the question. I'd never seen folks who talked so much at night and so little in the day.

At dawn the boys were up and dismantling the tent. Again I had only tea for breakfast, and we were underway after packing the animals. Packing was a long process though. For all the cargo that had been removed and stacked the night before had to be reloaded onto camels who protested loudly and were uncooperative as was their morning habit.

Taking its cue from the camels, my stomach began protesting also, for lack of food, as we took our first few steps eastward. Canonblitz' walking motion added to my misery. The elevator-like movement increased my hunger, and I had a case of saddle chafe.

But soon we could see the entire fiery ball of the sun. And as we were headed straight into it, it warmed our faces. Previous mornings on this journey had found me following the rising sun, but it wasn't really apparent until now. For out here there were no trees, buildings or mountains. I realized I was following the rising sun in a big circle, clear around the planet, and getting nowhere in the end. And just then it was all causing me to feel such hunger and soreness, I began to doubt the sanity of my troubadour mission.

The desert seemed a giant white apron that wrapped around the sun's waist. The sun was bigger than I'd ever seen it. It was easy to imagine that by noon we would surely reach it if it would only stay put, not shrink and not float into the sky beyond our reach. There was no wind now—just an eerie quietness that bewitched and fascinated. Drifting deeply into the bewitchment, I detached from my physical discomforts and they went away.

We stopped briefly at midday while they ate. These were smugglers and not very religious. So even during Ramadan, they ate both day and night. We moved on again, repeating a similar afternoon, evening and night as we had the previous day.

Each daybreak found me a little more famished than the previous one, but I began to feel better about being famished. With each glorious dawn, the warmth of the great fiery ball provided mental uplift, encouragement and therapy to my chilled, sore and tired body.

On many of the days my thoughts drifted onto Zoe and things about her I'd learned aboard ship. Surely she'd have enjoyed the beauty here, I thought. But the ancient mores of Arabian culture wouldn't have allowed her this experience. Further, I too would've refused to let her enter a situation where there might be nothing for her to eat. Still she'd have enjoyed it. And I imagined her riding along with me.

The afternoon of the eighth and last day, we passed the fresh corpse of an abandoned sheep, one of love's wooly ambassadors, lying in the shadow of a dune. It was a sign of civilization at last. Though it told a tragic story of growing old and weak, being unable to keep up with the rest of the flock, and for whatever strange reason being allowed to fall behind and find a place to die. It had chosen the shadow of this friendly dune where now a half-dozen vultures sat on it and were picking its flesh to the bone.

As Cannonblitz had fallen a few yards behind, I gently urged him forward. And he cooperatively trotted past the cargo group to his normal position.

As Ibrahim had predicted, we arrived at the souk of Nariha late that afternoon. He was an expert navigator, having known just where we were during the entire trip. My stomach had shrunk and no longer complained, though I was constantly dizzy and weak.

We stopped at the edge of Nariha. Everyone dismounted, and the quiet-mannered Ironhorse helped me untie the guitar and backpack. Saying goodbye to one with whom I'd traveled for so long was not easy. The task was compounded by my not being entirely present of mind. Without the goodwill of these young men, I might've perished like the sheep in the shadow. Yet I was about to shake hands cordially, say goodbye forever and walk away. I gave Cannonblitz a pat, and he responded with an affectionate nose nuzzle to my ear that surprised everyone and got a general laugh.

There was such a good feeling at that moment, I decided to take a small risk with them. I dug into my back pack and withdrew my small camera. They were delighted and quickly gathered for a group photo which I've kept and cherished over the years.

I shook hands with them all and turned away with a sad heart. For these kids were all right. Smugglers they were, and secretive about their destination and origin. But they were young men of goodness and honor. For they trusted me. They posed for that

Left to right, Khaled, Ibrahim, "Ironhorse."

photo without a second thought. It was important to them that I have a memento. Less important was the danger that I could've taken it to the Muslim authorities and used it to turn them in as hooch runners. Friendship is the greatest compliment that can be bestowed, but trust is certainly among the greatest. After walking for some minutes, I looked back at them. They'd mounted up and were moving farther to the south.

I walked to the gate of the American oil camp to see if they might be friendly. This wasn't a Tapline camp. It was owned by Aramco—the Arabian American Oil Company. Unlike the Tapline camps, it had Asphalt roads and parking lots. The gateman evaluated me in astonishment, for I was covered head to foot in fine white dust.

"You have been on a trip?" he asked.

"Yep. Would you please try and get me the superintendent on the phone?"

"Are you an Aramco man?"

"No, just an ordinary man."

Just then a pickup truck came along on its way into camp and came to a halt in front of me. The two American engineers in it were staring at me in astonishment.

"Don't be alarmed, gentlemen," I smiled, half aware of what I was saying. "My name is Casper, and I'm a friendly ghost. Can you take me to the superintendent?"

They told me to hop onto the back of the truck with my gear, and they took me along a smoothly paved road to the office of Superintendent H.C. Egy. A mellow man of kind inclination, he listened with rapt attention to my story and proposal to play a concert for my keep.

He reacted with such love in his face, I felt like a long lost brother returned. "That's a fair proposition. We'll get you in a room right now where you can clean up. Meet me in an hour, in the cafeteria, and I'll see that you get the finest dinner available. And it'll be on the house with all the trimmings. Then we'll figure a time for your performance. I'll be looking forward to this." He summoned a man who took me to a clean private room in the bachelor quarters. I quickly filled the bathtub and lay in it, sighing and exhausted.

A bath and delicious hot meal had never before felt so good. I felt much stronger and gave a 20-minute, pre-movie mini concert that night in their theatre. The group of fifty or so was appreciative and generous, and they took up a collection for me like they'd done in Badannah. I quickly made another wad of dollar bills and ten-rial notes. They decided to postpone the movie and gathered around me to talk. They'd all been flown in on company airplanes, hadn't seen the desert or met the Bedouins, and they wanted to hear about my experiences. I told them the camel ride had been hard only on the first and second day, and that I'd soon gotten used to the diet of tea.

Mr. and Mrs. Egy took me home and showed me their bathroom moonshine distillery. It was quite elaborate and innovative. He explained how the engineers prepared their bourbon scientifically—and dead seriously—on rigid weekly schedules. Tired on returning to my room, I slept soundly.

Mr. Egy put some of his regular work aside in order to arrange a schedule for me the next morning. Yesterday he'd been only my loving brother. Today he was that and more. He bloomed with cheer as I entered his office.

"You were a hit last night. My office has been flooded with phone calls about your doing a repeat performance. I've contacted

Mr. Duggan, social director, and Mr. Lafrenze, executive director of the Aramco Employees Association at our head offices in Dhahran. They're excited about you and are fixing appearances for you at our camps in Rastanura, Dhahran and Abquaiq.

"From now on you'll be treated as a proper showman and not be left to wander the desert on your own. Though, from your story, you apparently enjoyed it. But there's no desert left anyway. You've crossed it already. It's all blacktop road, smooth as glass, from here to the end of the Arabian Peninsula. You'll enjoy this road. It's a gift from Aramco to the people of Arabia."

He picked up a neatly typed paper and read to me from it. "At 12:30 tomorrow you'll be chauffeured to our head offices at Dhahran where you'll be met by Mr. Duggan at 2 p.m. You'll be shown to your room and rebriefed. At three o'clock you've an appointment with Mr. Lafrenze who's anxious to meet you. At 4:15 you're slated for an interview with the head of our passport department to have an extension of your visa requested under our official auspices, and at six o'clock you're scheduled to give a dining room concert for several hundred in the main dining room. Then at 8:15 . . ."

He sounded like an excited radio announcer as he read from my itinerary. I agreed to everything, grateful that complimentary, clean safe meals were in my future for the coming days, and I'd be given so many chances to play my music. That night, I gave a full evening concert for the entire Nariha oil camp of about 200. The affair was attended by His Highness, the shaikh of Hofuf, whose palace was nearby. The next morning, I was chauffeured in the Aramco Mercedes sedan along the smooth wide road built by the Americans. Thus I crossed the final 100 miles of desert to the Persian Gulf Coast.

The following week was a hectic but fun whirlwind of concerts, interviews, question-answer sessions, cocktail party shows, television appearances, a bit of tennis, and a refreshing reacquaintance with American accents. Dhahran was the largest completely American community that lived abroad anywhere on earth. When I played the dining room mini concert for several hundred and passed a tray, the greenbacks and rial notes came to more than 300 dollars.

A one-week extension was all the Arab government would allow. So the Americans arranged my visa for the nearby island emirate of Bahrain. And they successfully implored upon their shipping magnate friend, Aziz Kanoo, to give me a free cattleship ride across to it.

Several Americans came along to see me off, and I was very touched by this. The customs officer reviewed my affidavit, inspected the guitar, and added his signature and seal to the document. I sealed it inside the self-addressed, stamped envelope Mr. Parr had given me for this purpose, dropped it into their domestic mailbox, and stepped onto the cattleship bound for Bahrain—British Protectorate island of paradise—located in the Persian Gulf, with its palm trees, pearls and oil, a few miles from the Arabian Peninsula.

13

BECOMING A GUEST OF QUEEN ELIZABETH ON HER BATTLESHIP

Ramadan was almost over. The moment the new moon was seen by the priests at Mecca, the end of the month's fasting would be announced. A three-day period of festival and carnival fun would then begin. Those who could afford it would put on fresh new robes and eat until their bellies could hold no more, but not until the priests could see the moon. If the sky was overcast at Mecca, all the Moslem world would have to wait for better weather there—days or weeks if need be.

So there was tension in Bahrain's capitol city of Manama when I disembarked and went strolling through the murky back alleys of the waterfront to the colorful bazaar where I came upon a pearl merchant sitting semi lotus on a large cushion in his small booth.

Squatted before him, a blonde young Scottish sailor was buying a necklace for his lass who, as he was telling the merchant, lived far away in Edinburgh. He was stationed at the local British military stronghold, HMS Juffair Naval Base. Seeing me, he called out,

"I say! Is that a guitar?"

"Yep. So you come from Edinburgh? Have you ever been to the Fourth Dimension?"

He was surprised and smiled. "Why yes, I've been there a lot."

"What a small world. I've performed there. It's a fine showcase club."

We began chatting, and he took me to the local Gym Khana Club—one of a vast network of Gym Khana clubs for Europeans throughout the Middle East and India. He introduced me to the bartender who gave me a barstool and permission to play. The place was only half-full and rather quiet, so there was a chance to gather some ears.

I opened with a sprightly baroque study I'd only just been composing during my ride on the cattle barge. It was the first public performance for this little study which I now call *Gavotte*, and it proved itself worthy. For there was an energetic, very distinguished-looking man in his late twenties who was pleased with it, judging from the way he sat smiling and tapping on the table in front of him.

He wore a long bushy beard. His face looked exactly like that of the sailor on the trademark label of every package of Player's Cigarettes, a popular English brand. This impressed me. And as I played, I hoped I'd have the opportunity to find out if it was he whose picture it was. He obliged by standing up and inviting me to sit with him.

I gazed at his face. "You look just like . . ."

"Yes, I know." His eyes twinkled, and he invited me to dine with him. This was Peter Redding, jovial Englishman, sophisticate, art and music connoisseur, wit of the first water. He was mentally present, alert and kind, aware we had each waited all our lives for this moment of our meeting, and I was awed by it all.

"I've nothing to do with Player's cigarettes. Nor do I smoke them, even though their sailor happens to look like me. But everyone asks, and it's the shadow of my life."

He was an architect—assistant to Ronald Dashper of Compton House, Surrey, whose firm had been retained by a construction firm in Manama. He was also a philanthropist. Whenever he got a little money ahead, he always gave it to those poorer than himself.

"That's a beautiful philosophy," I said. "Where did you learn it?"

He mashed a small pile of over-boiled peas between the prongs of his fork and then stuffed the mash into his mouth with fork upside down. "The bulk of my wisdom I've gleaned from old men in pubs—most of them strangers. You can find many pearls among drunken hogwash. Separating and sorting them is a cultivated art."

During the process of our deciding each of us was good for the other, we were interrupted by the stocky middle-aged captain of a Polish merchant vessel who came over, introduced himself and sat with us. His accent was strong. "I like your playing on guitar. You are traveling?"

"Yes, sir, around the world on a guitar string."

"Ah, on a shoestring, aha. Maybe I can help. I would like that. My ship departs for Cape Town on Tuesday. You can come with us and play. You will be fed and charged nothing. Good?"

I felt excited and honored. "That's very nice of you. Thank you, though I've only today arrived in Bahrain and haven't made onward plans. May I think about it awhile?"

Looking pleased, he wrote his phone number on a scrap of paper he took from behind the belt of his skipper cap. Then he handed it to me with a loving smile.

Overwhelmed, I thanked him again.

He nodded graciously. "This is the best way to do things. Call me." Then, as though in a hurry, he rose and left.

Peter gazed at the scrap of paper and marveled. "That little chitty is a one-way ticket from Bahrain to Cape Town—worth a small fortune. How on earth do you do it?"

"I don't know. I just played and . . ."

"And presto, by jingo! That guitar of yours is like a magic wand!"

He was inspired by our encounter with the Polish skipper and decided to take me to a house where several of his bachelor friends lived.

"They're all employed by the Manama Branch Office of Kanoo Shipping Ltd. The house belongs to Aziz Kanoo, and they all live there rent free. They've many empty rooms. And being bachelors, they throw many parties where you can perform."

He drove me there in his car. A party was in progress when we arrived, and I played for the happy crowd of young people that included lots of pretty ladies. They gathered to hear me in front of the huge fireplace until the wee hours. A room was prepared for me, and I put my head down gratefully for the night. It was a grand house, and the Kanoo men proved to be kindred spirits.

A grapevine exists among a community of Europeans isolated on a tropical isle. Scuttlebutt, such as the arrival of a wandering troubadour, is quickly distributed.

At midday I was awakened by the butler with news that a Mr. Jon Trouton of Gray Mackenzie Shipping Lines (Kanoo's competitor) wanted me on the phone.

Jon spoke in crisp English accent. "I manage Gray Mackenzie Company, and I'm calling in behalf of Sir William Luce, Her Majesty's Political Representative at HMS Juffair Naval Base. Sir William is having a little dinner party tomorrow, and we thought it would be nice if you brought your guitar and played."

"Thank you. I'll bring my guitar and try."

"Good show, old boy. I'll be watching for you there." With a click he was gone. He'd not told me who the guests were, or I'd have been too excited for words.

That afternoon, Peter took me sightseeing. We attended an early-evening religious service in progress at the Muslim churchyard, kneeling with the multitude. Tension filled the yard. Will they see the moon in Mecca? Everyone knelt on the dirt floor beneath the tall muezzin tower.

"Allah Akbu," declared the Mullah.

All bowed and touched their noses on the ragged pieces of carpet stretched along the ground.

There was another cry, and all raised their heads again.

Then a new voice took over and announced the long awaited message.

"The high priests have seen the moon!"

People rushed to the doors, pushing, shoving, and shouting praises to Allah for bringing the moon and clear weather to Mecca, though it was overcast in Bahrain.

Brushing the dust from our clothes and straightening the dishevelment caused by tons of pushing humanity, we drove out of town to visit Hussein Yateem, billionaire oil tycoon friend of Peters, to celebrate with him the end of Ramadan. Even before we'd driven two blocks, we saw spectacular fireworks everywhere. Everyone was celebrating the end of a long, hard month of soul cleansing.

Hussein Yateem's mansion sprawled upon a very remote and exotically forested part of the island. Peter had called and obtained permission to bring me. We were taken into the house by a loving family servant and led through beautiful rooms, furnished with the finest carpets and gold ornaments, to an elegant sitting room. For the time being, I put my guitar behind the couch.

Hussein entered, his 22-year-old son with him. Both wore flowing robes and white silk headdress trimmed with cords of black satin. Peter introduced us.

Hussein asked, "So you are the one who came across the desert—on foot was it?"

"Not quite, sir. You see . . ."

He interrupted with a laugh. "What do you think of your fellow Americans and their homemade bourbon?" His gaze became intent and piercing.

"Well, we can say one thing for them. They can sure drink a lot of it and still get some work done."

He laughed again. It was a gleeful cackle worked up from within his thoughts. "Come. Let me introduce you to the other guests, and you can tell us of your adventures."

The other guests were Hussein's brother (His Highness, Shaikh Rashid), and Hussein's nephew, Prince Rashid. All spoke excellent English, were regal and sophisticated, and they peppered me with questions about my being a troubadour. I kept trying to redirect the conversation to general matters, but it was of no use.

"Now that is very interesting," said the shaikh, his hands folded on his knee. "So the end result is that your money purse is a one-way valve. It takes money in but doesn't give any out. And yet instead of making you selfish and unhappy, this makes you give more of yourself. Extraordinary."

"And I understand you folks employ this idea in the form of favor exchanges," I said.

"Indeed we do," he replied with enthusiasm. We can enjoy this form of barter because we trust. Americans are a mixture of races—minglings of half and quarter-breeds. That is why they cannot enjoy the mutual trusting we Bahrainians do. Being all of the same race, bound together over centuries of tradition, common culture, habits and folkways, we trust each other more deeply than you Americans could ever imagine."

He had a good point, and I nodded. "Granted. Though the highest form of trust is, I would hope, based on factors that transcend culture and habits."

He nodded and smiled.

The dinner of dinners was served on silver platters. Bahrainian food is very palatable to Western taste, and this was the finest. There were varieties of scrumptious seasoned rice, potatoes, baby leafy greens, deep-fried rolls with tempting things inside, olives, pickles, dates and countless additional offerings. They were prepared in unusual ways. This delectable cuisine was found nowhere but on the island of Bahrain, Hussein told me.

I got my guitar from behind the couch and enthusiastically presented the world of my composing. Hussein leaned back in his chair, waved his relaxed right hand as though conducting, and they all kept asking for more. During a long melodious samba, Hussein removed his headdress and sank more comfortably into his chair. Peter was pleased—actually electrified—at this, and later explained to me that his having removed his headdress in our presence was a compliment rarely shown to infidels such as ourselves.

The celebrations lasted into the next day, all over the little island nation, as people attended carnivals and flooded the beaches. At day's end, I managed to find an officer at the Gym Khana Club who was bound for HMS Juffair Naval Base. He took me through the guarded security gate to the impressive front entrance of the Political Residency of Sir William—a fine two-story chateau with its own swimming pool and squash court.

I was among the last guests to arrive. Sixty or so formally dressed people stood around the well-lit pool, hoisting cocktail glasses. Towering above them were lush tropical trees with leaves measuring several feet across.

There was a buffet dinner, and I sat with Mr. Trouton.

"I'm so glad you made it," he said merrily. "We were beginning to wonder." He was a short, imperturbable, very likeable Englishman's Englishman. His tie was of Scotch wool. He drove a Morris Minor with both hands on the wheel, and his face wore that dry humored look so charismatic when found in a pure Englishman.

My concert was held in the squash court where acoustics were perfect. There was a studied informality, and all sat on pillows and mats. I performed for an hour and tried to leave. But they would have none of that and kept demanding more. So I relaxed and played very late into the night, getting a good look at everyone, and spotted a few Royal Navy ship's captains with their four gold stripes. As I played my encores, I considered the transportation possibilities. Troubadours are especially interested in ship's captains.

I was finally able to take a break. The people divided into groups, and Sir William came over to shake my hand.

"Thank you," he said warmly. "So you're really a genuine troubadour and have just come across the Arabian Desert by camel. That's fascinating."

I told him I was looking for a way to play my way across the Persian Gulf.

"You'll never get a ride on one of Her Majesty's ships," scoffed a local British merchant who'd joined us.

Sir William became pensive. That old merchant was a stuffy know-it-all. I could see Sir William's mind working, making the decision to teach him a lesson.

"There are some Royal Navy skippers here. Let me go poking 'round and see what I can find for you."

Smiling an Alec Guinness smile, he pranced away clasping his hands behind his back. He bobbed from group to group, chatting with the skippers. The merchant was amazed. Mr. Trouton, who'd seen and heard everything, looked on in amusement.

"Is it possible?" I asked him.

He shrugged. "Sir William represents permission of the Admiralty. So if only one of these skippers is willing to take you, you're in."

In a few minutes, Sir William returned with the young-looking, debonair 33-year-old Commander Peter Campbell, skipper of HMS *Eastbourne*, Her Majesty's envoy ship and sometimes escort ship to the royal yacht *Britannia*.

"I'm afraid you'll have to play for us to earn your passage and fare," were Campbell's first words. He was smiling.

Sir William beamed.

"We're bound for Singapore," Campbell continued, "via Colombo and the Maldive Islands. You may disembark in Colombo and visit India or continue on with us as you wish." He stood and held his glass with aplomb, and he spoke with such polish as to rival James Mason portraying Captain Nemo. "If you choose Singapore, you'll earn your onward passage by entertaining Lord and

Lady Morley whom we're meeting at the Maldive Islands. You'll need to be aboard by 7 p.m. tomorrow. I like your guitar work."

I was awed. "Thank you, sir."

Having said all he wanted to say for the time being, he walked away and returned to his conversation with a pair of admirals.

Mr. and Mrs. Trouton were excited for me. "You're very lucky to be a guest on a navy destroyer. For it's absolutely against Royal Navy policy to carry civilians—even government VIPs. Even Lord and Lady Morely could be granted passage only by direct request of the queen."

The party ended, and the Trouton's took me in their Morris Minor to the Kanoo House.

The Kanoo men were thrilled for me, but quick to advise me what they'd do if confronted with my decision to go to either Cape Town, India or Singapore. Cockney scuba diver Bill McDougall, a mountain of muscle who called himself "Mac the doivah," was the most prone to advise me as he gulped down his can of "beah" for breakfast and then crushed the can with powerful fingers.

"Oi've been to India and will never go again. It's like an oven there—120 degrees in the shade. You'll die there sure as 'ell. Nobody has any money, and they die in the streets like flies and maggots. The urchins'll keep their distance until you collapse in the heat. Then they'll take your guitar and knapsack to hock, and dump your body in a ditch. Nobody cares about anybody 'cause there are too many people. I tell you India's a terrible place. Don't let the navy boys dump you there!"

While I was still cringing at Mac's use of the word "urchins" to describe fellow beings, the eldest, a middle-aged crewcut who bossed the household, was also quick to advise me while he ate his morning milk toast.

"That was charming of Sir William—most assuredly unusual. Still I wouldn't hesitate in going to Cape Town. In South Africa they'll understand your music. But in Colombo or Malaysia, you'll surely starve. The people are unbelievably poor there. It's shocking."

"Shocking," echoed the others. One couldn't hope to extract a supper from snake charmers, jungle natives and leprous mendicants, they said.

Peter came by to take me sightseeing again. Many influential people leaned on him for advice, including his boss. He took the news of Commander Campbell with surprise.

"This is fantastic. The Royal Navy has never done that for anyone on Bahrain. But now you have two free tickets going in diverse directions. What've you decided?"

"I haven't yet."

"I'd suggest you hurry it up a bit. You say the *Eastbourne* leaves tomorrow?"

"Yes, but I must be aboard by tonight at 7. They leave before daybreak."

He slapped his head. "Have you done anything about visas?"

"Uh, no." I'd been so engrossed with my decision, I'd almost lost my chances.

"Let's see. It's 2:45. You have two hours to get this done before the consulates close."

"Yes, but first I must decide."

"I hate to interrupt your thoughts," he said, handing me an envelope. "Hussein Yateem asked me to give you this. He says it is a token of his thanks for your music."

"But he has already thanked me more than enough with his hospitality."

"Well, you cannot send it back to him. It would be an insult."

The envelope contained a 100-rupee note. Yateem was certainly a thoughtful man.

We drove to a rocky oceanfront cliff where seagulls were squealing and scavenging. It's known that seagulls are nature-equipped to travel the world. They can rest while floating on the ocean, catch fish from the ocean surface, drink rainwater and catch jet streams. Yet it's also known that, unlike the albatross, they don't travel more than a few hundred miles. To me this is one of the great wonders of the world. Perhaps they just lacked the knack of deciding—like me right now.

Surely, I thought, there would be another ship in South Africa that would take me to India so I could see both places. But if I went to India now, it would require two ships to see South Africa and then get back onto my route around the world. I almost decided to go to Cape Town based on this logic. But the opposite decision came from my lips.

"Let's hurry to the immigration office," I said. "There's little time left."

So Peter took me around to some offices and quickly arranged the necessary stamps in my passport just as Colonel Chaveau had done in Ankara. For he knew all the people. And after a call thanking the Polish captain, and a farewell dinner with the Kanoo men, I went aboard HMS *Eastbourne* by 7 o'clock. For I wanted to cruise on a warship, and there would never be another chance.

Peter stayed with me all afternoon and evening, and took me to the ship. As we sat in his car saying goodbye, he seemed very moved by the importance of the moment—saying goodbye to a friend. He took off his wristwatch and handed it to me.

"I want you to have this. It's not a very good watch." He chuckled and said, "one day a maharaja will give you a proper one, but this one will serve you until then."

I was deeply touched, a bit amused at his making light of the gift with his mirthful reference to a maharaja, and couldn't refuse him. But I was destined to discover there was clairvoyance in his words.

Commander Campbell had radioed Buckingham Palace and gotten permission, directly from Queen Elizabeth, to take me aboard. As dawn mingled with the night, we left Bahrain behind the horizon. HMS *Eastbourne* cruised smoothly, as she was outfitted with stabilizing fins which could also make her heave and roll on purpose—as I was to find out—when we were simulating rough seas and training the gunners to shoot accurately under adverse conditions.

She cut through the water with classic poise.

She was among the most modern destroyers. A frigate capable of 32 knots or more, she could detect, overtake and reduce a nuclear sub to undersea rubble from considerable distance. Her motto was "detect and destroy," and she was kept spotless. One could eat from her deck, and she cut through the water with classic poise.

Before leaving the Persian Gulf, we stopped at the emirate of Abu Dhabi, a coastal community of Trucial Oman. Hordes of childlike desert folk stood on the shore and gaped at us as we anchored in the bay, admiring our sleek design and fearsome, bristling array of cannons, radar antennae and missile launchers.

"Scouts from British Petroleum Company have just discovered oil here," explained young Lieutenant Peter Dick, as we stood together gaping at the Abudhabians who were gaping back at us. "It's England's policy to send a power symbol on goodwill visit to such remote areas as these before drilling negotiations begin."

The Abudhabians certainly had seen fishing boats and old junks, but never anything like the *Eastbourne*. In turn, most of our sailors had never seen such a remote civilization. The mutual fascination lasted throughout our one-day visit, as both sides stared tirelessly.

Lining the beach were long low tents made of hemp and hand-worked skins. Alongside some of the tents were piles of dried, grassy-looking vegetation—perhaps seaweed. Lined up for half a mile along the shoreline were the teeming population with their camels and sheep, all having come to view the British spectacle.

Staring was particularly intent for the first hour. Then His Highness, Shaikh Shakhbut II bin Sultan Al Nahyan, ruler of Abu Dhabi, motored out to us in his royal boat. He'd been invited by the British Diplomatic Service and the British Royal Navy to come aboard with his immediate family, tour the ship and confer with Commander Campbell. His Highness had interpreted this to mean with all his male relatives, their sons and nephews.

There were about twenty of them—all colorfully dressed in fine robes, with cutlass and headdress, and they almost overwhelmed the royal boat's little cabin.

With its five-horsepower, one-cylinder inboard engine belching smoke, the boat motored laboriously toward us and came alongside. Though almost 70, His Highness mounted our rope-banister gangway stairs with energy, agility and dignity. He wore a magnificent robe with gold trim, and there was a stunning cord of gold satin around his headdress.

Our officers whistled him aboard, receiving him in parade dress replete with saber swords and white gloves, and rendered His Highness a perfect unison mass salute as he put his foot on deck. He shook hands with Commander Campbell, and they went below together to confer. The royal entourage was split into several sightseeing groups, each conducted by a pair of officers, and they went about in different directions.

I was penciled in to perform in the officer's wardroom for His Highness and the entourage, provided all went well and they decided to stay beyond the scheduled conference time. So I went to the wardroom to work with my guitar and hands. I found the room had been festively decorated. And there was a long table of punch, cookies and toothpick shishkebab. Chairs had been set in rows that faced the straight-backed armless chair on which I was to perform. I sat on it with my guitar and began to tune up.

Presently there was a wild yell from down the hall, a shuffle of running feet, and then a young warrior who leaped over the 7-inch-high threshold and landed in the wardroom with a bang that rattled the teacups. He too wore his nation's best dress, with shiny cutlass in his belt, for this was His Highness' 12-year-old grandson. His happy suntanned face exuded the excitement of being young, and his chest was inflated with the pride of being a guest on such a grand ship. The tactful steward waylaid him with

The boat motored laboriously toward us and came alongside.

some punch and cookies, and he settled at the head of the table chewing hungrily and smiling at me.

As the tour groups began converging on the wardroom, I played softly, setting a quiet tone to which they responded. When His Highness entered with Commander Campbell, a concert atmosphere was already established. They quickly and quietly took the front and center seats reserved for them.

I played a variety of studies—including my new *Gavotte*—to polite applause, and concluded with my latest Andalusian style composition, *Picadores*, that made use of rasqueada, legato, tremolo and snare drum effect. For this they applauded loudest, telling me this piece had a certain appeal unmatched by any other I'd yet written.

Everyone wore radiant smiles. His Highness shook my hand and spoke with me through his interpreter. He seemed to want to learn from my face and studied me as he asked the usual questions—how long had I been playing, how many hours did I practice and so on.

During my answers I studied him just as intently and was impressed with the dignity of his bearing that seemed to root naturally from a gracious nobility in his heart. One meets few such men. I asked him if he found the oil people helpful. He said he was very pleased with them despite many recent changes in the wake of the oil discovery. I was certainly glad to learn this and wished him all happiness.

The entourage was escorted to their boat, and we gave them a five-gun salute as they motored toward their mooring dock. When they reached it, we pulled anchor and began moving away, drawing farewell cheers from the happy Abudhabians lining the shore.

We cruised out of the Persian Gulf into the Gulf of Oman, and headed through the Arabian Sea out into the vast Indian Ocean. Vast to be sure, but HMS *Eastbourne* cruised at about 20 knots and made short work of it.

I was assigned the settee of the air-conditioned wardroom for sleeping and was issued a stack of bedding for this purpose. Each night, after all had retired, I could close the door, lounge there alone with a tall ginger ale on the rocks, and contemplate the day's events. I could even stick my head out the porthole to catch a sea breeze and listen to the ship's hull slide through the water. Having this big room all to myself at night was an unanticipated luxury, and I thanked the stars for my good fortune.

However I was lovingly obliged to arise by 6:45 each morning. For breakfast was served promptly at seven bells, and it was required of everyone to have all traces of slovenly slumber erased by then. The officers sat straight as ramrods, hands and faces washed, every hair in place, wearing their spotless, laundry-starched, white tropical uniforms.

At mid-table sat the first "leftenant." Beside him sat the next highest ranks and so on down to the ends of the long table. We ate baked beans with catsup—also bacon and stale eggs. Fresh eggs weren't to be found in Middle East ports.

Having attended both my concert at Sir William's and short performance for the royal family, the officers overwhelmed me with kind attention. They took turns taking me on tour of their posts and insisted I use their cabins and typewriters for daytime naps and writing articles for the ship's newspaper that was avidly read by all 250 crewmembers. They even produced a radio show with me for airing on the ship's closed-circuit radio.

My live concerts for the crew were carefully planned and promoted. The young officers planned their strategy so that my articles and radio show would be presented prior to the concerts, hopefully increasing interest and attendance. Separate live concerts were scheduled for the officers, chiefs and ratings.

Colin Forbes, a tall and diplomatic trainee officer, had a heart of gold. In charge of the Officer's Mess Fund, he fixed it so I wouldn't be assessed for food—so my performances would pay—allowing me to continue being a troubadour.

The youngest, 20-year-old, easy-smiling, Officer Trainee Richard Bridges, was an Eton graduate. He let me use his tape recorder so I could record some music for him and hear it played back. And he let me stay in his tiny cabin, during the nights when he had all-night watch on the bridge, so I could get a few extra hours' sleep for my shows.

Suntanned Officer of the Watch Roger Trussell gave me a tour of his post and taught me philosophy. "Sea life gives you space to figure out who you are why you're here. And there are the sunsets, when—if you're among the chosen—you can see a green flash upon the ocean as you watch the flying fish," he glowingly added. He and fellow officer Peter Dick spent patient hours teaching me navigation up on the bridge, demonstrating azimuth, altitude, the bubble sextant, and the "ping" system of underwater sub detection.

The sailors were given daily rations of beer and went about their work whistling. My show in the Chief's Mess was followed by a hootenanny of sailor songs. Coarse, bearded and shirtless, they hoisted froth-capped beer mugs and sang me the foulest, if gleefully delivered, selection of bawdy songs I'd ever heard. Their favorite was *The Alphabet Song*. With impressive baritones, they choadsed:

> G is for Gonorrhea, Goiter and Gout,
> And H is the harlot that spread it about . . .

But prior to the bawdiest part, one chief got up, stopped the singing and turned the pictures of the queen and Prince Phillip to the wall.

Commander Campbell lived the isolated life to which his position obliged him. He remained debonair, as he'd been at Sir William's, and occasionally emerged from his spacious three-room cabin-apartment to stand at the bridge railing, check our course and supervise training maneuvers. More often than not, he attended evening movies in the wardroom. He spoke just enough to be brief and cordial—no more. But he'd captured the crew's

Bawdy Songs (Illustration published with my story in the Kansas City Star, *April, 1962.)*

devotion, even among the lowest ranks. None ever spoke against him, and few griped of their lot. It was a happy ship.

After perhaps ten days of meandering at sea, circling in training maneuvers and rendezvousing with other British war vessels, we reached Colombo, the capitol of Ceylon—now known as Sri Lanka—a tiny island nation of many equatorial charms. Located at India's doorstep, the island was known for its fine tea plantations.

I had to choose now between India and Malaysia. Were I to go on with the *Eastbourne*, I could meet and entertain Lord and Lady Morely, see the Maldive Islands and be dropped off at Singapore. But if I wished to see India and find Zoe again, I would have to get off here and miss all that.

I began to hate the word, "decision." Decisions bound a man and took away his freedom. I decided this is partly what Zoe meant when she said in her letter, "no one is really free." For we're all obliged to decide things. Ironically, in situations where our freedom to make decisions is taken away, we're not free either. For then we're not free to decide.

Over the years, I've never been able to find an answer to this puzzle—how man could ever manage to be free to make decisions and then not have to make them.

The sailors were such a good bunch, the thought of leaving them before necessary made me sad. But India held Zoe. It was the land of Mahatma Gandhi and the great sages. It held sitars and tablas, painted faces and silver bangles, great Sanskrit literature, the setting for Rudyard Kipling stories, and the yellow striped tigers.

"But you'll starve in India," flatly declared the friendly steward and several officers. They extolled the virtues of Singapore. The more they talked, the harder it became until the kind and quiet Richard Bridges helped me do what I wanted most by referring me to his personal friend, the good Mr. Brownlee, director of the British High Commission in Colombo.

"If you must leave us, this will help ease the transition from ship to shore," he said, flashing his heart-rendered smile that had won him my friendship with its sincerity. He handed me a note of introduction he'd written for me. The envelope read: "Mr. Brownlee (kind Samaritan), #58 Sir Gregory's Road, Colombo." Bridges didn't talk a lot. But his feelings went deeper than those of most of the men, and he cared about things more than any of them.

We enjoyed a farewell lunch, and Commander Campbell shook my hand as I swallowed a lump in my throat and stepped onto the rope-banister gangway. The motor launch took me from the ship to the land of jungles, leeches, elephants and tea.

Sri Lanka was the jewel of the Indian Ocean—a garden of tropical splendor bathed in oven-warm humidity. Its rupee currency was so soft, even a Beirut money changer would balk, flinch and sigh unhappily before buying it at less than a tenth of its domestic value. Yet Sri Lanka provided the entire world with tea, in trade for which it could have hoarded an impressive treasury of gold-based currency were it not for corrupt officials who found devious means of squandering it for private gain.

Thus foreign goods were rationed. It was illegal to own a car newer than five years, no matter how rich the owner. And all Western-made radios, stereos and so forth, had to be shipped in as "replacement parts," completely dissected. Only the rich could afford refrigerators, air- conditioners and toasters, as they cost five times their value elsewhere.

Trained, English-speaking butlers could be hired for 20 rupees per week plus board and room. Twenty rupees were worth anywhere from two to five US dollars, depending on where and how one made his exchange. The black market thrived—patronized by both the noble and respectable as well as racketeers and public officials.

Mr. Brownlee was a proper, elderly Englishman—a widower, living in a fine house with three servants. He sat in his easy chair, peered at Bridges' note through his bifocals, and then studied me carefully through the upper lenses.

"Well, as you are a friend of Master Bridges and are from HMS *Eastbourne*, I must say I am honored by your visit. Master Bridges says here that you play splendidly. Please do play something."

While I prepared to play, he clapped his hands for a servant who came, went and returned quickly with lemonade and trimmed cucumber sandwiches. A large overhead fan cooled us as we sat together under the very high ceiling, and I played. He sat very still and became completely absorbed. The energy of his interest propelled me, and I played for an hour until he passed me the first trimmed and sculpted cucumber sandwiches I'd ever eaten in my life.

"I think I shall get you together with Harry Peiris," he said. "Harry is the biggest land baron in the nation, and Baroness Peiris has much to do with our Arts Center and local theatre. Would you like to give a concert here?"

I was delighted, and he phoned the Peiris' who were so taken by what he told them, they sent a chauffeur to come get me at once.

Baron Peiris was a pure Sri Lankan and lived in the sprawling Peiris Mansion at the foot of Peiris Road named after him. He was a gentle and loving man, distinguished by a lining of silver gray just above his ears. He had three sons and two very attractive daughters—all teenagers.

Mr. Brownlee had invited me to return to his home to stay, but Peiris wouldn't hear of it. "You must stop this uncomfortable moving around and stay in my home as long as you're in Colombo," he firmly insisted.

He dressed for coolness in loose, white cotton shirt, sandals and white baggy trousers, and conducted his business affairs each day by phone from the sheltered front porch. We enjoyed leisurely breakfasts on the mounted veranda that overlooked his tropical gardens and rolling manicured lawns that extended for a hundred acres. There were giant flowers that curled up and went to sleep by day and opened at night to issue forth perfume and display their beauty by moonlight.

A philosophy professor lived nearby and had breakfast with us each morning. And as we ate freshly cut pineapple rings and papaya, we discussed the politics of the latest government that had recently seized power by coup d' etat.

The baron wanted to send his oldest son to school in America, and I described American college life. The mansion's high ceilings, and the big electric fans hanging from them, made the humidity quite pleasant and endurable.

The professor contacted the director of Radio Sri Lanka who produced and aired a one-hour radio special I recorded in their excellent, air-conditioned studio. Then the professor phoned the local English-speaking newspaper, the *Colombo Daily News*, and a reporter and photographer came to get my story. A concert was set for me late the following week that was promoted in both the radio special and in the *Daily News* story which read in part:

> He is a wandering troubadour in strict keeping with the 12th-century code which goes with that profession, who does not demand money in the sordid manner of the professional entertainer. He has roamed the far corners of the earth, playing and receiving hospitality instead, from kings, nobility and peasants alike.
>
> Currently he is staying at the home of Baron Peiris. He gives a concert this Friday at 8:00 p.m. at the Art's Center, Guilford Crescent.

It worked. The Art's Center theatre was packed to capacity with embassy people, field representatives of large European business firms, plantation owners, shippers and tea tasters. They filled a box with cash for me and demanded many encores. Among the audience sat Baron Peiris and his family, proudly smiling.

As the applause was peaking, the baron rose, came onto the stage and spoke into my ear his suggestion that we donate the money in the contribution box to charity. He seemed so excited by the idea, I accepted with enthusiasm. He made the announcement, and the applause was overwhelming.

In a brief moment of glamour, I'd lost a very big box of rupees, probably a thousand dollars, and I swallowed hard I do confess. But I'm glad now. And I took comfort at the time by rationalizing that since I didn't use money anyway, there was no intelligent reason for being possessive with it despite Mac the Diver's bleak predictions about India.

And it worked out for the best, for the Peiris' became even more like a mother and father to me. Over breakfast in the morning, the baron suggested I take some time to travel around Sri Lanka as his guest, and he would see that I received complimentary air fare to Madras. He sent me off with a family friend, in a chauffeured Mercedes, to tour the island.

We visited the Temple of Bhudda's Tooth in Kandy, stayed with a family of tea growers near Nuwara Eliya who'd been in my concert audience, and I learned much in a few days.

Beyond the many mountainsides pregnant with tea bushes, my host found us a mahout, and we went by elephant through some of the countless giant ravines with their lush mini jungles of greenery.

Children ran around naked, and their parents wore only loin cloths. They lived in grass huts, and bare-breasted women labored by riversides, washing clothes by beating them on smooth rocks. Life was worry-free and relaxed, here where the jungle provided for all, and one sensed a happiness and completeness among this society of so-called "poor." If one wished to spurn "civilization" and go live in a happier place, he could do far worse than the jungles of Sri Lanka.

But the monsoon was coming. It moved from south to north, so at this time of year you needed to keep going north to stay ahead of it. Baron Peiris arranged for my visa and plane ticket which he pressed into my hand.

"India is very big," he warned. "It is unofficially a continent in itself. You must calculate your distances carefully and pace yourself for hard traveling." With a wistful face, he said, "I wish I were going with you. I have always wanted to rough it in India, but alas it is too late for me now."

I rode down Peiris road for the last time, sniffing the fragrant blossoms and heavy foliage.

14

Mystical moments with the maharaja of Sandur

Madras, now known as Chennai, was a large, rotten-smelling metropolis. It smelled bad even at the airport. The free airline bus put me off with the other passengers in front of a luxury hotel. But to the consternation of the bus driver, I took my gear and headed down the street—not into the lobby with the rest.

"Where are you going, sir?"

"To see Madras."

"But this hotel is where you must stay. All Westerners stay here." His superiors had instructed him to see that all passengers had safely been tucked away to bed before he left them. Madras was a hard city—no place for a giddy tourist to be gadding about with bag and baggage.

But as he was busy comparing stubs and luggage tags, I easily eluded him and wandered into the scurrilous heart of the rat-infested city. We were a good two hundred miles north of Sri Lanka, yet the humidity was as bad or worse. And it contained the odors of sewage and rotting flesh that drifted from every alley and wretched hovel.

The approach of evening brought the citizenry onto the streets for walkabouts. There were millions of them. They swarmed like bees into and out of every street, wearing dhotis—the fashion in India for centuries.

This was a lucrative time for beggars. They came out from their hiding places under bullock carts, from between garbage piles and out of urine-permeated gaps between buildings. Deformed, maimed, and often minus an arm or both legs, they dragged themselves along the ground like crippled rock crabs among the feet of the crowd. They grabbed at skirts and ankles, whining pathetic supplications to those approaching and hateful curses to those who walked by with nothing to give.

When a man of such caste felt moved to defecate, he often did so right on the sidewalk while pedestrians scowled and detoured. Small wonder that Brahmins, and those of higher caste, did everything possible to avoid the streets, taking to them only in carriages and automobiles.

Sacred cows roamed at will, and their rancid odor was everywhere. Often they would lie athwart train tracks, delaying freight and passengers, or clog an intersection in the heart of the city, causing accidents and long delays. They seemed to know they had the upper hand. The general desperation among the impolite traffic held up by trains that were in turn held up by cows, all in the triple digit heat, was agony to behold.

On some streets there seemed to be more beggars than those begged from. Small wonder then, that many a less aggressive beggar went without food for weeks until he fell into semi consciousness and his body was kicked into an alley, without mercy, by an angry policeman. And there he would lie until the smell of death, and a thousand flies, advertised his condition.

All this I witnessed at various stages within the short three hours between leaving the bus and hearing the toot of a Triumph sports car approaching from behind—a convertible with top removed. The driver was a young Englishman. He motored alongside, gazing at me in disbelief.

"What on earth—what country are you from?"

"California," I said, my stomach turning with sickness and disgust at what I'd been witnessing.

"Look, sir, are you mad? You cannot traipse about like you're doing—not in this part of town. You'll be attacked and beaten by urchins. Hop in, and I'll give you a lift to your hotel."

Once again cringing at that word, I told him I had no hotel, thanking him nonetheless.

"Well, hop in just the same. Blast it, sir, you cannot stay here!"

He was definitely worried for me, and I figured he might be right about the people he called urchins who did indeed seem otherworldly and consumed by hatred. So I put my gear behind the car's two seats and got in with him.

He drove erratically, honking at any pedestrians, cows, bullock carts or oxen we approached. And he shouted loudly, with alarming profanity, at every pedestrian who didn't jump like a grasshopper to make way for him.

"It's the only way to get along with these Indians. You have to whip, push and scrunch them," he yelled over the bleating of his horn. "Otherwise we'd be an hour making it to the next block."

I swallowed a lump in my throat. He was a visitor here like me. These streets belonged to our hosts whom he was terrorizing. And having climbed into his car, I was now his accomplice.

As we went through a particularly smelly area, he covered his nose and looked apologetic. "Sorry about that smell. When India became independent, Britain promptly donated thousands of outdoor privies. But instead of being used for their intended purpose, they got used as stalls to keep hay for the cows. Indians have been doing their toilet in the streets and gutters for centuries. You can't change them. There's no hope for them."

Filth was all he saw in India. I didn't argue and asked if he would please take me to the road that led to Bangalore. He did.

I stood on that road for a few minutes and got picked up by a squeaking, two-wheel cart drawn by a pair of water buffalo. The driver was a smiling, very wise old mahatma with soulful eyes. He quietly hummed a sweet and strange melody as he took me a few miles northwest to a lonely junction where he turned right and the road to Bangalore was straight ahead. There was filth and starvation in Madras, but beauty in this mahatma.

It was late at night here and very quiet. There were no "urchins" lurking in the bushes, as Mac the Diver had warned, so I lay in a patch of tall grass and went to sleep.

At dawn, as I awoke and walked out of the grassy area to the roadside, I felt something clinging to my lower leg. When I brushed it with my hand, it stung. Investigating, I found a gray-black leech imbedded and drinking to a vampire's content. I had no salt or match and didn't know any other way to discourage him. So I sat watching him in fascination, wondering how long a man could live with a leech on him that was over a half-inch long and growing.

I looked at Peter's watch to check the time, but it had stopped. The heat, humidity, and perhaps want of cleaning, had joined forces and brought the hands to a standstill. I carefully wrapped it in a sock and put it into my pack.

Several cars went by, all headed toward Bangalore. But none stopped. It wasn't the custom to pick up hitchhikers in India, and the custom always centered around and preserved the caste system.

But finally, in late morning, a big company truck stopped. The driver and cleaner were amused at my leech and gave me a match. I lit it and touched the leech with it. It went into spasm, withdrew its head, and I pulled it away.

They took me to the front gate of a beautiful and gracious home. It was all white and exuded an aura so peaceful as to capture my very soul They'd chosen this destination for me themselves, as I'd not asked to be let off at any particular place.

The gateman outfront watched as I climbed out of the truck. Drawn by his venerable smile, I couldn't resist chatting with him. He was a compassionate and loving old family servant of long standing. Very friendly, he gradually revealed this residence to be that of Shrimant Mamlukatmador Senapati, maharaja of Sandur, and phoned for permission to let me join the cocktail-hour party His Highness was hosting at that very moment in the backyard for some very gentle, middle-aged friends.

So kind were they all, so mild and quiet-mannered, I wanted very much to play for them. They gathered around me on lawn chairs in the gazebo. We were all so quiet that several huge, black, well-behaved ravens joined us by perching on the gazebo railing where round, bite-size crackers had been put out for them. But they didn't eat. They too were very quiet. They were so aware of us, so vigilant and intelligent, as to seem like feathered angels come to witness a magical event.

I played only for only 25 minutes or so, as I felt the need not to push my luck by requiring their loving attention for too long. But they were indeed a magical few minutes, for I had both birds and people listening to my music in that fine garden. For a few moments I sensed the presence and attention of millions of benign souls all around us. Excitingly, I had the feeling that everyone present was enjoying the same experience. Even the artful statues seemed alive. His Highness was so pleased by it all, he sat next to me as he chatted with us. Then as I rose to leave, he removed his wrist watch and handed it to me.

"I see you have no watch," he observed. "This one of mine is humble, but I would like you to have it. Please take it. I love your music so, and I want to give you something."

"But you gave me your attention. That is enough."

"Please take it," he repeated. Then he smiled. "There is a charm in it that will help you in your travels."

What could I do? So I accepted it and kept it for many years until it too, like Peter's, stopped working. Of course there was no conscious, benevolent conspiracy between Peter, the truckers and His Highness. How could there have been? But much evidence pointed to it.

And His Highness was certainly right about the charm. Because for many years, whenever I looked at his watch to check the time, I remembered him and the glow of that evening with him and his gentle friends.

Among the guests was a golfer who took me with him to his golf club and arranged that I play again that very evening on the club veranda. And it was here that I met young John Webb, an Anglo Indian whose father was the Mysore District distributor of Mercedes cars and trucks.

"Your music is beautiful," he said. He bought us each a late dinner, just before the kitchen closed for the night. The hour was so late we had the entire veranda to ourselves as we ate together. He explained, with youthful joy, that he was about to be married the following week. His apartment was unoccupied, save for the servants, because he was staying with his in-laws-to-be. But if I would only please stay in Bangalore a few days until his wedding, and perform as part of the ceremony, I could stay in his apartment. His maid and butler would prepare my food and look after me.

He was kind and gentle, like the Maharaja's guests, and very refined. I felt honored by his compliments and accepted his offer. It was an elegant apartment. I lived like a lord in it for almost a week and then played at his wedding. And he sent me to Bombay, now called Mumbai, as a passenger in one of his beautiful Mercedes trucks with two good drivers. The closer I got to Zoe, the better I felt.

We drove through the vast Mysore thickets where we saw elephants, monkeys and birds of paradise. The road was narrow, unpaved and somewhat obstructed by the roots of the roadside trees that were trying to reclaim it—their leaves drooping in hunger for the coming monsoon.

At a remote village, deep in the jungles of Poona, we found groups of near-naked men sitting on their haunches and smoking birris. The village was no more than a smattering of dank little huts. My two drivers found an empty hut in which to sleep. I was allowed to stay alone in the cab of the truck where I slept soundly.

At dawn I awoke with the feeling of being stared at. I opened my eyes, and my gaze was met by those of about 25 near-naked villagers both young and old. Dressed in loincloths and rags, they were sitting on the hood, clinging onto the sides of the cab, and staring at me entranced.

Happy and healthy-looking, they pressed their dirt-stained noses against the windshield and side windows. And they smiled, exuding overwhelming vibrations of brotherly love that made me laugh. For my breakfast they picked a scrumptious papaya and some small pink bananas from nearby trees—the quality and sweetness of which I'd never tasted. As I gratefully ate, a thoughtful youth climbed a very tall palm tree and landed several ripe coconuts which he then opened for me so I'd have safe water to drink.

Everyone watched as I sat on the ground with them, guzzled and ate. The coconut water was cooling, sweet and delicious. I nodded my gratitude and played them my new sonata in four movements. They grouped tightly around and smiled so broadly I could hardly concentrate on the music, the power of their love making me laugh almost continuously.

We watched village women arrive by the dozen, bearing large heavy urns and earthen jugs to the village well for their daily supply of water. Their foreheads were painted with red dots. Their beauty was accented with gleaming trinket jewelry that penetrated their nostrils and earlobes. Their saris were colorfully dyed, and they lowered and raised the very heavy well bucket with brute strength worthy of the legendary Amazon women. With the skill of professional furniture movers they wielded their filled, five-gallon urns onto their heads and wandered off in the directions from which they'd come, the deep red juice of the betel nut they constantly chewed oozing from the corners of their mouths.

My drivers returned and we drove on. The villagers waved as we pulled away. I'll never forget their love that made me laugh so. As we passed more monkeys and birds of paradise, we were hit by a pre-monsoon squall that muddied the road. Then the sun returned and baked the road mercilessly so that steam issued visibly from it. Sweat rolled from our bodies, and the water supply from our few coconuts was soon exhausted.

Dizzy with thirst, we came to a group of dhoti-wearing men drinking from coconuts in the shade of a mango tree. My driver stopped and gave one of them ten anas, about one cent in American money. He gratefully took the money, bowed, grabbed his machete, and climbed some trees from which he cut down six ripe coconuts. We sat and waited while he opened each and prepared them so that all we had to do was punch out the holes in the tops to get at the water. Having been kept insulated by thick skin around the shells, the water was cool. And it tasted sugar-sweet. I quietly speculated that Mac the Diver probably hadn't thought of this.

We stopped to rest, gorging ourselves on coconut water, bananas and mangos. There were some monkeys, and a school of colorful birds, cavorting. At last my stomach was being filled with delicious safe food, and I was beginning to like India very much.

We covered the 800 miles to Bombay in only three days. Since I didn't care where I was dropped, my truckers chose the American Consulate. And with a handshake and a wave, my home, and benefactors of three day's standing, disappeared down the avenue.

Suddenly feeling quite alone and lonely, I stood on the busy sidewalk, stroking my unshaven chin for about a minute until a well-dressed, very attractive American woman walked over to me.

"Excuse me," she queried with the warmth of a hospitable southern belle, "is that a guitar you have there?" Her drawl told me she was indeed a southerner.

"Why, yes it is, ma'am."

"Well, I was just walking to my car from the consulate, saw you and thought to myself, now there's an American-looking guitarist who can teach my 12-year-old son how to play. Do you teach?"

She was Mrs. Sidney Sober, married to the economic administrator at the consulate. Relaxed and open, as though greeting her own son, she invited me to her beautiful home and we drove off in her car.

It *was* a worldwide conspiracy to see that I got looked after! Logic demanded that it had to be! Yet to my knowledge, it was not.

I lived for three days with the kind Sobers, teaching guitar to their son. Then their friend, Dutch Consul General Peer J. Vandergag, invited me to stay with him while his family was vacationing in Holland.

I spent the mornings exploring. But each afternoon Peer took me sailing in his 12-foot fiberglass sailboat among the Elephanta Islands just offshore. We would ride to and from the boat in his long, black, air-conditioned, chauffeured limousine that had a hi-fi record player installed in the cupboards of the backseat cocktail bar.

Next to sailing, music was Peer's greatest love. He was a fan of Frederic Chopin as well as Mexican mariachis. So as we glided along in luxury, we heard extra-hi-fi Chopin and Trio Los Panchos recordings faithfully reproduced on full-range tweeters and woofers. We even had our own volume and equalization controls mounted in the arm rest.

As we sailed, I helped with the jib while he managed the mainsail and rudder. We talked of fools and kings, and of his amazing background as an Allied Underground agent during the Second World War. He was 55, suntanned, seasoned, and very happy with what he found himself to be. His chest was barreled and full. A role model for all men, his rich lifetime of loving, caring and self-sacrifice was clearly written on him.

The wind whipped salt spray upon us each afternoon as we sailed, and I peppered him with questions about his life during World War II. He explained how he'd faced death as a secret envoy between the Nazis and the exiled Dutch Parliament. His heroic actions saved Holland's dykes while Canadian forces were about to close in on the weakened 3rd Reich near the Eisel River—a dramatic story never told in the press.

The Elephanta caves were scattered among the main island's recesses. Some were vast caverns that contained twenty-foot carvings of goggle-eyed gods chiseled out of the granite walls by an old Hindu civilization. There was Rohu of the Seven Stars, and the trinity of Brahma, Vishnu and Siva. Rows of gods and goddesses were depicted riding hybrid animals of weird description. The quality of some of the work rivaled that of ancient Greek art.

I told him about Zoe. He was glad I'd found someone I felt was exciting, and he told me of women he'd known. I was deeply moved but gently told him none of them sounded as exciting as Zoe.

Amused, he arranged for me to meet his schoolmistress friend who was driving to Agra, about 1000 miles away. Agra was home to the great Tajmahal, one of the eight wonders of the world. A winsome Dutch woman, she was good company, and the 1000 miles went all too quickly. We arrived at the Tajmahal, Temple of Love, in the evening during full moon. It was so late at night we had the magic temple all to ourselves. It glowed and glittered for us until sunrise, teaching us the loveliness of India.

15

A GHOST HAUNTED A HIMALAYAN MANOR HOUSE, AND HE WAS REAL!

Delhi was only a short hitchhike away from Agra. And there was much tourist traffic on the Delhi-Agra road, including the winsome Swiss couple who delivered me to Old Delhi. They left me among the gharry wallahs, coolies and soft-drink sellers who chirped and yelled among the festering odorous mob of dhotied men and skinny, flea-infested fakirs and piedogs. The hot sun burned like an oven filament. Angry Sikh taxi drivers honked at fat women, sacred cows and jackasses that blocked the narrow streets where the temperature was 115 degrees.

There were old fortresses with weathered walls containing sinister and lawless slums where a Westerner's chances of living through a day's visit were even at best. Moldy and foul-smelling bazaar stalls made of mule's dung had grown like weeds around these rotted walls. And outward from them spumed the rest of Old Delhi. There was a kind of beauty in these dirty old walls. For they contrasted with the sun's purity, showcasing its richly golden rays and helping create a special mystique.

My Dutch woman had recommended I visit her Indian friend, Premila Premchand, a producer at Voice Of America. I found Premila at her office in Bahawalpur House and liked her at once, for she was a loving, serene and insightful young visionary. She was the wife of General Premchand, commander of India's military contribution to the UN forces in Africa. Her fine son Sunil was about my own age and destined to be my friend.

Premila decided to produce a radio show with me at her home, for airing on VOA. She was in a happy state of mind, and excited that I'd entered her life.

"My son Sunil and I are having a party tonight at the house," she warmly told me. "You can come and play for everyone, and I'll record you with a live audience. And as the guests are all young men and women from the university, we can record a challenging question-answer session. And you must, of course, stay with us while you are in Delhi."

She drove me in her car to her big new house in the Defense Colony where we found Sunil and a dozen of his student friends twisting to rock and roll records.

A tall and lean young turbaned Sikh—his never-shaven beard trussed up in cloth—was the life of the party, and he asked the most intelligent questions during the talk session after I finished playing. He was Kirit Singh, university student and budding connoisseur of fine food and women.

After the production was over, we gathered on the roof terrace for buffet dinner. One of the two charming ladies, who'd prepared and now served our meal, was Prime Minister-to-be Indira Gandhi's private secretary who lived in the nearby government compound. The other was her energetic if elderly mother who began telling us stories about her personal experiences with ghosts.

We were all too "sensible" to believe in ghosts, flying saucers and the like. But then the wrinkled, white-haired woman began weaving her tales of migrant souls, the moon shining on her face.

Her final account was the most stunning. "For some years," she began, "I lived at a large Elizabethan-era manor in the village of Simla, a pretty hill station among the Himalayas. The house had previously been occupied by the family of an old Hindu patriarch who'd recently died there on his bed in the master bedroom."

This caused a general gasp, and it was quickly explained to me that it was a violation of the Hindu faith to die on one's bed. Just prior to death, a man must get as close to the earth as possible, perhaps lying on the ground upon a straw mat or at least upon the floor.

Unruffled by this interruption, the old woman continued. "The house was sold to me very cheaply, for the sellers explained it was haunted. I cared little, for I was used to ghosts by that time and was unafraid.

"But this ghost was odd. At exactly seventeen past eight each evening, he would appear. He would land on the south veranda and begin walking audibly toward the bathroom. He would enter the veranda door of the bathroom, whether it be locked or not, and walk through the bathroom into the master bedroom where I slept. It was in fact the same bedroom where the old patriarch had died, and it contained the same bed."

At this, the group gasped again. For it's not customary to sleep in a bed where a dying man slept.

The old woman continued serenely, "at times I had neighbors and friends with me who heard the same footsteps. We could never quite see the ghost, but we could always hear his feet. They sounded as though he might be staggering under a heavy weight."

Premila, a pillar of rationality, was listening raptly without a trace of tongue-in-cheek.

The old woman stood up and pretended to be carrying a corpse on her shoulder. "The ghost would come to the foot of my bed and face me. After a moment of silence he would drop the body, and you could hear it drop. There would always be a moment or two of silence during which I could almost feel the ghost standing there at the foot of the bed watching me. Then he would turn and tromp out the same way he'd entered, his footsteps sounding much less labored. And he would be gone until the next evening at 8:17, the very time of the evening when the old patriarch had died."

We were all impressed. A fascinated and very brainy-looking student raised his hand to ask a question.

"Yes, what is it?" she asked.

He flexed his short nose and adjusted his thick glasses. "How long did you live there?"

"For two years."

"The ghost didn't scare you?"

"Of course not. I got rather used to him."

"And was he still visiting when you moved out?"

"Yes indeed. And so far as I know, he still visits that bedroom—the manifestation of a tortured soul."

The bespectacled young man's name was Nariche Kochar. "Tomorrow we should drive to Simla in Kirit's jeep and see this for ourselves!" he freely suggested. Everyone chuckled indulgently. But Nariche and I pressed the old woman about it later, and she gave us a note of introduction to her friends who'd bought the haunted house from her.

Just as Kirit was the life of the group, Sunil Premchand was the actual brains and promoter. Profound and smart—actually a bit clairvoyant and the son of an Army general—he controlled others with his ability to conceive and promote concepts derived from special visions. He sat considering Nariche's idea. And as the party thinned out, he chatted with Kirit, Nariche and me.

Simla was too difficult a journey, but we made travel plans beneath radiant stars out on the roof terrace. It was agreed that in a day or two we would undertake a local jungle trip in Kirit's jeep—and that I would be an invited guest, playing my guitar for my share of the gasoline and food. I sensed they were good men and accepted.

That night, I stayed with the Premchands. Sunil kept me up for hours with his story of a tiger-faced spirit visitor who attended to him at times.

The following night, I accepted Nariche's invitation to stay at his home. His Hindu mother was devoutly religious. And, as it happened, this was the time of year when Mrs. Kochar's holy man stayed with the family. He spent all his time traveling and staying in the homes of his disciples. Middle-aged and paunch bellied, he had all his hair clipped down to his pate, save for a strip in the middle which he retained so as to be pulled to heaven by it should he die.

He sat in lotus position, meditating all day upon a bare mattress in the main guest room, contemplating the divine at a level beyond the subconscious. His room adjoined the living room hall, and his door was never closed. Yet the daily bustle of family doings never disturbed him, and he remained motionless hour after hour.

But he emerged after supper, dressed in his spotless white robe and sandals. He sat near the hearth and instructed the family on matters of the soul. Mr. Kochar, an executive officer in the Indian Navy, sat and listened with attention and respect.

Nariche offered to interpret for me if I wished to ask the holy man a question.

"Thank you," I said. "Are ghosts and spirit visitors real?"

Nariche eagerly interpreted the question.

The holy man smiled and answered, "Ghosts and spirit visitors are as real as the fear and guilt that spawn them. When fear and guilt are strong and unchecked, then a ghost or spirit visitor becomes tangible."

This reply caused a murmur of concern around the room. Nariche interpreted it for me, blinking his eyes and flexing his nose in his struggle to find just the right equivalent English words.

We spoke of many things, including the worldly pursuit of eternal youth. The holy man told us our spiritual essence is indeed eternal and is all that matters. He said the paths to self-realization and heaven are like a maze of roadways on a mountainside. Some of the roads go to the top and some don't. Some spiral around the mountain. Others make shorter and steeper climbs. And one, that of the highest Hindu, goes straight up.

There was a good feeling at the Kochar home, and much of it came from the harmony exuded by this marvelous mahatma.

Morning brought with it Kirit and Sunil in the jeep filled with provisions. Nariche and I joined them, and we left for the jungles of Dera Dhun, deep in the Punjab. We visited small villages where gaunt fakirs sat under trees chewing betel nut. There was no big-city decadence in these villages, and we felt safe pitching our tent near them each night.

The first night, we sat around and talked with a sadhu Sunil had befriended. But on the second, we went to see the local source of public entertainment—a fight to the death between a cobra and a mongoose. The mongoose won, sinking his sharp teeth into the snake's head and shaking it in a death grip while the bloodthirsty village sadists watched with gleeful awe. The battle over, they went home happy.

The second-to-last day of our trip together found us temporarily lost, deep in a remote thicket, in our effort to find a shortcut to the Rajpura road. Kirit had unwittingly driven us onto a game preserve, and we didn't realize it until we saw the sign facing away from us when we found our way out later. Amid the preserve, a wounded pheasant staggered across our path. A second later his pursuer appeared—a handsome tiger who leapt and caught the bird with expert ease.

We saw him only for a moment, but I've never forgotten him. He was about 5 feet long, and he'd been so close we could almost feel his breath. Once you've seen a wild tiger in a forest, you never want to see him in a zoo or a circus. For a tiger in a cage is as far removed from his true state as is a butterfly that has been gassed and mounted on a pin. Jail is living death for a tiger.

We stayed with Kirit's family in Rajpura, and Nariche asked if I would please go to Simla, chase down the ghost and let him know if it still haunted that house. We still had the note of introduction from the old woman, and I too was curious. So Nariche enthusiastically gave me the address of his friend in Simla, Mrs. Sheila Rai, widow of the late Colonel Rai of the Indian Army, who lived there in a spacious home with her son and two daughters. He said he would phone Sheila about me as soon as he got home.

They put me on the road to Simla. As this was the hottest time of year, when those who were able escaped to such mountain villages, the road was well traveled. So I easily caught a ride in the car of a Catholic priest recently transferred to the Simla Parish.

For hours we scaled sheer cliffs, climbing hairpin turns on unpaved sections of narrow road at some points so steep it could barely be traversed. But it was worth the climb. For the air was cool in Simla, fragrant with the scent of fir trees and pine forests. The village commanded a spectacular view from its remote nest on the densely forested face of a dramatic Himalayan peak. Tentacles of the village wrapped around the side of the peak.

The ghost house was on my way to Sheila's. Ensconced in a clearing, amid a deep, dark pine forest, it was a gray manor house. Artfully built of stone centuries ago, it was illumined by a pale-orange afternoon sun. As I entered the brick courtyard, I could see the second-floor veranda used by the ghost as an "airport." The veranda door leading to the bathroom was just as the old woman had described.

Intricately sculpted pilasters adorned the entire facade of the house. The tall, fortress-like double front door, studded with massive nail heads, was flanked on each side by a pair of lanterns mounted on gracefully abutting marblestone brackets with lion heads carved on them. I began to feel a bit foolish as I approached, but I couldn't disappoint Nariche. I had to inquire at least. I'd come to Simla for the trip more than the ghost, I told myself.

There was a heavy wrought iron knocker ring on the door, and I gave it a gentle rap.

The door was opened with the undoing of a thick iron dead-bolt, and a cultured, friendly, turbaned Sikh gentleman stood there. I explained I'd been sent by the old woman, handed him her note, and he invited me inside. The pretty Indian lady of the house was dressed in a green sari with a red dot on her forehead. She spoke perfect English. Indians who lived in big houses usually did. Seeing my guitar and pack, she exclaimed, "ah, so you are the American guitarist interested in our ghost. Where is your friend?"

The old woman had phoned her, paving the way for Nariche and me, and had told her we'd be arriving together.

I told her Nariche couldn't make it but sent his best. They ushered me in to sit down and chat. They were both very hospitable—happy to receive me even though they'd hosted a number of curious callers like myself who wanted to experience the ghost for themselves. They enjoyed the attention, they said, for it gave them the opportunity to share the old house. They were Brahmins who didn't have to work for a living.

At supper we were served by the English-speaking household staff who confirmed the details of the story. On some evenings, the thumping and scuffling of the ghost's feet, and the dropping of the body, sounded very loud and clear. On other occasions, the sounds were very faint. But it was always at 8:17 p.m. So blasé had they become, they weren't bothered by it unless it got unusually loud.

Just after eight, we assembled in the master bedroom with our coffee. At 8:15 we stopped chatting and listened intently. I heard the landing—a soft scraping sound on the veranda—and then the footsteps, very faint this night. They were irregular, as though the entity was indeed struggling under a heavy weight. They came through the bathroom and advanced toward us.

There was no mistaking the sound of these footsteps for that of some quite normal phenomenon. There was just no possible alternative explanation for the sounds. With each step, the sound came closer until it reached the foot of the bed where it stopped for a second or two. Then I heard the clear sound of a body being dropped onto the floor.

I looked straight at the spot from where that sound had come, and then raised my gaze as though to look into the face of whoever was standing there who'd delivered the body. I felt no communication and saw nothing. But my knowledge that the entity might well be returning my gaze created a chill.

The entity stood there in silence for ten seconds or so before it began to walk away toward the bathroom, its footsteps more regular and rhythmic. It went out onto the veranda, and then the sound faded.

None of us moved. My hosts studied me, curious for my reaction. I asked them whose manifestation they surmised the entity might be. Could it be that of the old man delivering himself, or possibly that of a brother or dear friend also departed from this world? But they had no answers and said I now knew as much as they did.

I told them Nariche's mother's holy man had said it was all generated by guilt. "Whose guilt might've created it?" I asked.

They had no idea. After further thought, I suggested the staggering entity might be the person looking after the old patriarch who'd neglected to put him on the floor. That person, now also dead, was spending its afterlife putting the old man's ghost onto the floor in order to try and cleanse itself of guilt.

They both liked that, and we discussed why the sound might be audible to the rest of us. "Perhaps it is because the entities wish to teach us not to make that mistake when our own end is at hand," the Sikh gentleman suggested. He was quite philosophical.

I performed a short concert for them in their attractively furnished sitting room. They preferred my baroque-style compositions and requested these several times. The lady speculated that the reason she liked European baroque might be due to impressions upon her migrating soul during previous lifetimes.

They invited me to spend the night, which I did. India was certainly filled with mysteries, as the people were so very concerned with matters of the soul, I thought to myself as I dropped off to sleep.

Simla enjoyed more than its share of India's mystique. Furthermore it was very pretty here, so I decided to stay longer. After writing these kind people's names in my pocket journal, my one journal that was lost in subsequent years, I went to see Sheila Rai.

Sheila was also a Brahmin who needed not engage in enterprise for her living. She was the kindest and most pure-hearted woman I ever came across in my 50-nation tour. She'd suffered much at the hands of wrong-doers, wars and an alarming number of misfortunes, including the death of her husband, during her fifty-odd years on this earth. But in response she exuded inexhaustible warmth.

Love emanated from her every pore and was expressed in her words and deeds. Nariche had indeed phoned her of my coming, and as I approached her in her yard, she took both of my hands in hers and lovingly caressed them. Her hands emitted currents of love so strong as to tingle the heart.

As we sat at her dinner table attended to by her small staff of servants, we traded the stories of our lives. After dinner I performed a private mini concert just for Sheila and her children. She wouldn't stop loving me or my music and insisted I stay as a member of the family indefinitely. Her house enjoyed the prettiest of all Simla's Himalayan views. I was given my own bedroom and private bath. And Sheila's teenage son, Arun, accepted me like a brother as did his two very pretty teenage sisters, Aruna and Ahuna.

I stayed with them for many days, though all of us seemed to want to make it many years. Each day the Rais dropped some of their other activities and took me sightseeing. Sheila told me about the Indian people, culture, and matters of the soul. We toured many scenic roads in her car, visiting spectacular mountain gorges and rugged vistas.

On returning from one of the trips, I went to my room and found my soap container had been removed from my pack and was lying on the bed. I knew I hadn't taken it out. I'd felt so loved in this household, I had, just this one time, removed my chest pouch and buried it in my pack among the gear. It had felt good not to have to wear it. But now I could see the pouch had been removed and then replaced. For things were packed around it differently than I'd packed them. There was no question that someone had tampered.

I opened the pouch and counted the bills. All the dollars were there. But there had definitely been nine, five-pound English notes given me by the sailors aboard HMS *Eastbourne* in exchange for my Bahrain rupees. Now there were only eight.

Poking his head in to say goodnight, Arun found me sitting on the bed, recounting the eight bills and shaking my head in disbelief. He demanded to know the cause. I told him, and he insisted we tell Sheila at once.

Although we were all halfway to bed, we assembled in my room wearing bathrobes. Sheila sat on the bed holding my money pouch in one hand and the soap container in the other, a stern look on her usually loving face.

"How could this have happened in my house? It's not the loss of money that disturbs me, but the fact that it happened in my house!"

She ordered all the servants to come individually and be interrogated. The humble servants stood shaking and cowering, meekly answering her questions.

"Did anyone enter the house today?"

"No, Memsahib."

"Were you in this room at any time today?"

"Yes, but only to dust and sweep, Memsahib."

"All right, now we'll hear from the cook."

She conducted the formal procedure efficiently and doggedly but to no avail. So we went to bed without a single clue.

Whoever had taken the note must have rationalized that I was indeed a rich man to have all that money and would never miss a single five-pound note. He'd have been right too, if he'd only had time to replace the soap container. I might not have counted the money until months later. But perhaps we'd returned and entered the house before he could finish packing my gear exactly the way he'd found it.

In the morning, I found Sheila sitting smugly and pensively at the breakfast table.

Without a word, she produced a dirt-smudged paper napkin. Inside it was wrapped the five-pound note.

I was truly amazed. "Oh. Thank you. How did you . . ."

"The cook gave it to me this morning. He claims he heard something clanking near the trash pile during the night and got up to investigate. He found no one. But he fished through the garbage with his flashlight and found the note wrapped in this napkin."

"Hmm. That's just too bizarre. What do you suppose made him fish through the trash?

And if the note was inside the napkin, how did he see it, especially at night?"

"I don't know," she said, "but I intend to find out. We cannot abide a thief here."

She phoned the police, and the inspector arrived with his tough, massively built lackey. Both wore tight-fitting army-colored uniforms with knee-high leather riding boots and shiny brass buttons. They instructed us to stay in the house, and they conducted their interrogations out on the back lawn. We sat at the window with our lunches and listened.

The inspector was a slow-talking, profound and shrewd old man. With his lackey's help, he made sure the servants were kept separated. He questioned them one at a time. Then he took them in pairs and questioned them again. Sheila strained to hear every word. It was a tedious procedure. Finally the inspector narrowed it down to one of two servants—either the bowlegged old sweeper or the cook who said he'd found the money.

It was impossible to penetrate further without more "stringent" means, the inspector told Sheila. He sought her permission to take both to the police station for torturing until one of them confessed. She consented, though in tears because she loved her servants.

She thanked him for his kindness. Indeed, he'd given his whole afternoon to our problem, and now it would be his evening as well. The cook and sweeper whined and wailed, vehemently denying their involvement, as they were taken away.

I was tormented. "Please," I said, "the money's been returned. The matter isn't worth all this suffering!"

But Sheila wouldn't listen. Thievery, and secrecy about it among the servants, had to be nipped in the bud. She took me to her bedroom to explain why. Locking the door behind us, she took out a small jewelry chest from the closet and opened it. The pile of precious metal and stone reflected the overhead lamplight into her gentle face. Looking at the little treasure sent her into a state of pensive recollection.

"These are my little baubles," she said. And she sprinkled my palm with glittering rubies, diamonds and emeralds.

Then she told more of her story. She was born to a family in West Kashmir so wealthy it boasted 200 household servants and more than 1,000 field and farm hands to cultivate the tens of thousands of acres. Envious, Pakistan sent an invasion force. Her father threw vast resources into helping the Indian soldiers, but the Pakistanis couldn't be repelled.

They flooded onto her father's land, brutally killed him, occupied his houses, plundered, pillaged, destroyed and raped. The servants could offer no protection, for they would need to surrender at once when the Pakistani Muslims arrived at the door. Sheila grabbed these few handfuls of jewels from her father's huge treasure chest, concealed them in her clothing, and escaped with her life. These jewels were from the ancient treasures of Mogul emperors and great Khans. Their numismatic value was beyond estimate, making them far too valuable to be entrusted to a bank safe deposit box.

All her father's land became Pakistani soil. Sheila's fellow refugees borrowed a fortune in rupees from her and returned none of it. Prior to the invasion, everything had been done for her by her ladies-in-waiting. Since then she'd had to learn to brush her own hair, dress herself, and now to live in this quaint two-story cottage with only four servants and her late husband's Army pension.

So she'd be needing to sell a diamond or emerald occasionally in order to survive the coming years and couldn't afford to be robbed by her servants. Confronting them with police retaliation was the only way to insure her security and that of her children. India was a beautiful jungle but a vicious and cruel one.

I was saddened by this news, but suggested we put away the baubles and go look at an even greater treasure.

"What treasure is that?" she asked.

"Come on, I'll show you."

I led her downstairs to the terrace and opened my arms to her view that provided such a grand panorama as to inspire her bliss on bright days when the view was clear. As dusk approached, we sat and admired the view. I told her how lucky I thought she was despite all her losses. This visibly cheered her, and we smiled at each other all evening.

Just before we retired, she asked if she might borrow my chest pouch to study the zipper, the likes of which wasn't available in India. I was a little embarrassed, for the pouch was dirty, worn thin, and a little torn by the beggars in Tunis. But I let her have it. When I came downstairs for breakfast, she presented me with a brand new pouch. She'd been up half the night removing Mom's American zipper from the old pouch and installing it in this brand new one she'd made for me. It was beautiful work. I still have her pouch to this day and keep precious mementos in it.

I stayed on with her much longer than I'd planned. I can't remember now who it was that had taken the five-pound note. In fact I don't think it had yet been resolved the day I left for Calcutta. I was very sorry to leave and almost cried.

This deeply moved her, for she was sad too. "You've a home here as long as I am here," she reassured me with a husky voice. I was beginning to understand India had many charms. Sheila was among them.

I kept in touch and learned she left this earth some time ago. Otherwise I'd recommend to anyone precious enough to be reading this story, and planning a trip to Simla, that they at least phone her and convey to her my love.

⚜ 16 ⚜

Mr. Jan, the "richest man in Calcutta"

I found a ride as far as Delhi and went to see Nariche to report about the ghost. He was glad to see me, and we rejoined Kirit and Sunil to spend a day riding around town on bicycles. We passed a luxury hotel and saw a trio of crippled, topless dhoti-wearing lepers near its entrance. They rolled their shirtless bodies on the sidewalk to attract attention and arouse pity, and they cried like lunatics at the rich who entered and exited.

As they clutched their empty beggars bowls, flakes of wind-blown street dung, dust and debris, clung to the weeping red wounds on their decaying flesh. The respectable hotel guests were reviled at the sight, and none would go near enough to contribute baksheesh. So the lepers groveled there, helplessly dying slow, tor-tuous deaths. This world for them was grim and heartless indeed.

As we stood watching in horror, we saw a collision between a bicycle and an ox-driven bullock cart. The cyclist toted a pair of handlebar-mounted milk tanks with Delhi Milk Scheme printed on them. The milk spilled, making a puddle where the lepers had been groveling. But instead of moaning over his loss, the resource-ful cyclist removed his sweaty shirt, sopped up as much milk as he could with it, and wrung it back into the tanks. Then, with a cheer-ful whistle, he climbed back on his bike and rode on.

I later went back to that hotel and got permission to perform in the dining room.

Unfortunately the name of the airplane pilot I met there, and the name of that hotel where he always ate, are lost with my lost journal. He was an independent commercial pilot with his own DC-3 and a bit of an individualist. He knew I was a writer and asked me to never tell details about him. He probably ignored or bent a few regulations. But no one was cheated, and he took me a thousand miles to Calcutta.

Here was the city of action and violence—India's nucleus of unrest. Communists were strong here, and the U.S. Consulate was often picketed and vandalized. Two million of the city's human souls lived in the streets without food or shelter, and radicals planned their attacks in roach-ridden cellars beneath sewerless slums of unbelievable filth.

When I located the house of Zoe's parents on Chowringee Street, I was impressed. It was a grand place if empty. My inquiries at the British Consulate yielded no information other than that this was the residence of former officials who'd moved away. They wouldn't even verify the names when I offered them, much less give me a forwarding address. Embassies and consulates dispensed as little information as they could, which is how they'd survived so many years, I thought to myself.

Bitter at the apparent loss of Zoe, and angry with all diplomats worldwide, I combed Chowringee street once more to see if I could find a neighbor or friend of Zoe. I found nothing but a hotel, the Oboroi Grand, and walked in.

I showed the manager a feature story about me in the TIMES OF INDIA, a national newspaper whose reporters had discovered me playing for a group of child beggars in Bombay.

"Why, you're famous," he said. And to my delight he booked me to play in the Grand Showroom for meals and lodging.

The loss of Zoe made me so sad, I caught a virus. But the Oboroi was a grand place in which to convalesce. Ebony tables, inlaid with mother-of-pearl, were everywhere. The carved oak chair on which I performed was upholstered with a velvet cushion and embroidered with golden brocade. The clientele in the posh showroom was the choosiest in the province.

One evening, after my last show, a waiter visited my dressing room with a note written by a man requesting I join him at his table for a drink. I went out just to have a look at him—a short, fat, elderly Indian wearing an expensive suit. He saw me and motioned that I sit with him. I then had no choice, and he introduced himself.

"Good guitar playing," he said. "I am Mr. Jan. I am the richest man in Calcutta." He showed me his platinum wedding ring on which glittered a beautifully cut diamond the size of his knuckle. He wasn't being in the least bit facetious. This was his way.

I found him a bit comical and chuckled. "Tut-tut. I'm a troubadour. And because I'm free, I am the richest man in the world."

He chuckled too, but not genuinely. And he pointed again to his ring. "This ring is worth a half-million rupees."

I gazed at him quizzically.

"What is your favorite drink?" he asked, seemingly puzzled himself. Maybe he'd expected me to show more interest in his ring.

"Lemonade with cherry juice," I replied. "And I could well use some right now."

"But no. How about a martini, a bottle of champagne or . . ."

"No, thanks. I am a man of simple tastes. I like cherry lemonade."

He summoned a smartly outfitted waiter, issued the order, and the waiter glided off to obey. Mr. Jan showed much interest in me and impatiently questioned me about my career, demanding brief answers so there would be more time for other questions.

The waiter returned. "Excuse me, sahib. There is no cherry juice."

"Fine," I said. "I'll just have straight lemonade."

Mr. Jan was upset. "But you will not! He pouted and turned to the waiter. "Go out and get some cherry juice." He stuffed some bills into the waiter's pocket.

"Many thanks, sahib, but there is no cherry juice in all of Calcutta."

Mr. Jan's impatience grew to anger. "Then use some of that money and have a bottle flown in from Delhi. Surely there is cherry juice in Delhi." His chest puffed out indignantly.

"Very good, sahib. If we find some in Delhi, you will have it by tomorrow night." He bowed gracefully and glided off again.

I grinned at the situation. "Listen, I couldn't care less about the cherry juice."

Mr. Jan still fumed. "Yes, I know. But it is the principle of the thing. You will have your cherry juice tomorrow, or I will see that waiter fired."

Sighing helplessly, I suggested that his large tip for cherry juice might've been better spent buying shoeshine kits and setting up some of Calcutta's beggars in the shoeshine trade.

He laughed. This time it was genuine. "You are very naïve. You cannot give to these beggars. You give them a shoeshine kit and they'll only sell it and spend the money foolishly.

"On food perhaps?"

"Ah, it is clear you have not been long in India. You have not yet had time to learn the folly of helping the poor. They are untouchables. They cannot be helped because it is against God's will. We must all die in whatever strata we are born. But let us not speak of such things. What of your future. What are your plans?"

"Well, I'm headed east, following the rising sun around the world. So I suppose I will hike and/or hitchhike across Assam and along the Chindwin River to Rangoon—thence to Siam."

He looked surprised. "That is head-hunter country, and the monsoon is coming. You are an artist—not Tarzan. You would never make it."

"But surely others have done it. Besides, that's what folks have told me all along, prior to my journeys through Algeria, Arabia and India. You cannot do this, it's impossible to do that."

"But I will not hear of your going through Assam. I will see to it you have a complimentary ticket to Bangkok on an airplane. You are a troubadour. You can accept freely offered complimentary tickets and visas, yes?"

"Of course."

"Done," he declared, slapping the linen tablecloth.

He took out his pen and a large calling card and wrote on the back the name of a travel agency down the street. Then he added a brief note to the manager.

"Show this note to Sam," he said. "Sammy will give you a ticket, and any needed papers, and it will cost you nothing." The note read,

Sammy: This lad is a musician and a friend of mine and has played to me for his passage. Please attend to his needs and put him on the plane of his choice to Bangkok.

He rose, shook my hand and went out. Despite his fatalistic philosophy about the poor, I thought Mr. Jan a kind soul and was very moved and grateful.

His cherry juice never arrived. Perhaps they didn't have any in Delhi either.

But I took his note to Sammy, a short wiry man behind a littered desk in a noisy office.

"So," he said. "You have met Mr. Jan!" He was jubilant for me. "You are an extremely fortunate man." Any friend of Mr. Jan's was a friend of his. And he lovingly presented me with a visa and Royal Thai Airlines ticket to Bangkok, compliments of Mr. Jan.

As my plane flew over the heads of the head hunters, I reclined in my spacious first class seat and sighed in gratitude for Mr. Jan all the world's rich, kind Samaritans.

17

A command performance for HM King Bhumibol of Siam

If India was uncomfortably hot, Thailand was wretchedly so. The sultry monsoon weather was so heavy as to make breathing difficult as I trudged the few miles from the airport into Bangkok. My blue jeans were sweat-soaked as I entered the city and walked among friendly-looking, cherub-faced Thailanders. Weather-beaten, straw-hatted women cheerfully toted water buckets. Half-dressed men, glistening with sweat, pranced about happily despite the heat. Contentment, hallmark of the Siamese, was all around me, and I felt happy to be there.

The relaxed drivers of Bangkok's noisy three-wheel motor scooter taxis would take a native anywhere in the city for five baht—a tourist for ten. If his taxi was vacant, a driver would pull alongside a walking European and solicit patronage. Just across the road from the Royal Bangkok Sporting Club, they swarmed in great numbers in front of an architectural masterpiece. It was a tall, white, modern structure, air-conditioned throughout, called the Erawan Hotel.

I walked in, just to get out of the heat for a moment, and saw an attractive poster advertising a troupe of Bangkok's pret-tiest women dancing in authentic, ancient national costumes. They were called the "Thai Dancers," and they packed the hotel's Ambassador Room each night. Excited, I got out my newspaper story and showed it to the hotel manager, a friendly German who, without putting me through an audition, gave me a job as opening act for these young women in trade for my board and room—truly a lucky break.

A United States Information Service official was in the audience that first night. Not only did she arrange a concert for me at the U.S.I.S. Center for a large group of young Thailanders, but she wrote her own feature story about me that got printed, with a photograph she'd taken of me, on the society page of a local English-language newspaper, the *Bangkok Post*.

The story appeared alongside a big feature article about the latest activities of the royal family of Thailand. My story was headlined, "Troubadour Plays His Way To Bangkok," and it told how I'd revived the tradition of the troubadours who performed for royalty. I began wondering about the possibility of someone on Their Majesty's staff having seen it in process of reading about the royal family. There was only one way to find out.

Sticking the paper into my back pocket, I went over to the Grand Palace, an impressive labyrinth of glittering, sky-scraping golden domes and temples adorned with stained glass and shiny porcelain. The magnificent front gate was patrolled by the Grand Palace Guards.

A bunch of American tourists milled about, taking in the quiet harmony created by the splendid artistry in the statues and designs.

"Nothing like this back in Ohio," wheezed one potbellied excited husband to his wife. And he rewound his camera for another quick shot of her in her loud dress while she stood with her arm around a sitting Bhudda.

One of the Siamese castle guards watched them, horrified at their sacrilegious treatment of Bhudda's image. Finally the noisy busload of tourists left, and all was ghostly quiet save for the subtle tinkling of the hundreds of lovely glass mobiles.

So I went to the guard and asked to see His Majesty's private secretary.

His English was perfect. "What do you wish to see him about?"

I showed him my press card from the *Press Democrat* in Santa Rosa. "It's a private matter."

So he took me inside the gate and past a hundred yards of dramatic mural artwork to a tastefully appointed office where sat His

Majesty's private secretary Mr. K. Kitiyakara, a short, cheerful, chubby young gentleman wearing a suit of Thai Silk. He invited me to sit down and instructed the guard to wait outside.

Handing him the newspaper, I offered to play for the royal court.

He read the article, and his attitude was cordial if formal. "All right. I will try for you. But I must tell you that many musicians request audiences with Their Majesties, some of them quite famous. But Their Majesties invariably deny the requests, for the royal schedule is full. However if His Majesty grants you an audience, I will contact you."

He showed me to the door, and the guard walked me to the front gate. My prospects didn't look very promising, but I felt good about having offered my music. Also I had an inner feeling that something good would come of it.

And something very good did come of it. The very next morning, Mr. Kitiyakara pulled up to the impressive front steps of the Erawan in a chauffeured limousine. He got out, walked in to the amazed receptionist and asked to see "the troubadour."

I was still fast asleep in my room. My phone rang, and the excited receptionist told me the royal secretary was on his way up to my room. I had about a minute's notice.

I opened the door to greet him and he walked right in, still puffing from his exercise on the hotel steps, his cherub face brightly beaming. He presented me with his handwritten royal command to appear and perform for afternoon tea at Chitra Lada Palace the following Sunday.

"Is that acceptable with you?" he asked.

"OK," I said, both excited and amused by his news and bright face.

"Then I will be here at four o'clock to get you. I hope you will not fail me." He turned and snapped his finger at his assistant who quickly opened the door for him. "Please be ready by four o'clock. And please do not fail me," he repeated as he walked out.

King Bhumibol was the most loved monarch in Asia. Photos and images of him hung in every place of business and graced every item of currency and coin. News got around the hotel very quickly about the secretary's visit, and I was treated like nobility. When I told the hotel tailor about my command performance, he was excited and asked if I would please wear a shirt made for me by him. He would charge nothing. His payment would be that Their Majesties might see it.

Alone in my room with bubbles in my heart, I began mentally preparing. I wanted to play something special for the royal couple—something yet undiscovered. So I envisioned and taught myself to play a tune just for them—a tune more special than anything I'd ever written. It was a short ballad, for I didn't want to be grandiose. But despite its shortness, it was special. I decided to call it *Thespian's Ballade*.

Secretary Kitiyakara arrived on time, and by 4:01 we were in his limousine being chauffeured to Chitra Lada Palace. He coached me on protocol as we drove along.

"Never stand on higher ground than that on which His Majesty stands. Do not bow. Simply lower your head respectfully when His Majesty enters the room. Do not introduce yourself to His Majesty before His Majesty first greets you."

We glided along through the forbidden entranceway with a nod at the elaborately uniformed guards, and passed through acres of lawns, fruit trees and tropical gardens graced with the most beautiful of blossoms.

The scene of the royal tea party was a large and rather modern hall with a spacious, curtained, panoramic stage. The center aisle was flanked by pillars. Long, cloth-covered tables bore sterling silver platters of indigenous Siamese fruits and pastries that were ingeniously prepared. The hall was graced with splendid paintings and murals by contemporary Siamese artists and lit with modern lamps mounted around the pillars.

The secretary left me chatting with members of the large royal orchestra while he raced about attending to his duties. There were about a hundred guests, mostly government officials and their families. Servants and footmen moved quickly and unobtrusively, making last-minute preparations. They wore immaculate white with bright-colored trimmings and plumed hats.

As 5 o'clock drew near, some tension filled the hall. At 4:59 and thirty seconds, the room became very quiet. And at 5:00, the pair of eight-foot, relief-sculptured wooden doors at the head of the aisle were opened by a pair of plumed footmen—one man to each door. Then all servants and footmen got to their hands and feet and bowed their heads.

Their Majesties, King Bhumibol and Queen Sirikit, filled the doorway standing arm in arm. He wore a suit of Thai Silk. The queen, universally recognized as one of the world's most beautiful women, wore a white dress. They looked splendid and beautiful.

His Majesty's manner was all at once dignified, benevolent, intelligent and able. His was a high round forehead. His wise-looking if youthful, semi oriental eyes keenly surveyed us all as he walked with head erect and shoulders very relaxed. He was every bit the figurehead ruler of this happy nation with its ancient culture and unique beauty.

The queen was radiantly happy. Her face was purely oriental, though her other features reminded me of paintings of Egyptian goddesses I'd seen in museums. Her manner was so graceful as to upstage the king.

Her manner was so graceful as to upstage the king.

As he and the queen proceeded along the aisle, King Bhumibol's surveying of the guests became very keen, as though he might be taking a mental roll call. So occupied was I in observing the magnificent couple, I didn't notice the dwarfish secretary move in behind me. As he did so, Their Majesties stopped right in front of me as though given a signal.

"Your Majesty," said the secretary, "this is the troubadour."

King Bhumibol took my hand. "Welcome to Bangkok," he said cheerfully.

"Thank you, Your Majesty. I hear you play the clarinet like Benny Goodman."

"Rumors do get around in Thailand," was his modest reply. He was friendly, like a kind next-door neighbor of long standing. "What kind of guitar do you have?"

I was amazed at his informality, interest and attention. Using my hands to illustrate its size, I began describing the guitar as the royal photographer took our picture.

"We're looking forward to hearing you," said the queen. And Their Majesties walked on to our table where we sat with the prime minister and enjoyed a light Sunday evening meal impeccably served on trays of gold and silver.

His Majesty and myself comprised the entertainment. He and the orchestra began with modern jazz. He played brilliantly, on both clarinet and sax, with skill and finesse. His musical style was relaxed as he himself was, and I found his performance remarkably polished. His presence was calm, but powerful emotion came through his music.

He launched into a wild New Orleans Dixieland piece, bringing down the house with it. "Here is one king who, when working, really works. And when he plays, he really plays," said a government minister, gesturing at the king whose neck and cheeks were bulging as he put everything he had into a brilliant passage. Having lived in the USA, King Bhumibol lacked no orientation to American music.

He'd done me the favor of going on first. This helped relax me. As I went on, the queen, seated between her two ladies in waiting, smiled at me so sweetly I relaxed even more and debuted my new ballade for them. She appeared to enjoy it as well as my entire

His presence was calm, but powerful emotion came through his music.

program that preceded it. For she leaned forward to catch every note, applauded with effervescence, as did the rest of the audience, and brought me back for an encore. The entire hall became pindrop quiet as I mentally groped, deciding what to play. Her Majesty asked if I would please play *Danny Boy,* the pristine, richly melodic old Celtic *Londonderry Air* set to a touching, well known lyric about a young man gone off to war.

While I played it, the story in the lyric haunted me. And I suspect it haunted everyone in the hall. For yet unknown to the general public, the American military buildup in this little country had recently been escalated to 20,000 troops and well over a hundred F-107 jet fighter planes. It was a secret war—the beginning of the great Vietnam Conflict. It was June, 1962.

As I played this encore, the queen quietly left her seat and found an isolated chair closer to me—the better to hear and be alone with me and my guitar. She was such an earnest listener!

After I left the stage, the royal orchestra took up this haunting *Londonderry Air*. King Bhumibol surprised me by coming backstage to chat with me alone. We sat on a couple of folding chairs and faced each other. He wanted to talk about music. He had questions about the way I played, who'd taught me, and how I discovered my style and ability to compose. As I answered his questions, I complimented him on his own playing, suggesting in jest that we could be a duet and travel together.

This made him smile a little. But as we talked, I could see that he looked troubled about something. I suspected it might be the military buildup that was being kept from the news services as long as possible. I too had been saddened by it and decided to mention it. This indeed proved to be just what was troubling him.

I thought of Colonel Chaveau in Ankara. "Your Majesty, I've been told we're to be grateful for whatever befalls us—good or bad. Is this really true?"

He looked surprised. "Yes, I've heard that before. Yes, of course it's true."

Nothing more was said. But the Colonel's words had been helping me in my despondency about the militarism, and I felt better now that a king had validated the good colonel's words and might himself be cheered by them.

He told me about his royal bandmaster, Mr. Srikaranond Manratana, saying Mr. Manratana would try to arrange onward passage for me aboard one of the Royal Thai Shipping Line freighters as his guest. Then he shook my hand and retired, and Mr. Kitiyakara delivered me to the Erawan.

While Mr. Manratana was busy arranging my ship passage, I went on solo concert tour of the brand new American military bases in upcountry Thailand, including one that was dubbed "Green Latrine" by the GIs—historically masters of acronyms. It was so named because of the green excretion of the countless tiny "no-seeums" there that landed on your hands and face and feasted upon you day and night.

This tour had been set up by Colonel Holland, a director at the Joint United States Military Advisory Group (JUSMAG), who'd been coming to hear me nightly at the Erawan's Ambassador Room.

The hotel manager said I'd be welcome to return and continue playing for my food and lodging when the ten-day tour was finished. I was being given a chance to do something for my country, and it made me very happy.

Colonel Holland had enlisted the cooperation of Major General Weller who signed my travel orders. I had my own special helicopter flights, with jeep and driver at each terminus. Food and accommodation—sometimes primitive—were also provided.

"You're the first entertainer of our troops here," the colonel told me as he put me on my first flight. "Not even Bob Hope has been here yet."

This first flight was a cargo plane. I wore a parachute and sat next to a handful of GIs. There was a huge opening in the middle of the deck through which we could look down at the tops of the trees. We flew only a hundred feet above them, for we needed to stay low and avoid enemy radar. We were loaded with mortar cannons, jeeps, and a treasure trove of valuable equipment.

I stopped and played concerts at many camps, for audiences of one to four thousand GIs. They were the most appreciative audience I've ever had the pleasure of playing for. They clapped, whistled, stomped and hooted way out of proportion to the quality of my very poor performances in all that humidity upon stages built with a few rough-sawn planks.

I generally was given a tape recorder for a sound system. Makeshift mike stands were improvised for me out of tree branches stuck into the ground. Police car-quality tape recorder microphones were attached to the branches by simply wrapping the mike cords around a stem. There was no lighting but gas lanterns. And to power the tape recorders, there would always be a noisy generator that made more noise than I could—even with the 12-watt tape recorder amplifiers pushed to their limit.

My favorite of the shows was the one for about 1,000 GIs at Chengmai. For there was no tape recorder or generator—just a few small campfires. The jungle around us was serenely quiet. And better than half my audience had found seats high up in the surrounding trees. This way, were we to be surprise-attacked during my performance, our attackers would themselves be in for a rude surprise. For those in the trees were "packed"—armed to the teeth—as were those few hundred on the ground in front of me.

When I returned to the Erawan, Mr. Kitiyakara came by to get me once again. He took me to the royal recording studio where he produced a private album of my work to be enjoyed only by Their Majesties. I grew to like him very much, and he presented me with the above photographs to keep as a memento of my command performance at court.

The American Ambassador, Kenneth Young, invited me to play for him, his vice consul and both of their families at his Ambassadorial Residence near the Erawan. Here I met his teenage son Steve who arranged that I give a concert. He got it sponsored by the Bangkok Music Society, and it was held at the opulent Erawan Banquet Room.

Steve's friend, Ravi Manathasna of Madras, son of the Indian Ambassador, loaned me his spare racquet and played tennis with me at the Royal Bangkok Sporting Club. The two of us spent days meandering around the city, and he became my closest friend in Bangkok.

What I liked best about him was that he genuinely believed in miracles. He always looked as though he expected at any moment that perhaps a giant sunflower would appear, bend over and whisper a divine revelation into his ear. He's the only friend I've ever had who insisted on paying a photographer to take our picture together, and I still have my copy. He also gave me an autographed copy of *The Bhagavad Gita* which I treasure to this day.

Mac the Diver, in his dire predictions, had not accounted for the likes of the Peiris', Webbs and Sobers, the Vandergags, Premchands and Kochars, the Rais, Mr. Jan, King Bhumibol and Queen Sirikit, Colonel Holland and Ravi. Mac meant well, but I'm glad I disregarded his advice and went to meet these fine members of my worldwide family.

Mr. Manratana presented me with an open ticket to anywhere on a Royal Thai Shipping Lines Norwegian freighter. And on a starry tropical balmy night, we sailed with the tide out into the Gulf of Siam and the great China Sea beyond.

18

THE HEALING POWER OF FAITH

On my open ticket to anywhere as royal guest, the ship took me to several Far East ports where I played on national television shows and got featured in many magazines and newspapers. As the media attention began feeding upon itself and growing, it seemed harmless enough. It didn't occur to me that it might smother the delicate miracle in my adventures that it fed upon—that of love being discovered and reflected. The media attention was beginning to place me under a spotlight where true discovery rarely occurs.

But out on the China Sea, such worldly problems diminished in the wake of salty breezes and Bali Hai sunsets. I was given a luxury private cabin and felt deeply heartwarmed by the royal family's kindness. Our Norwegian captain beamed with an inner happiness. He was a friendly old salt and dined with us nightly.

But one night at dinner I felt weak and had little appetite. The captain remarked that my skin was turning yellow.

He gazed into my eyes with no small concern. "Your eyes are yellow as well as your face. May our ship's doctor visit you in your cabin and examine you after dinner?"

I was confused at this, for I had no history of health problems. "Sure, OK."

I returned to my cabin and looked at my reflection in the bathroom mirror. Sure enough, my entire body had suddenly turned to a deep yellow color.

As the media attention began feeding on itself and growing, it seemed harmless enough.

The doctor visited at once and administered a urine test. He was horrified. "Your urine is like molasses and sticks to the walls of the vial. Young man, you have hepatitis!"

He issued an order that I be quarantined in my cabin. Food was delivered to me there by the doctor, and none but him could touch my tray, utensils and dishes.

Our captain radioed a distress message to the nearest port, Naha, Okinawa, for permission to unload me and avoid a hepatitis outbreak aboard ship. Permission was granted, and we made an unscheduled stop at this beautiful island. A U.S. Army physician came aboard and examined me. I'd fallen so ill by then, I can barely remember him. But he determined I was definitely hepatitic. He had me put on a gurney and carried to an ambulance which took me to the Seventh Day Adventist Charity Hospital, a clean and modern facility.

I was taken to the x-ray room and x-rayed. Then they took me to a quiet room that looked out upon a pretty garden, and tucked me into a comfortable bed where I immediately fell asleep.

The doctor, a pleasant man in his forties, woke me at dinner time with warm food on a tray.

"Please eat if you feel able. I don't wish to alarm you, but I've examined your x-ray. Your liver is half gone." Tenderly, with much sympathy, he added, "it's quite amazing you're still alive, but I doubt if you'll live out the rest of the week. You might well die before tomorrow morning. Do you have a Last Will and Testament?"

What he said was so outlandish as to seem a bit of a joke. Death wasn't something I was into, so it felt like we were kids acting in a play.

"Is there nothing you can do for me?"

"I'm afraid not," he replied with sympathy so deep and powerful as to be a bit scary.

But I laughed inwardly, for I've always seen life as a game. Thus remaining calm, I replied that I had no Will, whereupon he produced a pad and pencil.

"I'd appreciate it if you would write some clear instructions as to how we're to dispose of your remains. Your instructions should include the names and contact information of your nearest relatives. Please go ahead and write this down for me, and give it to the nurse."

He walked out, leaving me to the friendly Oriental nurse. She was rather young, charming and very sympathetic, having heard the doctor's prognosis. She watched lovingly as I wrote out my Will. As I handed it to her, I asked if she'd please bring me a phone book and telephone. She quickly brought me these, and I began leafing through the Yellow Pages for a faith healer. Where medicine fails, faith often works. There was just one faith healer listed, and he billed himself as a Christian Science practitioner.

He was Bill Baxter, the Jaguar dealer on the island. He sold Jaguar cars duty-free to the American soldiers who ran them around the island and then shipped them home duty-free as used vehicles, saving thousands on the purchase price.

He picked up the phone. "Yes, this is Bill Baxter."

Rather spaced, I still felt like an actor playing a role and just spoke my line, "Bill, my name is Buddy Bohn, a troubadour touring the world with my guitar. I have some background in Christian Science study, and I'm here at the Seventh Day Adventist Hospital . . ."

Though I felt embarrassed to say it, for I somehow knew there was no way it would happen, I added, ". . . I guess I'm about to die, or so they've told me, and I'd sure like to talk with you about it if you have a minute."

Bill was a caring man, and that's all he needed to hear. "I'll be right over," he said, and hung up.

Okinawa was a small island, and he arrived quickly. Middle-aged, he was a sun-tanned American with dark glasses, Bermuda shorts, and a loud, loose-fitting Hawaiian shirt.

He carried himself with confidence and an invincible warm smile. Without saying a word, he closed the door to my room, took the chair from the corner, and brought it to my bedside.

Behaving like a long-lost friend, he sat himself and gazed at me with twinkling eyes and a grin. Delighted, I grinned back at him. With those grins, we instantly said volumes to each other.

Grounded in Christian Science, we both knew there was no substance in the medical claim of hepatitis. We were men who leaned on the power of infinity for our sustenance. This allowed us to indulge in powerfully positive thought—thought based on our faith that God created only good, perfect health and happiness. And God being the only creator, there's simply no room for anything contrary to exist.

So it was just a matter of our affirming what we both knew, and we affirmed my wellness out loud together.

"God didn't create disease," he said. "It's a false claim."

"I know."

"The little bug eating your liver has no power to hurt you because God made the little bug."

"Yep."

The things we said to each other didn't really matter. What was important was that we were, between us, building a positive thought trend. It felt like God's purpose that we meet on this island and affirm Him supreme over every false claim such as disease.

He sat hunched over my bedside. With adamance and purpose he began reciting, very slowly and deliberately from memory, Mary Baker Eddy's *Scientific Statement Of Being*. His understanding of the words was so deep and complete—and he was able to deliver them with such powerful transparency and clarity—I could understand the truth in them better than ever before.

"There is no life, truth, intelligence, nor substance in matter."

So my liver, being matter, had no actual substance, I thought to myself. For I'd been brought up to understand that man's only true identity is grounded in Spirit.

Bill continued, "All is infinite Mind and its infinite manifestation, for God is All-in-all."

I'd leaned on that affirmation since boyhood. But when Bill affirmed it, I recalled how my Sunday school teacher had taught me to think of allness as a flag of a single color—that of God—without so much as a single thread of another color. When we see the flag with only one color even for an instant, we're free—free of duality. This thought process had healed me of ear aches when I was twelve.

Bill went on, "Spirit is immortal Truth; matter is mortal error. Spirit is the real and eternal; matter is the unreal and temporal."

The real body, the one that was really me, was Spirit immortal—therefore impervious to disease.

"Spirit is God," he concluded, "and man is His image and likeness. Therefore man is not material; he is spiritual."

It felt like God was with us in this hospital room as we went over the fundamental facts of being, affirming our status as spiritual beings. There was infinite love both within and without this child of God who'd come to visit me. The love in me vibrated in sympathy with it, and I felt exhilarated.

"There is no power apart from God," he then said, quoting Mrs. Eddy in her textbook, *Science and Health with Key to the Scriptures.* "Omnipotence has all-power, and to acknowledge any other power is to dishonor God."

He added that If I would please hang onto that thought, he would go home and continue affirming the truth for me the entire evening until he fell asleep.

"You're in perfect health. At 9 tomorrow morning we'll tour the island in my Jaguar XKE, followed by lunch at my yacht club. How does that sound?" He smiled brightly.

That brought a lump to my throat. He was so kind and good!

"I'd like that very much."

I could see he was getting ready to leave, and I didn't want that. For there was an area of doubt I still wanted to discuss with him.

"Y'know, I've always wondered how, during this dream of human experience, we can truly receive God's Love and understand His Truth."

His face brightened. He laughed, reached out and touched my forehead. "Truth and Love manifest in you just as light passes through a window pane. Of course the light and glass don't mingle. But one who has kept watch on his thoughts and kept them pure is a cleaner lens for the light to pass through."

This very beautiful entity then said, "I'll see you at nine," and left me. I rolled over, pulled the sheet over my head, and joyfully wept at my good fortune of having met Bill Baxter.

I fell asleep without fear and with no thought of dying. For I'd already learned that God's Truth manifests in the body of one whose faith is strong. Feeling very loved, I found it easy to affirm God's omnipotence. As I did this, I also began recalling Mrs. Eddy's remarks in her book, *Science and Health with Key to the Scriptures*, that Bill had alluded to—her explanation of our ability to receive God's Love and understand His Truth.

> The manifestation of God through mortals is as light passing through the window pane. The light and the glass never mingle, but as matter, the glass is less opaque than the walls. The mortal mind through which Truth appears most vividly is that one which has lost much materiality—much error—in order to become a better transparency for Truth. Then, like a cloud melting into thin vapor, it no longer hides the sun.

I slept soundly all night. Birds, singing in the sunlit garden outside my window, gently woke me shortly before nine.

I felt hungry and full of energy for the first time in weeks. Popping out of bed, I went into the w.c. for relief. My urine was no longer molasses-like. It was perfectly normal for the first time in many days. I looked at myself in the mirror. My skin was normal—the whites of my eyes white and normal.

Chuckling, then belly-laughing not unlike my bony-chested, mad friend in the Arabian Desert, I went about packing my gear.

Bill showed up right at nine with his invincible smile and beheld my condition without a hint of surprise.

"Let's go for a drive," he said.

I picked up my guitar and backpack, and we began walking down the hallway. The nurse saw us and called the doctor who intercepted us near the hospital entrance.

"You cannot leave. You're deathly ill!" he told me.

This bewildered me a little, for he didn't seem to recognize that I was perfectly healed.

"Not anymore," I said. "I'm fine. We're just going for a drive to see the island."

He became livid. "If you walk through this doorway, I'm washing my hands of you. Do you understand?"

I was grateful for his hospitality and didn't want to hurt his feelings. "I hope that won't happen. I just need to get out in the air and sunlight, and spend some time with Mr. Baxter."

He glared at us both, started to open his mouth, but said nothing.

We waved at him and went out, climbed into Bill's Jaguar convertible with its top down, drove clear around Okinawa by midday, and lunched at his yacht club. We spent our time learning about each other. Neither of us felt a need to discuss the magical result of our faith, for we both considered it a very natural thing.

He took me to play an audition for his friend who ran the officer's club at Kadena Airbase. The man offered me money to play a short concert. So I agreed to return that night and give a one-hour performance while the orchestra took a double break.

Bill left, as he had some business. Neither of us said anything to anyone about the healing which we considered a personal and private matter. We knew that most folks, like the doctor, wouldn't have understood anyway.

I hung around the club, meeting friendly American pilots and ground personnel. During my performance that evening, I announced I needed a place to stay. The audience responded well to this, and about six officers and their wives entered my dressing room with offers to stay with them and their families.

I chose the couple who'd entered first and spent the night in their guest room.

Okinawa is a small island, so word quickly got around about my performance and where I was staying.

The next morning, that doctor showed up with a bottle of liver pills. Amazed and quite touched that he still cared about me, I tried one of the pills. It gave me a few minutes of indigestion. So I left the bottle in the food cabinet of my host's kitchen.

I gave other performances in Okinawa, including a private one for Bill Baxter, during the following days. Bill chose to have me play for him and some friends at an intimate Naha coffee house so old-worldly as to remind one of back-alley sangria clubs along the centuries-old alleyways near Madrid's Plaza del Sol.

My final performance was an afternoon concert for the local chapter of Freemasons who passed a plate among themselves and arranged visa and passage for me to southern Japan on a Ryukyuan junk-like sailboat of ancient design.

Though I shared a cabin with three young folks my own age, I spent most of my time seated alone at the absolute bow of the boat, watching the flying fish play with us like miniature dolphins as we quietly cut through the water. They swam slowly in front of us until we caught up. Then they flew, inches above the water, for a few feet to gain ground, swam slowly again, flew again and so on, never tiring of the game. They made small ripples on the water that reflected sunlight and dappled my mind as I privately, quietly, and very happily, celebrated being alive.

Bill had reminded me about God's Love, and I'd let it in. I decided it's hardest to remember Love when we're afraid, angry or hurting, but that's when it's most important to remember. For if we can only remember, and let it in, Love will fix everything.

19

HOW AND WHY MEDIA
INVASION SPELLED THE END

Continuing my journey through the Far East, I played for my supper in many private homes. One of them was that of *My Geisha Girl* film producer, Steve Parker, who was sitting in a Tokyo restaurant where I walked in and played. Steve had me give a private concert in his home, bought me a room at the Okura Hotel, Tokyo's finest, and influenced Royal Interocean Lines to put me on their ship, MS Tjiluwah, where I could play for my passage to Australia by giving concerts. A student among my concert audience at the American School in Tokyo arranged my visa through his dad who was director of public relations at the Tokyo office of Pan American Airlines.

After stopping at many Pacific Rim ports, we steamed into Sydney's Wooloomooloo Harbor on a clear, hot Summer afternoon in mid December. Leaving the ship, I went to have a look at the Australians. I found them sailboating, surfing and walking in the park. So I lingered to the park too, and sat next to a misty fountain to watch them. I found them delightful. They seemed more rugged than the Americans and the English—and more contented. It isn't how much a man has, but how contented he is with it that matters.

The front page of the local paper that day featured cricket matches. Politicians and public officials, such as Kennedy and Khrushchev, were secondary, back-page news.

A hearty, gray-haired man walked around passing out campaign literature and ballot forms. An election was being held.

I played for my supper in many private homes.

When he got to me, I regretfully told him I couldn't vote because I was a non-citizen having arrived in Australia only minutes ago.

"Not a citizen, eh?" His weather-beaten face beheld me with a smile. "Well, let's hope you soon are." He nodded and walked on. That was the very first social conversation I ever had with an Australian on his own soil.

I meandered and came across the Jazz Cellar on Liverpool Street. There was traditional Dixieland jazz of the highest order going on, played live by Graeme Bell's All Stars, the most famous jazzists in Australia. The music floated out the "Cellar" door and drew me in from a half-block down the street.

There was no door charge. I walked in and was sent to the ninth cloud of music. When the band took a break, I asked Mr. Bell if I may do a guest set. I was allowed to play and began with my *Alegria*, a flamenco piece I'd written. Most of the people were students, and they applauded extra long and loud, just as the American GIs had done. So I continued playing and began telling my story between numbers.

Aussies are among the few, if not the only folks, who like Americans as much as the Americans like them. Maybe it's because both nations are descended from Mother England.

People gathered around, smiling from ear to ear, shaking my hand and inviting me home. The first thing an Aussie wants to do with a stranger is take him home, "give him a feed," and put him up on the couch.

Graeme fought his way through the crowd and formally introduced himself, offering me a spot on his weekly television show, Trad Jazz—network on ATN-Channel 7. I stayed that first night in the home of the club owners, a fine young couple who'd only recently bought the club.

Within a week I'd signed to appear with Graeme on television, and he'd introduced me to the directors at Festival Records who'd signed me to record an album—my first-ever record contract. Then I walked into the Chevron Hilton Hotel and got myself a spot opening for Vicki Carr at their penthouse showroom, the Silver Spade, in trade for supper and lodging.

Veteran writer, Malcolm Forsyth, wrote a clever feature article about me in the widely circulated *TV Week* magazine. It read in part,

> Once upon a time there was a wandering minstrel who had a great wish to play his music before a king. So one day, guitar in hand, he found himself at the gates of the Royal Palace outside Copenhagen.
>
> "I would very much like to play for the king," he said to the palace guard.
>
> "Alas, I am afraid that would be impossible," the guard replied. "His Majesty is not in the habit of admitting mere minstrels to the confines of the palace."
>
> But the troubadour did not lose heart. He began playing for the guard. His music was so appealing that the guard, after hearing for a time, gave way and smiled.
>
> "Very well, you may pass through the gates, but you must not say that I let you through."
>
> Soon the troubadour was in the palace kitchens playing to the cooks and kitchen maids, and it happened that the king heard him from the royal apartments.
>
> He was so delighted he ordered the troubadour be given food and lodging for the night, and that a hamper be packed to see him on his journey the next day.
>
> Sounds like something from Hans Christian Andersen? But in fact it happened only a few months ago at the palace of King Frederic

IX of Denmark. The troubadour was 22-year-old Buddy Bohn of Bodega Bay, California, who wandered into Sydney last week from Hong Kong.

Buddy will feature on Sydney TV screens soon as guest artist on ATN 7's *Trad Jazz.*

The story caused a lot of interest, and I was invited to appear several more times on Trad Jazz. Then I appeared on Bandstand, Lionel Long and other network shows. Reporters from a score of newspapers and magazines began looking me up, in the private homes where I was circulating, in order to photograph and interview me. I've never, before or since, had so much attention.

One sunny day I eluded a group of reporters by ducking into the private, membership only, White City Tennis Club. Members of the New South Wales Tennis Association were holding an outdoor luncheon out on one of the beautiful grass courts. I was

I've never, before or since, had so much attention.

drawn to them and joined their group, much as I'd done with the International Council of Europe. I found a chair, sat at the head of the long table and began playing.

No one challenged me, and I performed for a half-hour or so, finishing with my new high-energy flamenco piece, *Picadores,* that had worked so well aboard HMS *Eastbourne.* There was a solid round of applause. I got up and walked off in order to return my guitar to its case that I'd left inside the clubhouse with the young and pretty receptionist.

I'd put the guitar away and was chatting with this pretty lady when I felt a hand on my shoulder. I looked around to see a smiling man who introduced himself as Mr. Fox, managing director of Dunlop Sporting Goods-Australia and president of the New South Wales Tennis Association. Amazingly he called me by name. He knew me, he said, from having been in the audience at one of my tennis matches back in America.

"Are you playing any tennis?" he wanted to know.

"No, I am only here in Australia to play my guitar and look around. I'd love to play, but I've no racquet or tennis clothes. I live out of this Kelty pack here."

He grinned with a knowing, inner glow. "Well, if that's all that's stopping you, I think we can arrange some free equipment for you."

The next afternoon in his office, as we chatted waiting for my racquet to be strung, one of Australia's finest tennis players, Max Anderson, poked his head in. Mr. Fox had arranged this and introduced us. Max was an extroverted, brightly smiling, powerfully built athlete in his thirties.

A man of action, he immediately took me to White City Tennis Club as his guest and we played. I'd never played on grass before, but I liked White City's lawn-surfaced courts. And though out of practice, I enjoyed a bit of beginner's luck often experienced by a player on his first day back. It was almost impossible for me to miss a shot, and I found myself serving for the first set at 5–2.

I couldn't believe it. Doubt began creeping in. For Max was well known, having beaten his good friend Rod Laver consistently during Rod's teenage years. A battle-wise court general, Max sensed my doubt. He dug his toes in, raised his game and came after me like a freight train. He broke my serve and leveled the score at 5–5, at which point we entered into a see-saw battle which he finally won 19–17 (We didn't have tie-breakers in those days). Then he grabbed my hand and said, "My friend, if you weren't such a lollygagger, you could give me a decent game."

He said I was "oroite" though and took me home for "stike 'n aigs." We played again, he connected me with other players who also wanted to play repeatedly, and my golden days at White City Tennis Club were underway.

I enjoyed those days. But reporters were all over me, and I needed to get out of town.

Physical escape was my only choice, for I didn't understand celebrity life. When "success" happens so very fast, you don't feel you know what you're doing. No one's footing seems to be on the ground any more than your own. People generally aren't "real" with you anymore. "Real" was what I wanted to discover, which is why I was traveling.

So I hitchhiked into the hills—way up into and beyond the Blue Mountains to the great Australian Outback. Here I was invited to stay at a remote ranch and was taken by my host to play for a large group of Aborigines at a camping place where they gathered. They listened quietly and didn't applaud, much like the enchanting ravens in the Maharaja's garden. This fascinated me, and I planned to meet with them again.

But I was soon tracked down by a detective service hired by the Melbourne TV show, In Melbourne Tonight. Producer Bill Beams radio-phoned me person-to-person. His voice glistened like that of a polished radio personality.

"We've read about you in *TIME* magazine," he said—all friendly and excited. "We want you on our IMT Show. We'll fly you to Melbourne and give you fifteen pounds."

"No, thanks," I replied with all sincerity. "I'm enjoying the Australian Outback. That's what I've come to Australia to see—not television studios."

There was a pause. "We'll double it. We'll pay you thirty pounds!"

I swallowed hard. "Uh, no."

"We won't go any higher than thirty. But we can throw in two free nights of food and lodging at the Southern Cross Hotel."

"But I'm not trying to dicker with you. It's just that . . ."

"We'll even throw in a free trip to Tasmania all expenses paid. How about it?"

He'd found my weakness. I'd always wanted to see Tasmania. "One way or round trip?"

"Round trip!"

Beams sent a car to get me at the Melbourne airport and provided free taxi service between the luxurious Southern Cross Hotel and the TV studio.

My appearance was successful. More than a hundred phone calls flooded the GTV Channel 9 switchboard from Melbournites of all kinds offering bed and board in their homes if I would bring my guitar and play like I had on television. The switchboard staff stopped logging them after 110. But I had 110 numbers I could call and get free lodging.

I never called any of them back. It would have made things too easy—taken the challenge out of finding ways to be discovered. Television is to the troubadour what a fishing net is to a fisherman. With the net he catches far more fish than he can ever eat. And he misses his opportunity for individual, mutual discovery with each soul.

Mr. Beams wanted me to appear again and again, and I also appeared on other Melbourne TV shows. Beams introduced me to his friends, Mr. and Mrs. Braddock, who took me home to stay indefinitely. They lived just down the road from Kooyong Tennis Stadium, destined home of the Australian Open Championships for five years from '82 to '87. They sent me there to see if I could find someone to play with.

I entered the stadium at about 2 p.m., on or around Valentine's Day, and found an impressive row of impeccably maintained grass courts—the grass in such pristine condition you didn't want to walk on it for fear of disturbing a lady bug. There was no one there but Margaret Court, the famous Wimbledon champion, her partner having pulled a muscle just as I walked in and limped home to put ice on it. She sat alone at courtside, pensively searching her grip bag for her car keys.

It's known as being in the right place at the right time. I walked over and said, "Excuse me, I've come to find someone to hit with, and you're the only person here. Would you like to hit some?"

The world's most accomplished tennis player surveyed me and smiled. "Sure," she said.

We didn't introduce ourselves right away. We were just two tennis players, and that's all that mattered. She had beautiful strokes, and the artistry in them was pure joy to feel from across the net. And I sensed she could feel my enjoyment of her art. I suppose this made her feel good about her artistry, for she began indulging it at a deeper level.

She hit her shots crisply and perfectly, inspiring me to do the same, raising my game with the incomparable beauty of her own. I decided to join her—to become one with her—to be an artist in my own right and be a happy part of the machine we made together. We became a pair of motors, functioning as a team in perfect synchronization and harmony.

So there was no sense of competition. Though on opposite sides of the net, we were on the same team, helping each other keep it all going.

With only this happening, we played for three hours without vocalizing. We didn't need words. We spoke in the superior language of good strokes—an unvoiced, eloquently beautiful language wordlessly transmitted and understood in the upper artistic stratosphere of sport. I saw the wisdom of remembering this feeling of being on the same team with my opponent and summoning it whenever I played. For it was very relaxing and helped me play better.

At five o'clock she suggested we return tomorrow and rally like that again from 2 to 5.

"I really enjoyed just rallying like that—just engaging in the art of hitting the ball," she said with the sweetest, most radiant smile I'd seen in a long time. I decided she was one of the world's most beautiful women, even prettier than her photos that graced the front covers of many tennis magazines.

We met there each day at two, immersing into the same delightful "zone," speaking only with the artistry of our shots. Words cannot describe a tennis player's exhilaration when communicating with good strokes. Each day our three hours transpired in what seemed a few minutes. And we adjourned full of energy, wanting more tennis instead of feeling tired and needing rest.

Her coach, Harry Hopman, began showing up and watching us by the hour. He never spoke or disturbed us in any way.

Only once did Margaret use her vocal cords. It was toward the end of the first week. She stopped playing and asked with alluring charm, "Would you please hit me some shallow backhands? I'd like to practice stepping into them."

Truly excited to be of service, I hit her some of these. After a few minutes she said, "OK, that's enough," and we resumed our freeform indulgence in the art of hitting—our machine still very much intact.

Harry was in touch with Margaret by phone each evening. He told her we should take that first weekend off to "reconstitute." Neither of us liked his idea. For being in our early twenties and playing in the "zone," we felt immortal. But this living legend of a coach had his loving and unobtrusive way of getting obeyed without discussion.

So we took the weekend off and resumed for another five days on Monday, during which I appeared on television by night and played with her by day.

But sadly for me, she had to leave for Europe the following weekend to play in a tournament, and I never saw this exquisite lady again. Missing her terribly, I spent the afternoon after her departure wandering around Melbourne's port area and caught the scent of fine cooking from aboard a ship called the Wave Prince. I followed my nose up the gangplank, found a dinner party in progress, and spoke to one of the ship's officers.

"Oh, yeah," he said. "Oive read about you in the paypuhs." And he set up a place for me to play and get some of that good food.

I was badly blood-bathed. Conversations drowned out my music almost completely. But there was one tall smiling guest who listened. He was the first officer of the Australian submarine destroyer HMS *Anzac*, escort ship to Her Majesty's royal yacht *Britannia* while she sailed Australian waters. The *Anzac* was moored alongside the *Britannia* on the next pier. He introduced himself.

"Good on ya, mate. How would you like to serenade the queen?"

My life had turned into a fairy tale, and I just rolled with it. I consented, and he took me in a chauffeured military car through the wooden barricade and rows of security police to spend the night aboard HMS *Anzac*. Lining the barricade were tens of thousands of Australians who'd been lined up for hours to catch a fleeting glimpse of their queen as she and the Duke of Edinburgh rode by in their Rolls Royce to go aboard HMS *Britannia*.

The royal couple came through the barricade shortly after we did. Awed by the splendor of royalty, thousands remained at the barricade gazing all night at the royal yacht.

The queen and duke lunched aboard their yacht the following noon, during which I performed a half-hour mini concert, scarcely a coin's toss away, for fifty sailors on the *Anzac*'s top deck. Just behind them was the queen's open porthole—the perfect setting for a royal serenade.

This got into the local papers, several magazines and even the international news services, adding fuel to the fire. And the Festival Records promotion department arranged that I film ten music videos for general network airing throughout Australia—also a 90-minute television special—at TVT Channel Six in Hobart, Tasmania. So I used the ticket Mr. Beams had given me and flew to Hobart.

The work at TVT-6 was done under the guidance of their dynamic and talented producer, Peter Richman—himself an actor with a flair for the dramatic. He sent me with a camera crew to the excitingly wild and beautiful Tasmanian rainforest for some of the scenes.

Then the crew built us a fishing pier inside the studio where Peter donned an old skipper's cap, wielded a fishing pole, smoked a pipe, portrayed an ancient mariner I'd met there, and challenged me on camera with spontaneously conjured questions. I illustrated my answers by playing improvisations on my guitar. We had no script and just made it all up as we went along. With subsequent editing, it became a cohesive piece of work that enjoyed several airings. While still in Hobart, I gave a sellout concert at their luxury hotel, the "Wrestpoint."

Returning to Melbourne, I played the IMT show yet again for Mr. Beams, and among the hundred or so new callers was Zoe!

I called her back. She was married but wanted me to wait there until she arrived in her car. She truly wanted to see me. While awaiting her arrival, I decided that finding her like this was the most thrilling miracle of my entire journey.

Looking more beautiful than ever, she entered the greenroom and hugged me. She wanted to hear what had happened to me. I wanted to hear what had happened to her. Finally I had to go first. Then she related her adventures:

"My father in Calcutta died within a week. My mother was too feeble and morose to live alone in Calcutta. So I uprooted her and took her to her sister in Northumberland. While there I met Ian, my handsome plucky Australian. He swept me off my feet so completely I could think of nothing and no one else. I married him within a month and flew with him here to Melbourne."

She could see that hearing about Ian made me sad, but she insisted on taking me home to meet him. I felt happy for Zoe that he seemed a giving and compassionate man. Such men are rare, and I couldn't feel the slightest jealousy. He too was incapable of jealousy.

"Had I abandoned the troubadour code and flown straight to Calcutta, I wonder if things would've turned out different," I said.

"Who knows," they both laughed, and I felt secure with them.

Zoe and Ian took me to all my appointments and appearances—even to the famous "Powerhouse," a rock-'n'-roll palace, where I was part of a pop concert.

The most bizarre of my new television offers was from the producer of a BBC public affairs talk show. He invited me to be one of a panel of three "experts" and talk for an hour on the subject of "world leaders—their whims and prejudices."

Zoe was as amazed at the insanity as I was. As we sat together in her writing room, I played her *My Own Song*, the tune I wrote at age seven.

She entered a semi trance as I played. "I've never heard this, yet it feels familiar."

I shrugged and admitted, "You might've heard it aboard the Lydia. But when a strange tune feels familiar, maybe that's because it's somehow just as much part of you as it is of the composer."

Our souls met in delight while she worked on her story about me for Copley News Service. "Any guitarist who's played privately for two princes, a knight, an ambassador, two consuls, two kings, a duchess, a cabinet minister, three shaikhs, two billionaires, a baron, a maharaja, an emir, a sultan, two queens, a baroness, a roomful of parliament members, a prime minister and a duke—this is a guitarist people should know about," she giggled, pointing to her copious notes and practicing her lead paragraph.

Our tongues were in our cheeks, for we'd learned a little about the media. We knew that while my having recently come from a California vineyard and played for these luminaries was selling ad space and making me famous, it was a self-defeating kind of fame. For in order to capitalize on it, I would have to stop living the kind of life that was the source of the media attention that kept the fame alive.

And unbelievably, my agents, club managers producers and promoters, like so many money bugs, were so busy setting up to profiteer that they couldn't see it was a dead end street. Such pitiful frailty among grown men.

City people were beginning to take me into their homes because I'd been on TV and in the newspapers, and less because they liked and wanted to hear more of the music they'd heard from a homeless adventurer. My environment was becoming a superficial showbiz world with less genuine contact—no more talks with folks like Mrs. Kochar's holy man.

I did go ahead and make an album for Festival, and it sold well for them. But I didn't feel experienced enough yet to make a record commensurate with my potential and began looking for an offer to go to South America where I would be unknown and could start over again. I contemplated taking a raft down the Amazon River to Rio and hitchhiking overland from there to Bodega Bay.

But having read of me in *TIME* magazine, the principles of P&O Orient Lines invited me to give concerts for my passage aboard their SS *Orsova* via the South Seas to Oakland, California.

Somehow it seemed right to take this offer as the final leg of my trip. It would secure the success of my original plan to circle the world by the troubadour code. I felt embarrassed by the media attention because it had robbed me of that very adventurous life for which it was crediting me—that very spirit of the hunt that had kept my travels alive for me.

During my last days in Sydney, I began spending my time with college students. I liked them best of all the Australians. They invited me to perform full-length concerts to packed halls at Sydney University and at the University of New South Wales. Being far more "real" with me than their parents, they put me up in their dorm rooms, stayed up until the wee hours chatting with me, and a pair of them took me windsurfing.

The day of departure from Sydney, I went aboard ship both triumphant and sad—sad to have lost Zoe and my adventures were over, but happy I'd made it around the world without even once using money as a means of exchange. I was indeed a troubadour.

Zoe enjoyed a good cry now and then. She drove all the way up from Melbourne to see me off, and we stood together on SS *Orsova*'s main deck, hugging and kissing a lot.

"Like Candide the optimist, you deserve to be in Eldorado where the streets are paved with gold," she cried.

I gazed at her in amazement, for she'd been constantly surprising me with such declarations of her love and concern for me though she was now married to another.

I swallowed a tear and replied, "Well, I've seen our world here, traveled its roads, and found them paved not with mere gold but with love."

She was comforted by that, I think. For she stopped crying for a moment, smiled a little, and gazed deeply into my eyes.

I went to the ship both triumphant and sad.

The *Orsova*'s smokestack bleated the final all-aboard signal, and Zoe had to hastily disembark with the last few non-passengers.

She stood on the dock, waved at me, and we cried at each other as the ship pulled away.

During the month-long transpacific voyage, I nursed regret at losing Zoe and reflected on my long journey. I felt warmed by the way folks had been so strongly moved to help me. There had to be a reason. I decided it was because they saw a young man enjoying a lifestyle we all want to experience but rarely do, being caught up in the quicksand of our involvements and our fear of living a life seemingly more exposed to the fickle whims of happenstance. Contemplating this, I realized my travel experience had shown me it's not our lifestyle so much as the way we perceive life that dictates our happenstance.

Mom and Jack came to meet my boat in Oakland. What a joy to see them after my long two-year journey! I decided to make my very first expenditure of money in two years by taking them to a Chinese restaurant in San Francisco's Chinatown. Chinese was always Jack's favorite food. As I was putting my pack into the car trunk, Mom gazed at it and marveled that it had held up so well.

EPILOGUE

MY OWN SONG

Through the backwoods of a golden season,
Sings a troubadour who's come my way.
Have I gone astray?
With visionary things to say,
And with a song he says I wrote, he serenades me—
With my own song enchants me—
This gypsy troubadour in me.

Singing my own song
Within my heart
He's leading me home so reverently.

He has traveled far to find me wandering
From my castle in a golden age—
This kindly sage.
A friend for reasons he won't say,
His wealth in Shangri-La is in the richness of . . .
The song he sings—the peace he brings—
This gypsy troubadour in me.

ILLUSTRATIONS

ABOUT THE AUTHOR

After growing up in the California towns of Carmel, Laguna Beach and Los Gatos, Walter Moro ("Buddy") Bohn, professionally known since 1975 as Moro, a one-name composer/ guitarist, began touring with his guitar and knapsack during his Principia College summer breaks. On receiving his BA in Drama/ Journalism in 1961, he knapsack-toured clear around the world as a guitarist-troubadour, never once using money as a means of exchange. He wrote about his travels for several newspapers. His adventures were covered extensively in the media, and he performed on many television shows and in nightclubs and concert halls throughout the world.

While in Los Angeles he played his guitar nightly at Paul Newman's own private, membership-only nightclub, The Factory. He also played in Las Vegas, at Howard Hughes' own nightclub, the Cabaret Room. He toured with the New Christy Minstrels and was guest soloist until he became engaged to Princess Simine of Iran and went to live with her at her beach villa in the south of Spain. She died tragically, and he went to London where, as Buddy Bohn, he composed and recorded for Deep Purple's label an LP that contained his first international radio hit, *Vermouth Rondo*, performing it with the London Philharmonic Orchestra produced by his good friend Jerry Lordan, composer of the multimillion-selling *Apache*.

He settled in Bodega Bay, California, and released eight albums of his compositions including *Hosanna Blue*, the world's most aired solo guitar recording from 1981–84. As of this writing, he's the recipient of 31 consecutive annual ASCAP Awards for airings of his compositions. His music can be found at www.moromusic.com.